# Local Politics and Social Policy in China

Due to uneven economic reforms, Chinese provinces have developed distinct approaches to governing that impact social policy priorities and policy implementation. Ratigan shows how coastal provinces tended to prioritize health and education and developed a pragmatic policy style, which fostered innovation and professionalism in policy implementation. Meanwhile, inland provinces tended to prioritize targeted poverty alleviation and affordable housing, while taking a paternalist, top-down approach to implementation. This book provides a quantitative analysis of provincial social policy spending in the 2000s and qualitative case studies of provinces with divergent approaches to social policy. It highlights healthcare but also draws on illustrative examples from poverty alleviation, education, and housing policy. By showing the importance of local actors in shaping social policy implementation, this book will appeal to scholars and advanced students of Chinese politics, comparative welfare studies, and comparative politics.

Kerry E. Ratigan is Assistant Professor of Political Science at Amherst College. She has published articles in journals including *World Development*, *China Quarterly*, *International Political Science Review*, and *Studies in Comparative International Development*, among others.

# Local Politics and Social Policy in China

## *Let Some Get Healthy First*

Kerry E. Ratigan

*Amherst College*

Shaftesbury Road, Cambridge CB2 8EA, United Kingdom

One Liberty Plaza, 20th Floor, New York, NY 10006, USA

477 Williamstown Road, Port Melbourne, VIC 3207, Australia

314–321, 3rd Floor, Plot 3, Splendor Forum, Jasola District Centre, New Delhi – 110025, India

103 Penang Road, #05–06/07, Visioncrest Commercial, Singapore 238467

Cambridge University Press is part of Cambridge University Press & Assessment, a department of the University of Cambridge.

We share the University's mission to contribute to society through the pursuit of education, learning and research at the highest international levels of excellence.

www.cambridge.org
Information on this title: www.cambridge.org/9781009066020

DOI: 10.1017/9781009067409



First published 2022
First paperback edition 2024

*A catalogue record for this publication is available from the British Library*

ISBN 978-1-316-51247-0 Hardback
ISBN 978-1-009-06602-0 Paperback

To my grandparents:

Ray "Lefty" Ratigan (1926–2013)

Grace McClary Ratigan (1926–2016)

# Contents

# Figures

# Tables

# Acknowledgments

In the winter of 2003–4, I was in Beijing with my future husband, Kurt, a Canadian citizen who was feeling ill with a mysterious low-grade fever and persistent fatigue. I accompanied him to doctors' appointments, blood work, and a lumbar puncture to rule out leukemia. A doctor at a second hospital recommended repeating the lumbar puncture, but Kurt refused. To mediate between the recalcitrant patient and the doctor, an American doctor was called. She explained that he was infected with Epstein–Barr virus, causing mononucleosis. He was treated with rest and traditional Chinese medicine. Mononucleosis among young adults in their twenties is highly unusual in China and suggests an underlying condition related to the immune system, hence the lumbar puncture. Another American doctor used Kurt's case to explain to a panel of local doctors that, in some countries, exposure to Epstein–Barr virus can occur later in life. Local doctors studied this case with interest, listening carefully to his experience, as they were preparing to host the 2008 Olympics and wanted to be ready for an influx of foreigners. Several aspects of this experience stuck with me: the care and attention of the providers, concerns about SARS, fever clinics, long lines of patients, and – perhaps most notably – the amount of cash changing hands. Despite China's communist political system, healthcare seemed extremely expensive for ordinary people. I continued to puzzle over China's healthcare system when I arrived in Madison, Wisconsin, for graduate school. I was grateful to find a dynamic intellectual community that supported me in the research that has become this book.

Writing a book would not be possible without the guidance and encouragement of professors, colleagues, and friends. Melanie Manion's consistently incisive and comprehensive feedback – at all hours of the day and night – challenged me to strive for excellent research at the dissertation stage and beyond. Her keen analytical critiques helped me to clarify my arguments, and her patient encouragement has provided much-needed support.

Ed Friedman always reminded me to think big. I shall be forever grateful for having the opportunity to learn from him and his mind-bogglingly diverse experiences. I am in awe of Ed's wisdom, kindness, and generous spirit.

I thank Christina Ewig for being willing to engage so deeply with research outside of her geographic region of expertise; her critiques pushed me to think about China in a broader comparative context.

I am incredibly thankful for participants in the Chinese Politics Workshop at the University of Wisconsin–Madison, organized by Melanie Manion, for their thoughtful comments and camaraderie every step of the way. This vibrant community of China scholars included Meina Cai, Dominic DeSapio, Timothy Hildebrandt, Brandon Lamson, Ning Leng, Ruoxi Li, Dalton Lin, Jinjie Liu, Naya Mukherji, Leah Rabin, Kristin Vekasi, Samantha Vortherms, and Cai (Vera) Zuo.

The research and writing of this book benefited from substantial financial support from Amherst College, the Chiang Ching-Kuo Foundation, the Department of Education's Foreign Language and Area Studies Fellowship program, a National Science Foundation Doctoral Dissertation Research Improvement Grant, and a Harvard–Yenching Library Travel Grant, as well as the Department of Political Science Summer Initiative and the Vilas Travel Grant program at the University of Wisconsin–Madison.

I am incredibly grateful for the generosity of my Chinese colleagues, research assistants, interviewees, and friends in supporting this project. Special thanks go to Gordon Liu at Peking University, whose tenacity is both infectious and inspirational. Without his continued support and encouragement, the obstacles to conducting this type of research may have been insurmountable.

I thank Dominic DeSapio, Siqing Liu, Alice Yang, and Yichi Zhang for assistance with data collection. I thank Andy Anderson for support with ArcGIS. Many thanks go to Kelly Dagan for her exceptional library and research support at Amherst College.

A number of other friends and colleagues greatly contributed to this project through their intellectual and emotional support. I would like to thank Adam Auerbach, Ryan Biava, Jess Clayton, José Luis Enríquez Chiñas, Lacy Ferrell, Kyle Hanniman, Rachel Jacobs, Yujin Kim, Brett Kyle, David Nelson, Geraldine O'Mahony, Saemyi Park, Jennifer Petersen, Marc Ratkovic, Camilla Reuterswaerd, and Emily Sellars.

I am grateful to the Amherst College Political Science Department for creating such a vibrant and supportive intellectual environment. Many thanks to my incredible colleagues Amrita Basu, Kristin Bumiller, Javier Corrales, Tom Dumm, Jared Loggins, Pavel Machala,

Eleonora Mattiacci, Jonathan Obert, Ruxandra Paul, Austin Sarat, William Taubman, Ronald Tiersky, and Princess Williams. I am especially thankful for the brilliant Vanessa Fong, who was willing to entertain multiple conversations about the book and offer feedback on sections of the manuscript.

This book benefited from feedback at a book manuscript workshop supported by Amherst College. I am greatly indebted to Nara Dillon, Mark Frazier, and Prerna Singh for their thoughtful feedback and to Amrita Basu for helping me navigate the workshop and revision process.

I am thankful for comments and feedback from many other generous scholars including Rikhil Bhavnani, Carla Freeman, Mary Gallagher, Krista Gile, Justin Gross, Mary Alice Haddad, Alex Jingwei He, Xian Huang, Lauren McCarthy, Andrew Mertha, Jessica Pearlman, Dorothy Solinger, Jessica Teets, Ezra Vogel, David Weimer, Yuhua Wang, and Joseph Wong.

Special appreciation goes to Theresa Laizer and Steve Laizer for their unparalleled administrative support to our department.

I thank Tami Parr and Elena Abbott for copyediting, as well as Cambridge University Press editors Robert Dreesen and John Haslam and two anonymous reviewers for their exceptionally thoughtful and constructive comments. Many thanks to Wade Guyitt for outstanding copyediting and to the production team at Cambridge University Press.

This research would not have been possible without my collaborator, Leah Rabin, and her exceptionally supportive and patient husband, Zach.

While many people contributed to this book, I alone am responsible for any errors or inaccuracies.

Thanks also go to my friends, colleagues, and students at Teda International School in Binhai, Tianjin. Because of them, my extended fieldwork in China was far more entertaining than it might have been.

I am also very lucky to have wonderful friends who were willing to either listen to the latest trials and tribulations of research or take my mind off them, as necessary. Special thanks go to Meredith Carey and Sarah Cheeseman Barthel, for whom time zones are no barrier.

This project would not have been possible without the support of my mom, Maureen Ratigan, and my grandparents, Ray and Grace Ratigan, who all worked tremendously hard so that my generation could pursue our passions. I am incredibly grateful for my mom's love and support during this long process.

I am deeply grateful for my loving husband and children. Kurt Marchl and our children, Benjamin and Finley, have had unwavering faith in me. Kurt's contributions to this project ranged from emotional to intellectual to logistical. Finley and Ben were always willing to offer lots of hugs and opportunities to learn about giant squids and outer space. I appreciate our kittens, Eartha and Spot, whose antics have provided crucial entertainment in the final stages of the project, especially amid a pandemic. A key collaborator on this project, who nearly survived the entirety of the process, from graduate school to book, was our unusually cosmopolitan cat, Dusty (2006–20). Had she been alive to see the book in hard copy, she surely would have sat on it.

# 1 Introduction

By early 2020, the significance of local government had become tragically apparent as the world was on the cusp of the COVID-19 pandemic. Local officials in Wuhan had suppressed reports from doctors regarding human-to-human transmission of a respiratory illness, allowing the virus to spread. The delays in recognizing human-to-human transmission of the novel coronavirus cost lives. After acknowledging the outbreak, the Chinese Communist Party (CCP) marshalled significant resources to support healthcare workers in Wuhan and other affected areas. Nonetheless, Wuhan had begun the pandemic at a disadvantage, with a hospital system that was already strained by a difficult flu season. If SARS-CoV-2 had first appeared in a Chinese city with local officials who placed expertise over politics, might the outcome have differed?

China is governed by a Leninist-style party-state with a hierarchical structure and a strong central government. Thus, we might assume that the omnipresent Chinese party-state would have a homogenizing effect on policy implementation on the ground. By this logic, local officials would be interchangeable cogs in the machine; we would expect a similar response to warnings about an infectious disease in Wuhan or Shanghai or Lanzhou. Although we cannot know if local officials in another city would have responded differently to the novel coronavirus, my research suggests that there is significant variation in how local officials behave in China's various regions, which could have implications for response to a crisis like the COVID-19 pandemic.

When I conducted interviews on healthcare in rural China from 2009 to 2012, acute differences emerged in how policies are interpreted and implemented. I consistently asked county officials for mundane information about local health policy, such as reimbursement rates for rural health insurance. In one province, officials would readily supply the information, proudly declaring that it was publicly available (*gongkaide* 公开的) on their website (and it usually was). In another province, officials would provide basic information, but, when pressed for more detail, they would prevaricate (e.g., *buhaoshuo* 不好说) or say that they would send me the specifics via e-mail (and they never did). And in a third province, officials would claim that the same information was classified (*baomide* 保密的) and refuse to divulge anything of substance, while regurgitating central government rhetoric. I observed variation not only in how forthcoming local officials were but also in how most policies were implemented. As other scholars have noted, during the Hu Jintao government of 2002–12, policy implementation was highly decentralized. The central government would set out broad national strategy, but there was substantial room for local government to interpret national priorities and policies at the implementation stage.

This book explains how local politics can undermine central policy by showing how Chinese provinces govern differently, as well as the consequences of these differences for social policy. In the first wave of economic reforms, the central government selectively granted coastal localities access to the global economy, and reformer Deng Xiaoping signaled acceptance of inequality by declaring: "let some get rich first."[1] These coastal provinces gained not only wealth but also greater autonomy vis-à-vis the central government. Concurrently, all provinces were tasked with funding and implementing social policy amid hard budgetary constraints. Distinct forms of governing emerged. Coastal provinces were forced to rely on locally generated revenue to fund social policy. Luckily for the coast, their coffers were relatively full, and their early exposure to foreign investors had encouraged the development of relatively functional governing institutions. Thus, coastal provinces developed a *pragmatic* policy style, which fostered innovation and professionalism in policymaking.[2] Because pragmatic provinces were self-funding many social policies, they were also more likely than others to shape central policies according to their local interests and to further decentralize policy implementation to counties and cities. As a result, they sometimes subverted the center's goals. By contrast, poorer inland provinces eventually received earmarked fiscal transfers from the central government for social policy, which reinforced a top-down governing style that I refer to as *paternalist*.

As an authoritarian party-state, China is often portrayed as monolithic. In this book, however, I show that approaches to governing in Chinese

[1] In 1978, in his speech at the closing session of the Central Party Work Conference prior to the Third Plenum of the Eleventh Party Congress, Deng Xiaoping stated: "In economic policy, I think we should allow some regions and enterprises and some workers and peasants to earn more and enjoy more benefits sooner than others, in accordance with their hard work and greater contributions to society." (Deng, Xiaoping, "Emancipate the Mind, Seek Truth from Facts and Unite as One in Looking to the Future," Selected Works of Deng Xiaoping, 1975–1982, Beijing: Foreign Languages Press, 151–163, 163.) Deng expressed a similar sentiment in subsequent speeches.

[2] Only one inland province is classified as pragmatist: Chongqing. All other pragmatist provinces are coastal. On provincial policy styles, see Chapter 3.

provinces – each of which is as populous as a European nation – can vary as widely as governance in different countries. While previous research has demonstrated the significance of decentralization in reform-era China, none has provided a framework for understanding the specific ways that provincial governing styles differ or the implications of these differences for social policy. Ultimately, understanding the prevailing governance styles among Chinese provinces sheds light on both the resilience of the Chinese Communist Party (CCP) at the national level and the uneven provision of social welfare at the local level.

In the following chapters, I use a "policy-style framework" to show how pragmatic and paternalist approaches to governing have influenced and shaped social policy implementation in China. While focusing on healthcare, I also utilize illustrative examples from other types of social policy – by which I am referring to the laws, regulations, and programs that the Chinese party-state implements (or claims to implement) to address problems related to health, education, poverty, and housing. Although nonstate actors may be involved in policy implementation and, occasionally, in the creation of new programs, the predominant actor in China's social policy is the party-state. Thus, I focus on state-led action in this book. Where appropriate, I acknowledge the role (or lack thereof) that nonstate actors play in the policy process.

Throughout, I discuss different levels of the Chinese party-state. I use the term "subnational" to refer to any level of government below the central government, including the village committee (which occupies a liminal position vis-à-vis the party-state because it is not officially part of the government). I use the term "provincial" government when referring to any of the thirty-one provinces or province-level cities in China.[3] I use the term "local" or "locality" to refer to any level of government below the province (cities, municipalities,[4] counties, townships, districts, and villages). Figure 1.1 provides an overview of the levels of government in China and their competencies regarding social policy. I also discuss "fiscal transfers" in this book, a term referring to funds that a higher level of government sends to a lower level of government (e.g., the center to the province). These transfers are also sometimes called "conditional grants."[5] Here, I focus on fiscal transfers

[3] The four provincial-level cities administered by the central government are Beijing, Tianjin, Chongqing, and Shanghai.

[4] Municipalities, also sometimes translated as "prefectures" or "prefecture cities" (*dijishi* 地级市), constitute a relatively large administrative unit one level below the province. One municipality comprises counties, towns and townships, and villages in rural areas, or cities and districts in urban areas.

[5] World Bank and the Development Research Center of the State Council, the People's Republic of China, *Urban China: Toward Efficient, Inclusive, and Sustainable Urbanization* (Washington, DC: World Bank Group, 2014).

earmarked for implementing social policy, meaning that the funds have been designated for use for a specific policy or program.

## The Welfare State in Developing Countries

Social scientists have developed three major paradigms to explain why social policy differs across countries and over time: economic development strategy; levels of democracy and democratization; and relative strength of internal social forces. In the first case, Nita Rudra and others have argued that whether or not a country's strategy for economic development is export-driven can affect welfare state development.[6] This logic leads to classifying developing welfare regimes as either productive (using social policy to support economic growth) or protective (using social policy to protect vulnerable sectors of society). In regard to democratization, many developing countries have expanded or reformed their social welfare systems at the same time as their transition to democracy. In some cases, democratization can lead to new constituencies, which in turn may incentivize political parties to promote welfare expansion. Finally, strong internal social forces like workers' unions or doctors' professional associations often shape the timing and content of social policy expansion by putting pressure on political elites to advance specific interests. Yet most of the research related to all three of these paradigms focuses on the nation-state as the level of analysis, with little attention to subnational variation. While these theories have advanced our understanding of the variation in welfare states across developing countries, they provide few tools to explain subnational differences in social policy in a country with an authoritarian political system.

Gøsta Esping-Andersen's seminal "worlds of welfare" framework is a useful point of departure to understand welfare reform.[7] Esping-Andersen argues that there are three distinct approaches to social policy that reflect the economic and political conditions of a country: liberal (United States, Canada); corporatist (Germany, France); and social democratic (Sweden). This framework, however, relies on a state-centric model in which the majority of workers are employed in the formal sector. While Esping-Andersen's approach advanced our understanding of welfare regimes in developed countries, analysis of social policies in developing countries has required new models to capture how economic

[6] Nita Rudra, *Globalization and the Race to the Bottom in Developing Countries: Who Really Gets Hurt?* (New York: Cambridge University Press, 2008); Nita Rudra, "Globalization and the Decline of the Welfare State in Less-Developed Countries," *International Organization* 56, no. 2 (2002): 411–445.

[7] Gøsta Esping-Andersen, *The Three Worlds of Welfare Capitalism* (Princeton, NJ: Princeton University Press, 1990).

and political environments affect social policy. By definition, developing economies rely more heavily on the agricultural sector and the informal economy. In addition, state–society relations in these nations may be clientelistic or even predatory, often leaving nonstate, nonmarket actors – such as families and communities – to provide a social safety net. Ian Gough and Geof Wood advanced this research by differentiating between the welfare state regimes of developed countries and the systems observed in developing countries, the latter of which they classified into categories of informal security regimes and insecurity regimes.[8] Informal security regimes are characterized by uneven economic development, a weak state, and pervasive patron–client relations but with some state support for social policy at the community level. Insecurity regimes, by contrast, are characterized by predatory states with no commitment to social policy or stability, leaving most of the population vulnerable.

While Gough and Wood's typology advanced Esping-Andersen's research by distinguishing between social policy regimes in developed and developing states, further research has deepened our understanding of how social policy provision among developing countries has diverged. In 2005, Evelyne Huber and John D. Stephens classified Latin American countries based on whether their social policies were aimed at developing human capital, such as education, or protecting workers from the market, such as pensions and social insurance.[9] This distinction has been further developed by Rudra and, subsequently, Juliana Martínez Franzoni and Jennifer Pribble.[10]

Rudra groups developing states into three dominant types: productive, protective, and dual welfare states.[11] These three types are determined by the country's economic development strategy. In a productive regime, developing countries that pursue an export-oriented industrialization strategy tend to invest in social policy that will improve human capital (health and education) while keeping the cost of labor low in order to attract foreign investors and keep the costs of exports competitive (e.g., South Korea). By contrast, Rudra's protective welfare regimes emphasize

[8] Ian Gough and Geof Wood, *Insecurity and Welfare Regimes in Asia, Africa and Latin America: Social Policy in Development Contexts* (New York: Cambridge University Press, 2004).

[9] Evelyne Huber and John D. Stephens, "State Economic and Social Policy in Global Capitalism," in *A Handbook of Political Sociology: States, Civil Societies, and Globalization*, edited by Thomas Janoski et al. (New York: Cambridge University Press, 2005), 607–629.

[10] Juliana Martínez Franzoni, "Welfare Regimes in Latin America: Capturing Constellations of Markets, Families, and Policies," *Latin American Politics and Society* 50, no. 2 (2008): 67–100; Jennifer Pribble, "Worlds Apart: Social Policy Regimes in Latin America," *Studies in Comparative International Development* 46, no. 2 (November 2010): 191–216, https://doi.org/10.1007/s12116-010-9076-6; Rudra, *Globalization and the Race to the Bottom in Developing Countries*.

[11] Nita Rudra, "Welfare States in Developing Countries: Unique or Universal?" *Journal of Politics* 69, no. 2 (2007): 378–396.

shielding workers from market fluctuations by providing benefits such as subsidized housing, generous pensions, or ample unemployment insurance. Protective welfare regimes tend to develop this priority due to their state-led development strategy, such as attempting to replace imports with goods produced domestically through import substitution industrialization (ISI). Thus, developing countries systematically diverge in the development of welfare regimes that are themselves in large part a reflection of the economic development strategy pursued by leaders.

Martínez Franzoni expands on Rudra's work by incorporating a new category, nonstate familiarist, in order to capture those societies that rely mainly on the community for social support.[12] Additionally, Pribble argues that the process of industrialization has interacted with both the nature of marginalized groups' political incorporation and the proportion of ethnic and racial minorities to create four distinct social policy regimes in Latin America.[13]

While this research has advanced our understanding of social welfare regimes in developing countries, these frameworks do not explain local variation within one large developing country – especially in the context of China, where one political party dominates politics. In this book, I build on the insights of existing research and provide a new approach for examining subnational variation in social policy implementation. Previous research often emphasizes the role of multiple political parties, but China is ruled by a single party. In Rudra's typology, moreover, countries where the state sector plays a crucial role in the economy tend to develop protective welfare systems. Yet while state-owned enterprises are nearly ubiquitous in China, not all Chinese provinces exhibit protectivist tendencies. Thus, I have developed an original measure to capture differences in Chinese provinces' approaches to governing to shed light on local differences in social policy.

As research on developing welfare states has evolved, so have the research subjects – the countries themselves. Social policy reform, particularly the phenomenon of welfare state expansion in developing countries, is often linked to processes of democracy and democratization. From a cross-national perspective, democracies are more likely to expand social policy than nondemocracies.[14] In the case of more recent democracies, the transition away from authoritarianism can provoke social policy expansion. As the process of democratization enfranchises new constituencies and provides space for the

12 Martínez Franzoni, "Welfare Regimes in Latin America."

13 Pribble, "Worlds Apart."

14 Stephan Haggard and Robert R. Kaufman, *Development, Democracy, and Welfare States: Latin America, East Asia, and Eastern Europe* (Princeton, NJ: Princeton University Press, 2008).

inclusion of new societal actors in policymaking, political elites may expand social welfare benefits as a strategy to garner support with key groups, as was the case in South Korea and Taiwan.[15] Not all democratic transitions facilitate social welfare expansion, however. Some Latin American countries faced seemingly insurmountable obstacles to expanding social policy programs after democratization, including the dominance of an austere economic paradigm and the institutionalization of former authoritarians' political power. These obstacles were overcome by encompassing major societal actors' peak associations in cases such as Chile, but not in Brazil, where fragmentation among key actors prevented cohesive reform.[16]

The degree to which a country incorporates the needs of social forces such as workers' unions and medical lobbies impacts the timing, nature, and effectiveness of social policy reform and implementation. On the one hand, previous research contends that the presence of strong left-wing parties will facilitate welfare expansion because their political platforms tend to emphasize a strong social safety net. On the other hand, excessive veto players, such as powerful industries who may oppose increased taxes, can stymie attempts at expanding social policy. For example, Stephen J. Kay demonstrates how the interactions between institutions and interest groups can explain variation in social security privatization in South America. While the Argentine executive branch successfully dominated the process, resulting in full pension privatization, the Uruguayan anti-privatization coalition managed to utilize institutional features such as plebiscites to hold the government to a partial privatization. Brazil's labor-led coalition also blocked similar privatization efforts.[17]

Further research has shown that when the state includes social groups in the policymaking process, the resulting policies are more likely to effectively address societal grievances and improve the social safety net. Effective redistribution also hinges on whether the state can manage to maintain sufficient autonomy to implement policy without succumbing to clientelistic relationships. At one end of the spectrum, for example, Christina Ewig has found that the exclusion of social actors in the Peruvian reform process resulted in a "piecemeal" reform.[18] At the same time, Kurt Weyland argues that the previous capture of state

[15] Joseph Wong, *Healthy Democracies: Welfare Politics in Taiwan and South Korea* (Ithaca, NY: Cornell University Press, 2004).

[16] Kurt Weyland, "'Growth with Equity' in Chile's New Democracy?" *Latin American Research Review* 32, no. 1 (1997): 37–67.

[17] Stephen J. Kay, "Unexpected Privatizations: Politics and Social Security Reform in the Southern Cone," *Comparative Politics* 31, no. 4 (1999): 403–422.

[18] Christina Ewig, "Piecemeal but Innovative: Health Sector Reform in Peru," in *Crucial Needs, Weak Incentives: Social Sector Reform, Democratization, and Globalization in Latin*

agencies by societal groups prevented successful reform in Brazil.[19] Strong medical lobbies have also impeded redistributive policies in Latin America.[20] In Korea, Huck-ju Kwon observed that advocacy coalitions were instrumental in putting health reform on the agenda after democratization.[21]

The presence or absence of participation by vulnerable groups also has implications for social policy expansion. Pribble posits that variation in the degree of female participation in the labor force resulted in different levels of women's mobilization in Chile and Uruguay and, thus, divergent approaches to social policy.[22] In Chile, the dictatorship was able to suppress mobilization and social pressures around social policy, thereby further institutionalizing policies that maintain gender inequity. Moreover, the presence or absence of links between the state and society matter for the content of social policy. Marcus J. Kurtz, for example, argues that the state will generally opt for a social assistance model rather than a universality approach to social policy when there are not linkages connecting state actors to society.[23] Similarly, conditional cash transfer programs often constitute a politically viable, but minimal, approach to social policy because they require less significant spending. They also target the poor and are therefore less likely to be the target of political opposition.[24] As an unintended consequence in a democratic context, however, Judith Teichman has found that cash transfer programs may have mobilized civil society groups to advocate for more comprehensive programs.[25]

In broad terms, China lacks the type of interest groups and societal coalitions that would pressure the state for healthcare reform in

*America*, edited by Robert R. Kaufman and Joan M. Nelson (Baltimore, MD: Johns Hopkins University Press, 2004), 217–246.

19 Kurt Weyland, "From Leviathan to Gulliver? The Decline of the Developmental State in Brazil," *Governance* 11, no. 1 (1998): 51–75.

20 Joan Nelson, "The Politics of Health Sector Reform: Cross-National Comparisons," in *Crucial Needs, Weak Incentives: Social Sector Reform, Democratization, and Globalization in Latin America*, edited by Robert R. Kaufman and Joan M. Nelson (Baltimore, MD: Johns Hopkins University Press, 2004), 23–64; Kurt Weyland, *Democracy Without Equity: Failures of Reform in Brazil* (Pittsburgh, PA: University of Pittsburgh Press, 1996).

21 Huck-ju Kwon, "Advocacy Coalitions and Health Politics in Korea," *Social Policy and Administration* 41, no. 2 (2007): 148–161.

22 Jennifer Pribble, "Women and Welfare: The Politics of Coping with New Social Risks in Chile and Uruguay," *Latin American Research Review* 41, no. 2 (2006): 84–111.

23 Marcus J. Kurtz, "Understanding the Third World Welfare State after Neoliberalism: The Politics of Social Provision in Chile and Mexico," *Comparative Politics* 34, no. 3 (2002): 293–313.

24 Judith Teichman, "Redistributive Conflict and Social Policy in Latin America," *World Development* 36, no. 3 (2008): 446–460.

25 Ibid.

a democracy. Moreover, collective action is strongly discouraged and often met with repression.[26] In terms of possible lobbying groups, there is no strong autonomous medical association to affect policy, as the medical profession is controlled by the state.[27] Hospitals are still predominantly public, and hospital directors are appointed by the Communist Party. Like other developing states, China is affected by some of the factors identified by Rudra and others, but they exist in a nondemocratic institutional context. Uncertainty and vulnerability related to globalization are certainly salient issues in China. However, Rudra's "social reactions to the market" are filtered through Chinese political institutions.[28] There are channels for societal grievances to reach state actors, but they are neither transparent nor public.

In stark contrast to democratic contexts, Chinese villagers and other marginalized groups must traverse a political minefield to express their grievances. In the Hu Jintao era, dissent was channeled through myriad, sometimes diffuse, outlets, such as protests, the petition system, and investigative ("watchdog") journalism.[29] Nonetheless, social unrest may affect policy in China, as both central and subnational levels of government pay particular attention to protests, petitions, and sometimes even media reports as indicators of social "instability."[30] Through these informal channels, rural residents' grievances have, to some extent, been reflected in policy changes made by Beijing. Indeed, the central

[26] For a recent example of a violent clash between protesting villagers and local police, see James Pomfret, "Special Report: Freedom fizzles out in China's rebel town of Wukan," Reuters, February 28, 2010, www.reuters.com/article/2013/02/28/us-china-wukan-idUSBRE91R1J020130228, accessed May 27, 2013.

[27] Officially a "charity," the Chinese Medical Doctor Association (CMDA) was formed in 2002 but does not control licensing or have the capacity to mobilize doctors as an effective lobbying group. Xuebing Cao provides an excellent analysis of the CMDA's potential as an actor in health policy debates. See Xuebing Cao, "The Chinese Medical Doctor Association: A New Industrial Relations Actor in China's Health Services?" *Relations Industrielles* 66, no. 1 (2011): 74–97.

[28] Rudra, "Welfare States in Developing Countries," 381.

[29] Benjamin L. Liebman, "Watchdog or Demagogue? The Media in the Chinese Legal System," *Columbia Law Review* 105, no. 1 (2005): 1–157.

[30] Thomas P. Bernstein and Xiaobo Lü, *Taxation without Representation in Contemporary Rural China* (Cambridge: Cambridge University Press, 2003); Yasheng Huang, "Research Note: Administrative Monitoring in China," *China Quarterly* 143 (September 1995): 829–834; Isabelle Thireau and Linshan Hua, "One Law, Two Interpretations: Mobilizing the Labor Law in Arbitration Committees and in Letters and Visits Offices," in *Engaging the Law in China: State, Society, and Possibilities for Justice*, edited by Neil J. Diamant, Stanley B. Lubman, and Kevin J. O'Brien (Stanford, CA: Stanford University Press, 2005), 84–107; Yuezhi Zhao and Wusan Sun, "Public Opinion Supervision: Possibilities and Limits of the Media in Constraining Local Officials," in *Grassroots Political Reform in Contemporary China*, edited by Elizabeth J. Perry and Merle Goldman (Cambridge, MA: Harvard University Press, 2007), 300–324.

government was aware of concerns related to mounting inequality in the 1990s and put social welfare and healthcare on the agenda by the early 2000s.

The Hu Jintao government notably increased state investment and engagement with healthcare and other social policies, but the implementation of these policies was filtered through the realities of local government. As Xian Huang has found, local fiscal resources and social risk impact how local officials implement social health insurance.[31] As a result, central policies that seek to mitigate inequality can lead to significant local divergence in their implementation. This book expands on Huang's findings to examine how provinces may develop different approaches to social policy.

In addition to local resources and needs, the local sense of community can shape social policy provision. Lily L. Tsai, for example, examines how informal solidary groups, such as lineage or fraternal organizations, can encourage public goods provision, such as paved roads.[32] Tsai finds that solidary groups can hold village leaders accountable, resulting in improved governance relative to villages without these groups.[33] Similarly, Prerna Singh argues that regions in India with a sense of "subnational solidarity" are more likely to excel at providing public goods.[34] While other research has suggested that ethnic divisions can undermine public goods provision, Singh shows that local elites in some regions of India developed a strong shared identity of "subnationalism" that supported health and education. Juxtaposing Tsai and Singh's findings with the argument of this book, I speculate that solidarity in the community could mitigate the effects of policy style on local leader behavior, although such an interaction is beyond the scope of this study.

I build on the insights from Tsai and Singh but focus on the role of provincial politics in shaping social policy in a nondemocracy. I show that provincial policy styles help explain how uniform national policies are implemented very differently across China and, in extreme cases, even subverted by local leaders despite national targets. While Tsai focuses on the microfoundations of public goods provision,

[31] Xian Huang, "Four Worlds of Welfare: Understanding Subnational Variation in Chinese Social Health Insurance," *China Quarterly* 222 (June 2015): 449–474, https://doi.org/10.1017/S0305741015000399.

[32] Lily L. Tsai, *Accountability without Democracy: Solidary Groups and Public Goods Provision in Rural China*, Cambridge Studies in Comparative Politics (New York: Cambridge University Press, 2007).

[33] Ibid.

[34] Prerna Singh, *How Solidarity Works for Welfare: Subnationalism and Social Development in India*, Cambridge Studies in Comparative Politics (New York: Cambridge University Press, 2016).

acknowledging that solidary groups are distributed more or less randomly, my study moves the level of analysis up to examine how the provinces shape social policy provision. Singh advances our understanding of social policy by focusing on how shared local identity can facilitate health and education provision. By contrast, the policy-style framework used in this book reveals some of the structural features that can shape leaders' behavior and cultivate enduring habits despite the strength of local solidarity.

Through a policy-style framework, this book unpacks how national policies are shaped, and sometimes distorted, by local government. It builds on the cross-national research seeking to classify welfare regimes as well as those that explain welfare expansion. I show how pragmatist provinces are more likely to leave space for their localities to shape central policy, sometimes by innovating and sometimes by subverting central directives. By contrast, paternalist provinces are more likely to implement social policy in alignment with central guidelines, although these provinces may suffer from corruption and other deleterious effects on policy implementation. Furthermore, pragmatist provinces tend to prioritize universal policies such as healthcare and education, while paternalist provinces tend to prioritize targeted policies such as poverty alleviation and housing. In these ways, provincial politics lead to a collection of welfare states in China rather than one cohesive welfare regime.

## The State and Social Policy in China

By the founding of the People's Republic of China in 1949, the overall well-being of the population was abysmal by any measure, and social welfare institutions were in shambles due to the tumult of the early twentieth century. In the second half of the twentieth century, the role of the state in social policy provision fluctuated with the vicissitudes of Chinese politics. After establishing the People's Republic of China in 1949, the CCP reconstituted many of the prewar social policy institutions that had been devastated by China's civil war and war with Japan, and it made some important innovations.[35] For example, the government established public health campaigns that dramatically improved

[35] AnElissa Lucas, *Chinese Medical Modernization: Comparative Policy Continuities, 1930–1980s* (New York: Praeger, 1982); Ka-che Yip, *Health and National Reconstruction in Nationalist China: The Development of Modern Health Services, 1928–1937*, Monograph and Occasional Paper Series 50 (Ann Arbor, MI: Association for Asian Studies, 1995).

hygiene, reducing the incidence of preventable illness. However, the gains of the early 1950s proved difficult to sustain amid the subsequent political oscillations of the Maoist period, including Mao's aversion to technical expertise, the famine caused by the Great Leap Forward, and the political fervor of the Cultural Revolution. Moreover, the CCP funded social policy regressively, favoring a small minority of cadres and urban employees in the state sector, thereby creating a stratified social welfare system.[36]

Yet in the early 1950s, the new regime did make major gains in a variety of sectors. For example, the health of the population improved significantly, not just because of the stabilization of the country and the end of civil war but also because the CCP instituted basic healthcare, such as vaccination programs. The CCP also improved health through heavy-handed political campaigns that mobilized the masses to eradicate illnesses plaguing the population, such as schistosomiasis. This emphasis on primary health and hygiene served as inspiration for developing countries internationally.[37] In education, the new regime emphasized the importance of basic literacy for the whole population. To this end, the CCP created a simplified version of Chinese characters to facilitate literacy (*jiantizi* 简体字) and standardized the Romanization of the ideographic language with *pinyin* (拼音). Regarding poverty alleviation, the communist regime privileged urban workers in state-owned enterprises (SOEs). These coveted positions were available to only a small minority of the population, but they came with a so-called "iron rice bowl": a robust basket of benefits including larger food rations, improved schooling for children, improved housing, and pensions. The CCP focused social welfare benefits on the elite: urban SOE employees and cadres (party members with an official government position). As a result, many social policy programs were exceptionally regressive, even during the Maoist period. For example, health spending for cadres in the early 1950s comprised an estimated 19–25 percent of all health spending, although cadres accounted for less than 2 percent of the population.[38]

By contrast, although they comprised the majority of the population, farmers did not have access to these benefits. In rural areas, the party-state

[36] Nara Dillon, *Radical Inequalities: China's Revolutionary Welfare State in Comparative Perspective*, Harvard East Asian Monographs 383 (Cambridge, MA: Harvard University Asia Center, 2015).

[37] Vojin Djukanovic and Edward P. Mach, eds., *Alternative Approaches to Meeting Basic Health Needs in Developing Countries: A Joint UNICEF/WHO Study* (Geneva: World Health Organization, 1975), 49.

[38] Bizhao Zhen, *Population and Health Policy in the People's Republic of China*, Occasional Monograph Series 9 (Washington, DC: Interdisciplinary Communications Program, Smithsonian Institution, 1976), 24.

socialized agriculture by the late 1950s. Farmers were grouped into larger and larger collectives that culminated in communes of thousands of households working to satisfy central agricultural targets, often without success. Farmers did not receive individual remuneration, since the commune was expected to provide food and social welfare for its members. The commune system produced variable results, especially since communes typically received inadequate support from the central government and lacked expertise to provide services such as healthcare for their members.

Paramount leader Deng Xiaoping opted for a pragmatic approach to policymaking during the economic reform period beginning in 1978. Deng prioritized economic growth over ideology, advocating gradualism and a do-whatever-works strategy. He signaled this shift away from ideology through a well-known proverb: "It does not matter if a cat is black or white, as long as it catches mice."[39] China's remarkable economic growth in this period has been touted as the most effective poverty reduction program in human history. Nonetheless, state retrenchment in social policy meant that inequality rose dramatically, access to adequate education became highly variable, and healthcare became unaffordable and inaccessible.[40] Subsequent efforts to expand social policy, such as pension reform, also resulted in heightened inequality.[41]

China's current welfare system consists of some policies that are universally accessible and others that are targeted and means-tested. About 90 percent of children attend public schools, and most prestigious universities are public.[42] Over 90 percent of rural residents and 77 percent of urban residents participate in a state-subsidized health insurance plan, and key healthcare providers are state-run.[43] By contrast, access to poverty alleviation through the Minimum Livelihood Guarantee (MLG)

[39] Deng Xiaoping, *Selected Works of Deng Xiaoping (1938–1965)*, trans. by the Bureau for the Compilation and Translation of Works of Marx, Engels, Lenin, and Stalin Under the Central Committee of the Communist Party of China (Beijing: Foreign Language Press, 1992), 293. The original translation from Deng's 1962 speech "Restore Agricultural Production" reads: "'It does not matter if it is a yellow cat or a black cat, as long as it catches mice." I use the more common translation of "black or white."

[40] Jane Duckett, *The Chinese State's Retreat from Health: Policy and the Politics of Retrenchment* (New York: Routledge, 2010).

[41] Mark W. Frazier, *Socialist Insecurity: Pensions and the Politics of Uneven Development in China* (Ithaca, NY: Cornell University Press, 2010).

[42] William C. Smith and Devin K. Joshi, "Public vs. Private Schooling as a Route to Universal Basic Education: A Comparison of China and India," *International Journal of Educational Development* 46 (January 2016): 153–165, https://doi.org/10.1016/j.ijedudev.2015.11.016.

[43] Min Su et al., "Comparing the Effects of China's Three Basic Health Insurance Schemes on the Equity of Health-Related Quality of Life: Using the Method of Coarsened Exact Matching," *Health and Quality of Life Outcomes* 16, no. 1 (March 2018): 41, https://doi.org/10.1186/s12955-018-0868-0.

and affordable housing programs is conditional on means testing and targeted at the poorest members of society.[44] Thus, poverty alleviation and housing policy are highly redistributive, whereas education and healthcare are not.

Two features of the Chinese institutional context shape citizens' access to social policy in China: the residence permit system and decentralization. Since the founding of the People's Republic, social welfare has been segregated between urban and rural residents through a system of residence permits, or the *hukou* (户口). Each citizen is issued a *hukou* at birth and can only access social services in their official place of residence, which is determined by their parents' *hukou*.[45] Moreover, it is very difficult to change one's *hukou*, particularly to move to coveted, top-tier cities like Beijing or Shanghai. Reforms to the *hukou* system were underway as of the writing of this book, but these residence permits restricted mobility in a meaningful way in the early 2000s.

The second feature that shapes citizens' access to social policy is that, since the reform era, social policy provision has been highly decentralized. While the central government sets broad policy priorities, local governments are responsible for implementation and about 70–80 percent of the funding.[46] This decentralized structure results in widely divergent policy outcomes in health, education, and welfare. Despite observed subnational variation in social policy provision in China and beyond, subnational analysis of social policy continues to be an emergent and overdue line of inquiry.

## Decentralization with Chinese Characteristics

Despite its current Leninist-style party-state, China actually became more decentralized over the reform period until the mid-2010s. This

[44] Note: the MLG translates as *zuidibaoshenghuobaozhang* (最低生活保障) and is commonly known as *dibao* (低保). Youqin Huang, "Low-Income Housing in Chinese Cities: Policies and Practices," *China Quarterly* 212 (December 2012): 941–964, https://doi.org/10.1017/S0305741012001270; Dorothy J. Solinger and Yiyang Hu, "Welfare, Wealth, and Poverty in Urban China: The Dibao and Its Differential Disbursement," *China Quarterly* 211 (September 2012): 741–764.

[45] Kam Wing Chan, "The Household Registration System and Migrant Labor in China: Notes on a Debate," *Population and Development Review* 36, no. 2 (June 2010): 357–364, https://doi.org/10.2307/25699064; Kam Wing Chan, "The Chinese Hukou System at 50," *Eurasian Geography and Economics* 50, no. 2 (2009): 197–221; Kam Wing Chan and Will Buckingham, "Is China Abolishing the Hukou System?" *China Quarterly* 195 (September 2008): 582–606.

[46] Christine Wong, "Fiscal Reform: Paying for the Harmonious Society," *China Economic Quarterly* (June 2010), 20–25; World Bank, *China National Development and Sub-National Finance: A Review of Provincial Expenditures* (April 9, 2002), http://documents1.worldbank.org/curated/en/111911468240901599/pdf/multi0page.pdf.

decentralization is not a surprise. China has a long history of regionalism extending back as far as the dynastic period. Nonetheless, the relationship between the center and the provinces (or regions in earlier times) has been fraught with tension for centuries.[47] The center needs the provinces, as governing a territory as large and diverse as China would be unwieldy without officials on the ground with in-depth knowledge of local conditions. Likewise, the provinces need the center to coordinate tasks such as distributing state resources, maintaining security, and facilitating interprovincial trade and relations. Nonetheless, the center and provinces have different interests and time horizons, which can lead to tension. As Linda Chelan Li finds, the provinces use a variety of tactics to advance their interests, including bargaining for favorable policies, seeking exemptions from national policy, and implementing policies according to flexible interpretations of the center's intent.[48]

At first glance, a decentralized approach to governance might be unexpected in the context of an authoritarian regime with a strong central state. The observed subnational variation is less surprising, however, in the context of the personalistic, agency-based nature of Chinese politics. Rather than developing a consistent institutional structure that would constrain policymaking, Chinese leaders have opted for a "guerrilla" policy style inherited from the Maoist era.[49] This approach to policymaking includes an emphasis on experimentation and adaptability, in opposition to the constraints imposed by stable institutions. In terms of division of labor, the central leadership is responsible for grand strategy, while lower levels are charged with implementation. Ideally, this system offers the potential for local leaders to tailor policies to suit their community's needs.

Despite the hierarchical party-state, what Kenneth Lieberthal has described as China's "fragmented authoritarianism" provides multiple opportunities for subnational officials to advance their interests.[50] Many administrative decisions require support from varied state agencies,

[47] David S. G. Goodman and Gerald Segal, *China Deconstructs: Politics, Trade, and Regionalism* (New York: Routledge, 1994).

[48] Linda Chelan Li, *Centre and Provinces – China 1978–1993: Power as Non-Zero Sum*, Studies on Contemporary China (Oxford: Clarendon Press, 1998).

[49] Sebastian Heilmann and Elizabeth J. Perry, eds., *Mao's Invisible Hand: The Political Foundations of Adaptive Governance in China* (Cambridge, MA: Harvard University Asia Center, Harvard University Press, 2011).

[50] Kenneth G. Lieberthal, "The 'Fragmented Authoritarianism' Model and Its Limitations," in *Bureaucracy, Politics, and Decision Making in Post-Mao China*, edited by Kenneth G. Lieberthal and David M. Lampton (Berkeley: University of California Press, 1992), 1–25; Andrew Mertha, "'Fragmented Authoritarianism 2.0': Political Pluralization in the Chinese Policy Process," *China Quarterly* 200 (December 2009): 995–1012, https://doi.org/10.1017/S0305741009990592.

and the importance of ideological conformance was greatly reduced in the economic reform era.[51] These institutional changes engendered a flexibility within the party-state that provided an opening for subnational officials to assert themselves. As a result, Chinese provinces have become relatively powerful vis-à-vis the center – particularly as compared to other unitary systems – and the center has been unusually tolerant of localism.[52] Thus, the center often finds itself "playing to the provinces," to use Susan Shirk's apt phrasing.[53] Furthermore, as Mingxing Liu, Victor Shih, and Dong Zhang find, the CCP's Central Committee after the Cultural Revolution was largely composed of provincial leaders who fiercely advocated for their interests and achieved greater fiscal decentralization until central authorities increased their representation on this crucial body, balanced the power of the provinces, and instituted some centralizing policies.[54] Similarly, but at a more local level of analysis, David Bulman and Kyle Jaros show that cities benefit when local leaders hold concurrent positions in the provincial government.[55]

Previous research on decentralization focuses on individual leaders and whether local government can assert its autonomy vis-à-vis the center. This book builds on these insights to offer another perspective: provinces that were early movers in economic development have been able to generate their own revenue and, thus, have more autonomy in social policy implementation than provinces that depend on earmarked fiscal transfers to provide these services. As a result, provinces with locally generated revenue have developed a distinct way of governing, with implications for social policy provision.

China's form of decentralization differs from federalist democracies and from the Soviet Union, although the latter was also a Leninist party-state. First, the Chinese constitution does not empower provinces with the rights of states, as does a democratic federalist system. In China, the Communist Party supersedes all other interests, including provincial autonomy. Chinese provinces, for example, cannot litigate against China's central government. Second, Chinese local institutions take

[51] Lieberthal, "The 'Fragmented Authoritarianism' Model and Its Limitations"; Mertha, "Fragmented Authoritarianism 2.0."

[52] Heilmann and Perry, *Mao's Invisible Hand.*

[53] Susan L. Shirk, *The Political Logic of Economic Reform in China*, California Series on Social Choice and Political Economy 24 (Berkeley: University of California Press, 1993).

[54] Mingxing Liu, Victor Shih, and Dong Zhang, "The Fall of the Old Guards: Explaining Decentralization in China," *Studies in Comparative International Development* 53, no. 4 (December 2018): 379–403, https://doi.org/10.1007/s12116-018-9267-0.

[55] David J. Bulman and Kyle A. Jaros, "Leninism and Local Interests: How Cities in China Benefit from Concurrent Leadership Appointments," *Studies in Comparative International Development* 54, no. 2 (June 2019): 233–273, https://doi.org/10.1007/s12116-019-09279-0.

a multidivisional form (M-form) as compared to the unitary form (U-form) of the Soviet Union.[56] Derived from the study of corporations, the M-form describes an organizational structure in which each province is structured as a semi-autonomous unit with its own specialized offices, such as its own Departments of Commerce, Security, Education, Natural Resources, and others. By contrast, the Soviet Union was structured with a U-form of about sixty specialized ministries, such as Defense or Railroads, that were responsible for their policy portfolio throughout the country.[57] Eric Maskin, Yingyi Qian, and Chenggang Xu explain how the M-form enables competition between localities because each province has its own offices dedicated to various policy domains, whereas the accomplishments of the Ministry of Railroads in the U-form could hardly be compared to those of the Ministry of Foreign Economic Relations.[58] By some accounts, interprovincial competition then contributes to economic growth and entrepreneurship.[59] Third, although the M-form description advances our understanding of how institutions foster competition between provinces, it fails to capture the ways in which the Chinese central government interacted differently with coastal and inland provinces in the late reform era. Although all provinces generally have the same institutional structure, the degree of fiscal and political autonomy afforded them by the central government differs substantially, as will be discussed in the case study chapters.

Fragmented authoritarianism and powerful provinces have created a nation within which local politics vary tremendously from place to place. This variation necessarily shapes policy implementation. As a result, initiatives from the center can become significantly distorted or ignored when carried out on the ground. For example, we would expect that fiscal transfers and targeted poverty-alleviation policies would reduce inequality, but these efforts have yielded mixed results at best.[60] In fact, the provinces with the greatest reductions in inequality in the early 2000s were those that did not benefit from central support in these areas.

The provinces have significant autonomy in a broad array of policy areas. In the economic reform period, provincial authorities decided

56 Eric Maskin, Yingyi Qian, and Chenggang Xu, "Incentives, Information, and Organizational Form," *Review of Economic Studies* 67, no. 2 (2000): 359–378.

57 Ibid., 360.

58 Maskin, Qian, and Xu, "Incentives, Information, and Organizational Form."

59 Gabriella Montinola, Yingyi Qian, and Barry R. Weingast, "Federalism, Chinese Style: The Political Basis for Economic Success in China," *World Politics* 48, no. 1 (1996): 50–81.

60 Leslie McCall and Christine Percheski, "Income Inequality: New Trends and Research Directions," *Annual Review of Sociology* 26 (August 2010): 329–347, http://dx.doi.org/10.1146/annurev.soc.012809.102541.

how policies would be implemented, in contrast to the Maoist period, when localities within the provinces played a greater role.[61] Of course, they are much more constrained in politically sensitive policy areas, such as the draconian family planning policies that were relaxed in 2015. Nonetheless, provincial governments – and sometimes lower levels of government – have significant authority in deciding the details of how to implement policy in most cases. For example, a change in provincial leadership in Ningxia meant a change in the province's approach to education policy.[62]

Figure 1.1 provides a simplified depiction of the division of labor for Chinese levels of government in policy implementation. The central government determines national goals and broad strategy, as well as fiscal transfers from the center to the provinces or other forms of support. Provinces, including centrally administered municipalities, then determine how to implement national policy. Provincial governments may choose to take the lead in implementation by standardizing or regulating policy features, or the province may delegate the specifics to the localities. Localities may include prefectures, cities, counties, townships, or villages. There are, however, complexities that Figure 1.1 obscures for the sake of simplification and focusing on the dynamics of policy implementation. For example, provincial officials often bargain with the center to shape policy or receive exemptions to unfavorable regulations.[63] Mass unrest at the lowest level can also influence central policy.[64] Cities increasingly vie for power vis-à-vis the province, and there is substantial diversity in the role and power of the various subprovincial units.

As the CCP has been unusually tolerant of localism, Chinese provinces have developed distinct approaches to governing depending on local economic and political conditions. The provinces have exhibited both pragmatist and paternalist tendencies during and prior to the founding of the People's Republic of China, as will be discussed in the following chapters. As provinces gained greater relative autonomy in the economic reform period, they diverged in their dominant policy style. Provinces that opened up to the global economy earlier, in particular those along China's coast, developed a relatively *pragmatic* approach to governing. In pragmatic provinces, the provincial government delegates to local

[61] Joseph Fewsmith, "The Elusive Search for Effective Sub-County Governance," in *Mao's Invisible Hand: The Political Foundations of Adaptive Governance in China*, edited by Sebastian Heilmann and Elizabeth J. Perry (Cambridge, MA: Harvard University Asia Center, Harvard University Press, 2011), 297–320.

[62] Tingjin Lin, *The Politics of Financing Education in China* (London: Palgrave Macmillan, 2013), 72–73.

[63] Shirk, *The Political Logic of Economic Reform in China*.

[64] Bernstein and Lü, *Taxation without Representation in Contemporary Rural China*.

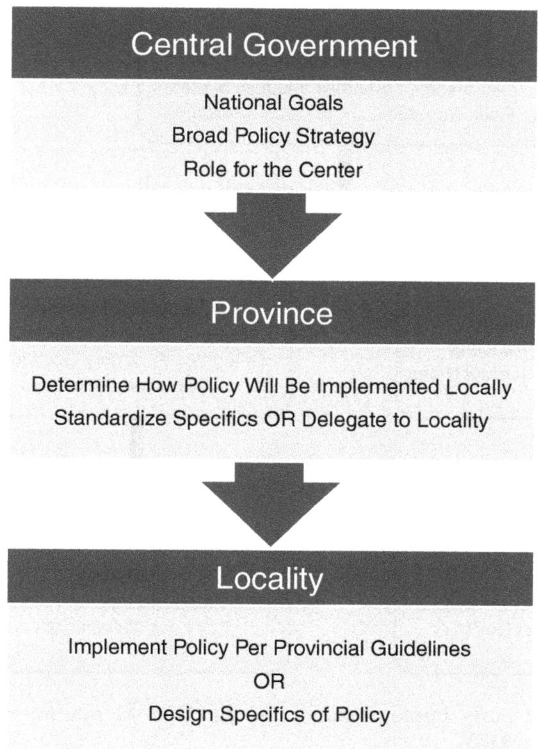


Figure 1.1 Levels of government in the Chinese party-state and policy implementation.

government, the private sector, and nonstate actors to implement social policies that support economic development. Provincial leaders task lower-level officials with social policy implementation, thereby allowing greater within-province variation. By contrast, provinces that are economically reliant on fiscal transfers from the central government for social policy exhibit a more restrictive policy style, taking a *paternalist* approach to the policy process. These provinces micromanage policy implementation and prioritize targeted social policy, such as poverty alleviation and housing, to appease restive groups. *Mixed* provinces exhibit elements of each of these two approaches.

The CCP's unusual brand of communism has allowed these distinct provincial policy styles to flourish or fester, depending on one's point of view. These governing styles impact policy implementation and can

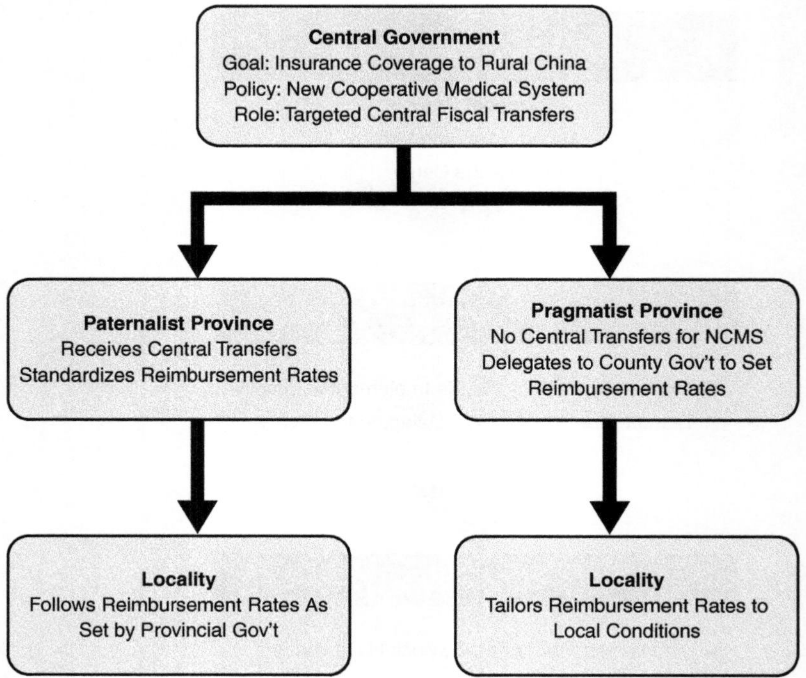


Figure 1.2 Early implementation of the New Cooperative Medical System (NCMS).

even have feedback effects for institutions. Local innovators may devise successful new policies that the center decides to spread nationwide.[65] But other subnational officials might pervert policy, divert fiscal transfers, or squander funds. Bad behavior among local cadres impedes good governance and can undermine the party-state as a whole.[66] Figure 1.2 shows how China's decentralized approach to policy implementation plays out using the example of the New Cooperative Medical System (NCMS), a government-subsidized rural insurance program that will be discussed in greater detail in the following chapters. After a pilot project stage, the central government set the goal of full insurance coverage

[65] Sebastian Heilmann, "Policy-Making through Experimentation: The Formation of a Distinctive Policy Process," in *Mao's Invisible Hand: The Political Foundations of Adaptive Governance in China*, edited by Sebastian Heilmann and Elizabeth J. Perry (Cambridge, MA: Harvard University Asia Center, Harvard University Press, 2011), 62–101.

[66] Fewsmith, "The Elusive Search for Effective Sub-County Governance."

for rural China through the establishment of the NCMS. The center provided earmarked funds for the program to central and western provinces, but not to the coast. As recipients of earmarked central transfers, paternalist provinces tended to standardize policy implementation within their borders. For the NCMS, they enacted provincial regulations to standardize the program's funding structure and establish consistent reimbursement rates for various services. Meanwhile, the pragmatist coastal provinces relied on funds from the province and county to fund the NCMS, and they often delegated the details of the NCMS implementation to county governments. Over time, the NCMS became more standardized nationwide, but the benefits offered to villagers differed significantly both across and within provinces for some time.

Several models seek to capture the relative power of the local state vis-à-vis the center in China to explain how and why the central state has retained significant power over time despite decentralization.[67] While the nature of Chinese decentralization and its implications for the power of the local state relative to the central state continue to be contested issues, scholars generally concur that certain competencies were devolved to the subnational level over the course of the reform period and that decentralization resulted in dramatic local variation in many different policy areas. Decentralization peaked during the Hu Jintao government, the period under study in this book. By 2012, President Xi Jinping began to reverse course and centralize power, although distinct policy styles have persisted.

China's decentralization has been identified as a cause of various phenomena ranging from economic growth to corruption to authoritarian resilience.[68] Some scholars argue that the central and local governments can each serve different and important functions. For example, Sebastian

[67] Vivienne Shue, *The Reach of the State: Sketches of the Chinese Body-Politic* (Stanford, CA: Stanford University Press, 1988); Le-Yin Zhang, "Chinese Central–Provincial Fiscal Relationships, Budgetary Decline and the Impact of the 1994 Fiscal Reform: An Evaluation," *China Quarterly* 157 (March 1999): 115–141; Jae Ho Chung, "Reappraising Central-Local Relations in Deng's China: Decentralization, Dilemmas of Control, and Diluted Effects of Reform," in *Remaking the Chinese State: Strategies, Society, and Security*, edited by Chien-min Chao and Bruce J. Dickson (New York: Routledge, 2001), 46–75; Andrew C. Mertha, "China's 'Soft' Centralization: Shifting Tiao/Kuai Authority Relations," *China Quarterly* 184 (December 2005): 791–810; Yumin Sheng, "Central-Provincial Relations at the CCP Central Committees: Institutions, Measurement and Empirical Trends, 1978–2002," *China Quarterly* 182 (June 2005): 338–355; Andrew H. Wedeman, *From Mao to Market: Rent Seeking, Local Protectionism, and Marketization in China* (New York: Cambridge University Press, 2003).

[68] Montinola, Qian, and Weingast, "Federalism, Chinese Style"; Hongbin Cai and Daniel Treisman, "State Corroding Federalism," *Journal of Public Economics* 88, no. 3–4 (March 2004): 819–843; Heilmann and Perry, *Mao's Invisible Hand*.

Heilmann finds that, while local governments devise innovative policy solutions, the center plays a crucial coordinating function in disseminating information about successful experiments so that they may spread to other areas of the country.[69] Similarly, Jessica C. Teets and her coauthors find that, in implementing water pollution policies, assigning some tasks to the center and some to the local government is most effective in reducing water pollution.[70] This book builds on this previous research on decentralization to examine how local politics shaped social policy implementation in China in the early 2000s.

In cross-national research, the dominant approach of using national means to conceptualize welfare regimes obscures significant variation and falsely implies the existence of an "average" or "typical" province. While a national-level analysis would paint China in shades of purple, metaphorically speaking, I argue that a closer look reveals red provinces and blue provinces. In China, average provincial spending on education is 16 percent of the provincial budget, social welfare and pensions is about 13 percent, and housing is about 3.5 percent. But no single province spends exactly in this way. Not one province exhibits this "average" behavior. Rather, as per central government directives, local authorities shape social policy priorities according to local conditions, resulting in significant variation in welfare provision. For example, wealthy coastal Zhejiang spends about 20 percent of its provincial budget on education, while Tibet spends only 11 percent. The sparsely populated northwestern Qinghai spends almost 9 percent of its provincial budget on subsidized housing, whereas the northeastern municipality of Tianjin – where housing costs are much higher – spends less than 1 percent. Moreover, beyond spending data, qualitative analysis of social policy reveals further unexplained variation. By examining subnational policy styles, this book reveals the implications of China's unusual approach to decentralization for social policy implementation on the ground.

## The Policy-Style Framework

How can we systematically analyze something as amorphous and multifaceted as the way a state governs? Moreover, how do we elucidate links between governance and policymaking? Cross-nationally, previous

[69] Sebastian Heilmann, "Policy Experimentation in China's Economic Rise," *Studies in Comparative International Development* 43, no. 1 (Spring 2008): 1–26, https://doi.org/10.1007/s12116-007-9014-4.

[70] Jessica C. Teets et al., "The Promise of 'Payment for Ecosystem Services': An Analysis of Watershed Eco-Compensation Policy Design in China," conference paper, Association of Chinese Political Studies (2018).

research suggests that political regime type and economic development strategy might be good candidates for explaining subnational variation. Within China, however, we observe ample variation in local social policy provision without corresponding differences in regime type or political party, as the Chinese Communist Party monopolizes political power. While distinct local economic strategies offer some clues to local social policy priorities, the predominance of state-owned enterprises in the economy weakens the explanatory power of economics alone.[71] Moreover, significant qualitative differences in policy implementation across localities requires attention to political factors as well.

To resolve this issue, I conceptualize the ways that provinces govern using a policy-style framework. I argue that distinct approaches to governing, conceptualized here as policy styles, lead Chinese provinces to emphasize some types of social policy over others and to implement policy in different ways. Comparing the different dimensions of provincial policy styles reveals patterns across provinces that impact policy implementation.[72] These patterns suggest that the subnational variation in China's social policy is not random, nor does it simply reflect local needs or access to resources. Rather, local political and fiscal circumstances lead the provinces to take different approaches to policymaking and social policy.

A policy style is a framework used to elucidate how those involved in the policymaking and implementation processes govern. In characterizing Chinese policy styles, I consider the following questions: Who makes policy decisions? How are those decisions made? Is the process inclusionary or exclusionary? How do formal and informal institutions constrain or support the policy process? How do norms about problem-solving shape policy implementation?

Insofar as they suggest a distinct and stable set of practices, one may conceive of policy styles as "standard operating procedures," following Jeremy Richardson and his coauthors' work on public policy in Europe.[73] While this analogy helps ground the concept, however, it may also mislead a student of Chinese politics. By design, standard operating procedures comprise a specific set of rules or procedures written down in detail to ensure conformity. In China, however, with few exceptions, formal rules and institutions constrain behavior about as well as a torn

71 Kerry Ratigan, "Disaggregating the Developing Welfare State: Provincial Social Policy Regimes in China," *World Development* 98 (October 2017): 467–484, https://doi.org/10.1016/j.worlddev.2017.05.010.

72 I use the term "policy process" to refer to any actions or decisions taken during the process of policymaking and throughout the process of implementation.

73 Jeremy Richardson, Gunnel Gustafsson, and Grant Jordan, "The Concept of Policy Style," in *Policy Styles in Western Europe*, edited by Jeremy Richardson (London: George Allen & Unwin, 1982), 1–16, 2.

net catches fish. Many of the habits of China's provincial policy styles reveal routinized norms of behavior that are not written down. In some instances, local officials in different provinces follow the same laws and regulations yet interpret policies quite differently. Therefore, we must go beyond an examination of formal institutions to discover the norms that shape actors' decisions throughout the policy process.

In this book, I focus on provincial policy styles in China during the Hu Jintao government: 2002–12. I speculate that provincial policy styles are likely to impact politics after 2012, as these governing practices may be somewhat path-dependent. According to Gary P. Freeman, the policy-style approach presupposes "persisting, systematic national differences in the way policy is debated, decided, and implemented. Anyone who has spent any extended time and effort comparing public policymaking in at least two countries can appreciate certain characteristic ways of doing things."[74] While Freeman is referring to cross-national research, one could make the same assertion about Chinese provinces regarding enduring habits of governing. A policy-style framework suggests that some provinces will deal with exogenous shocks differently than others.

Although policy-style frameworks typically appear in policy research on Europe and developed countries,[75] this approach resonates with the concept of *zuofeng* (作风), or "work style," found in Chinese political discourse.[76] Sebastian Heilmann and Elizabeth J. Perry brought the policy-style framework to China studies by arguing that, at the national level, the CCP has a "guerrilla" policy style characterized by adaptability.[77] By the end of the 1990s, Jiang Zemin, central leader from 1989 to 2003, explicitly criticized cadres for their work style. Jiang discussed their shortcomings in several communications, but the most notable was his October 2000 speech at the Fifth Plenary Session of the

[74] Gary P. Freeman, "National Styles and Policy Sectors: Explaining Structured Variation," *Journal of Public Policy* 5, no. 4 (1985): 471.

[75] Monica Battaglini and Olivier Giraud, "Policy Styles and the Swiss Executive Federalism: Comparing Diverging Styles of Cantonal Implementation of the Federal Law on Unemployment," *Swiss Political Science Review* 9, no. 1 (April 2003): 285–308, https://doi.org/10.1002/j.1662-6370.2003.tb00408.x; Jürgen Feick, "L'Analyse Comparative Des Politiques Publiques: Un Chemin Vers L'Intégration Des Résultats? [Comparative Analysis of Public Policy: A Path Towards Integrated Findings?]," *L'Année Sociologique* 40 (1990): 179–225; Freeman, "National Styles and Policy Sectors"; Michael Howlett and Evert Lindquist, "Policy Analysis and Governance: Analytical and Policy Styles in Canada," *Journal of Comparative Policy Analysis* 6, no. 3 (December 2004): 225–249; Berthold Rittberger and Jeremy Richardson, "Old Wine in New Bottles? The Commission and the Use of Environmental Policy Instruments," *Public Administration* 81, no. 3 (September 2003): 575–606, https://doi.org/10.1111/1467-9299.00362.

[76] Heilmann and Perry, *Mao's Invisible Hand*.

[77] Ibid.

Fifteenth Central Committee of the CCP, "On Improving the Party's Work Style" ("关于改进党的作风").[78] The CCP periodical *Qiu Shi* subsequently published an excerpt from this speech. Furthermore, at the Sixth Plenary Session of the Fifteenth Central Committee in 2001, the CCP published a decision with guidelines for cadres to improve their work style, with their recommendations closely following Jiang's speech.[79] Jiang maintained that a good work style would be crucial for modernization and for the party to maintain a positive "image" (形象) and a close relationship with the masses.

> Formalistic and bureaucratic work style is a scourge that is devastating our party. The entire party and nation must take strong measures against the bad tendencies of formalistic and bureaucratic work style. Cadres and leaders at every level should insist on being practical, speak the truth, do concrete things, seek practical results, and promote the work style of being earnest and down-to-earth. We should all follow the central party's guidelines and policies with determination [and] strive to innovate by integrating [central guidelines] with each of our work tasks. [We should worry about] what the masses worry about, be concerned with the difficulties the masses are facing, seek [to provide] what the masses need, concretely resolve urgent issues that threaten the stability of our reforms for development and the masses' life and work. We should establish our credibility among the masses through showing tangible actions in improving our work style.[80]

Notable themes in Jiang's speech include an emphasis on pragmatism, honesty, and achieving tangible results. While acknowledging the importance of central guidelines, Jiang also states that cadres should "innovate." He emphasizes the importance of cultivating a positive relationship with "the masses." Hu Jintao subsequently followed Jiang's lead in encouraging cadres to improve their work style.[81] Mao Zedong, Deng Xiaoping, and Xi Jinping have all also been quoted on work style.[82] Thus, a policy-style framework has the added benefit of resonating with discussions of work style in Chinese political discourse.

In my analysis, I identify three dimensions of policy styles to help us understand how local officials approach the policymaking process in

[78] "关于改进党的作风 ["On Improving the Party's Work Style]," www.cctv.com/special/733/-1/47004.html, accessed June 28, 2017.

[79] "中共中央关于加强和改进党的作风建设的决定(全文) [Decision of the CPC Central Committee on Strengthening and Improving the Party's Working Style (Full Text)]," www.people.com.cn/GB/shizheng/16/20011007/575835.html, accessed June 28, 2017.

[80] "关于改进党的作风 [On Improving the Party's Work Style]."

[81] See quotes under Hu Jintao headings at "开展群众路线教育 大力加强作风建设 [Carry out Mass Line Education and Strengthen Construction of Work Style]," accessed June 29, 2017, www.miit.gov.cn/n11293472/n11293877/n15329799/n15369909/index.html.

[82] "开展群众路线教育 大力加强作风建设 [Carry out Mass Line Education and Strengthen Construction of Work Style]."

Table 1.1 *Dimensions of policy styles*

| | Description |
|---|---|
| Local State Resources | Size of provincial budget<br>Capacity of local state<br>Relationship to central government |
| Institutional Approaches | Decentralized vs. standardized<br>Degree of attention to corruption<br>Degree of transparency |
| Patterns of Policymaking | Top-down vs. bottom-up in the policy process<br>Degree of innovation<br>Inclusion/exclusion of nonstate actors |

China. Table 1.1 summarizes these dimensions. First, "local state resources" refers to the size of the provincial budget and the human capital available to local government offices. Wealthier provinces have larger budgets and are more likely to find well-qualified professionals to work as public servants. Poorer provinces rely heavily on central-government transfers and have more difficulty finding talented staff. Moreover, when a poorer province relies on earmarked central transfers for social policy, local officials are more likely to be compelled to follow the "letter of the law" when implementing policy. Provinces that raise their own funds are more likely to creatively interpret or resist central policy since they are not completely beholden to central funds. Second, although all provinces have Communist Party institutions, their approach to the policy process differs substantially. Some provinces implement policy through provincial regulations, thereby standardizing the policy across the province. Other provinces allow lower levels of government, such as the city or county, to work out the details of policy implementation. For example, rural health insurance premiums and reimbursement rates were standardized by some provinces, whereas others allowed the county government to determine these rates. Provinces also differ in how they handle corruption and how transparent they are. Finally, local officials vary in their patterns of behavior in policymaking. Some provinces foster local government innovation and partner with nonstate actors in policy implementation, while others exhibit more exclusive habits of policymaking.

Although this book is about regional variation, we must keep in mind that formal institutions encourage conformity among local governments in China. Local actors must all work within the Chinese political system. The CCP's monopoly on political power has created formal institutions that affect policymaking across the country. The Communist Party governs through a system of parallel hierarchies in the government and party, with a government and party body at each level of the state. The CCP coordinates across this complex system through overlapping directorships: leaders often hold posts in both the party and the government, particularly at the highest levels of the state. Thus, the omnipresence of the Communist Party at each level reduces the ability of local states to maneuver independently, particularly in politically sensitive policy areas such as family planning.

Another pair of institutions constrains local actors: personnel management (*nomenklatura*) and the evaluation system for government officials (*ganbu kaohe* 干部考核). Higher levels of government determine the prospects for officials' advancement through detailed personnel files and a point-based evaluation system with specific targets for local government.[83] Although the CCP portrays the system as meritocratic, personal connections impact officials' career trajectories in addition to competency. Nevertheless, evaluation systems matter. Due to this hierarchical system of oversight, local policy rarely contradicts Beijing's broad strategy; at best, local officials may implement a creative interpretation of central policy. Instead, local government generally envelopes whichever policies are adopted at the local level in the current rhetoric from the center. In some respects, therefore, we may not observe as much variation in policy style across provinces as we do with cross-national comparisons. Nonetheless, while the central government determines broad strategy, local government decides many of the details of policy design and implementation, resulting in local variation that impacts the lives of many people.

The term "authoritarianism" has been used to describe a wide range of regimes. Scholars have sought to specify myriad types of authoritarianism and their impact on regime longevity. Yet the study of subnational variation within authoritarian regimes is rare.[84] My approach offers a means of examining how different governing tendencies exist within an authoritarian regime. The variants of authoritarianism, particularly in large countries with some degree of decentralization, can be better understood by disaggregating approaches to governance at the local level rather than

[83] Maria Edin, "Remaking the Communist Party-State: The Cadre Responsibility System at the Local Level in China," *China: An International Journal* 1, no. 1 (2003): 1–15; Melanie Manion, "The Cadre Management System, Post-Mao: The Appointment, Promotion, Transfer and Removal of Party and State Leaders," *China Quarterly* 102 (June 1985): 203–233.

[84] With the exception of China and some studies of Mexico under the Institutional Revolutionary Party (PRI).

focusing solely on the configuration of elites at the national level. Moreover, hybrid regimes and procedural democracies may exhibit some democratic institutions, while governing practices reveal authoritarian tendencies. Attention to the policy process at the subnational level can elucidate distinct authoritarian (or democratic) tendencies within a polity.

## Structure of the Book and Methodology

In this book, I explain how local approaches to governance shape social policy implementation in China, sometimes undermining the goals of central policy. This book presents an original conceptual framework with which to understand provincial governance styles. First, using data that I gathered on China's thirty-one provinces, I classify and characterize each province as primarily exhibiting one of three policy styles. I then explain the impact of local governance style through in-depth analyses of three provinces, with references to other provinces that exhibit similar tendencies. I reveal how different ways of governing shape the policy process in healthcare. I also provide illustrative examples of how these dynamics impact policy implementation in education, poverty alleviation, and housing. The analysis focuses on the Hu Jintao government (2002–12), when decentralization in policy implementation was in its heyday prior to Xi Jinping's recentralization of power. I draw on my fieldwork in five provinces, including a survey of over 1,000 villagers and village leaders, coupled with government documents and secondary research. I provide greater detail on research methods and challenges in two methodological appendices.

Chapter 2 discusses how central policy toward health policy has evolved from 1949 to the 2000s. This chapter focuses on the central state's approach to healthcare, but similar trends have been observed in other areas of social policy. I develop a framework of policy styles and illustrate how these styles operate to produce divergent social policy outcomes in Chapter 3. I operationalize these policy styles by examining variation in provincial-level political indicators. Political indicators include spending on the public security bureau, number of media outlets, number of registered nongovernmental organizations, number of corruption cases, and an original measure of fiscal transparency. I explain the metrics used to classify provinces by policy style briefly in the following chapter and in greater detail in Appendix A.

I use the province as the level of analysis for both principled and practical reasons. As noted, each Chinese province is a large unit, housing as great a population as a European country. The thirty-one provinces each also exhibit as much heterogeneity as different countries, a characteristic also found in other large, developing countries like India or Brazil. In China, many of the decisions regarding social policy allocations occur at the provincial level. The provincial government sets the tone for local government decision-making and how much autonomy these lower levels will have, such as whether localities have discretion over policy implementation. Provincial officials can act as filters for how central policy should be implemented within the province.[85] The role of lower government levels can be significant in shaping social policy, but the extent of their involvement in the policy process varies across provinces. In some cases, social policy may vary widely between cities in the same province, but the same policy may be more standardized across cities in a different province. The provincial government essentially acts as a gatekeeper for funding, as well, whether funds originate from the province itself or from the center. By focusing my analysis at the province level, I balance nuance and parsimony. There are thirty-one provinces but about 3,000 counties in China. Classifying counties as subnational welfare regimes would suggest that counties (or other smaller units) have more autonomy than the empirical evidence suggests.

I illustrate how these styles operate to produce divergent social policy outcomes through three in-depth cases studies in Chapters 4 through 6. Following John Gerring, I use case studies as "an intensive study of a single unit for the purpose of understanding a larger class of (similar) units."[86] I use site-intensive methods that balance breadth and depth to develop a theory of subnational authoritarianism.[87] As data on social policy implementation is not systematically available, I triangulate using official statistics, survey data, and semi-structured interviews.

The case studies chapters focus on Jiangsu (pragmatist), Yunnan (paternalist), and Hubei (mixed), respectively, with references to other provinces that exhibit similar tendencies. I purposefully chose three

[85] Wen-Hsuan Tsai and Nicola Dean characterize provincial party secretaries as the "linchpin" in a system of central–local relations and a crucial determinant of the whether the province pursues political reform. See Wen-Hsuan Tsai and Nicola Dean, "Experimentation under Hierarchy in Local Conditions: Cases of Political Reform in Guangdong and Sichuan, China," *China Quarterly* 218 (June 2014): 342. Susan Shirk also establishes the political power of the provinces. See Shirk, *The Political Logic of Economic Reform in China*.

[86] John Gerring, "What Is a Case Study and What Is It Good For?" *American Political Science Review* 98, no. 2 (May 2004): 342.

[87] Benjamin L. Read, "More Than an Interview, Less Than Sedaka: Studying Subtle and Hidden Politics with Site-Intensive Methods," in *Contemporary Chinese Politics: New Sources, Methods, and Field Strategies*, edited by Allen Carlson et al. (New York: Cambridge University Press, 2010), 145–161.

provinces that vary in their levels of economic development, given the importance of economic conditions in social policy implementation. For each case study, I examine the policy process in the areas of health, education, poverty alleviation, and housing. Analyzing *how* policies are implemented provides an important perspective on the impact of local governance and social policy. While tracing spending patterns and provincial-level quantitative metrics is valuable, complementing the quantitative analysis with qualitative evidence enables me to triangulate and get at the *how* and *why* of variation in social policy provision in a way that would be difficult to quantify.

The evidence for the case studies is comprised of qualitative and quantitative fieldwork, laws, regulations, other government documents, and secondary research. First, I conducted semi-structured interviews with local officials and villagers in Jiangsu, Hunan, and Gansu from 2009 to 2010. Then I conducted a survey of over 1,000 villagers and village leaders in 2012 in Jiangsu, Hubei, and Yunnan with Leah Rabin. I explain the methods used during fieldwork for semi-structured interviews and the collection of survey data in Appendix B.

Chapter 7 concludes the manuscript by examining the broader implications of provincial policy styles for our understanding of inequality, center–local relations, and Chinese politics, as well as for practitioners in the fields of development and social policy. I show how the logic of the argument can be applied to other political systems with decentralized social policy implementation, including the United States and the European Union. In these cases, a national (or supranational) state also seeks to advance social policy, but local politics shaping implementation on the ground often results in unintended consequences.

# 2 China's National Health System

## Ideological Oscillations and Incomplete Reform

Since 1949, the Chinese state's approach to administering healthcare policy has fluctuated with the vicissitudes of politics, oscillating between overall neglect and an instrumental use of healthcare to promote state legitimacy.[1] Due to the country's postwar stabilization and eventual economic growth, significant gains were made in healthcare outcomes, but the gains came largely in spite of central government policy rather than because of it. During the Maoist period, two main factors hindered the erstwhile Ministry of Health in improving health services: budget constraints; and political oscillations that reduced the ministry's independence, favoring political fervor over a technocratic approach to health policy. After Deng Xiaoping initiated market reforms in 1978, healthcare and social policy were subordinated to economic growth, effectively debilitating the Ministry of Health. As a result, local-level health facilities that had functioned intermittently during the Maoist period were undermined both financially and politically.

It was not until the late 1990s that local governments began working with researchers to experiment with new policies, laying the groundwork for future healthcare reform. However, central leadership was still lacking in terms of funding new policies and disseminating them nationwide. In 2003, the Hu–Wen administration responded to the crisis caused by severe acute respiratory syndrome (SARS) by putting public health on the national (and international) agenda and initiating a national health reform. This reform represented a compromise between various proposals from state and nonstate actors, seeking a middle path between state and market solutions. The timing and nature of this reform was contingent on changes in the policymaking process in post-Mao China.

Historical and political context is necessary to understand preexisting health systems and institutions, embedded interests in healthcare, and the expectations (or lack thereof) that villagers may have for healthcare based on their lived experiences and previous interactions with state health institutions. Accounts of contemporary healthcare reform and current

[1] For more on the pre-1949 legacy in health policy, see Lucas, *Chinese Medical Modernization*; Yip, *Health and National Reconstruction in Nationalist China*.

policy evaluations tend to ignore or misrepresent the reality of healthcare during the Maoist era, thereby failing to appreciate how historical context affects current reforms. Moreover, cursory examinations of post-Mao-era state retrenchment in healthcare exaggerate the importance of market reforms and the role of the SARS crisis while underestimating shifts in domestic elite politics, state–society relations, and international discourse regarding the role of the state in healthcare provision.

In this chapter, I examine how health policy evolved in China during the economic reform period. I start by briefly reviewing healthcare during the Maoist period (1949 to the 1970s), then delve deeper into health policy in the context of market reforms and state retrenchment (1980s to early 1990s), culminating in the state's reengagement with healthcare policy from the late 1990s to 2013 (including the ongoing reform initiated in 2009). Although this chapter focuses on healthcare, similar trends occurred in other areas of social policy during these periods.

## The Maoist Period: Ideology and Fragmentation

The healthcare system under Mao Zedong is often touted as having dramatically improved the health of Chinese people through its emphasis on providing access to basic healthcare for most of the population, but the reality was more complicated. Although life expectancy increased dramatically after the CCP's victory in 1949, most of the gains in population health should be attributed to the end of the civil war and the stabilization of the country rather than to policies initiated by the CCP. Nonetheless, the CCP took important steps for improving population health in the early 1950s. First, the new government reconstituted health systems with substantial investment in health infrastructure. The CCP also implemented hygiene campaigns that mitigated pervasive scourges such as schistosomiasis.[2] Indeed, if divorced from Mao's ideological fervor, some initiatives – such as the barefoot doctors and the CCP's emphasis on hygiene and prevention – can be seen as progressive and innovative for the time, as they provided inspiration for community-based medicine on the international stage.[3]

[2] Yushang Li, "The Elimination of Shistosomiasis in Jiaxing and Haining Counties, 1948–58: Public Health as Political Movement," in *Health and Hygiene in Chinese East Asia*, edited by Angela Leung Ki Che and Charlotte Furth (Durham, NC: Duke University Press, 2010), 204–227.

[3] See, for example, Djukanovic and Mach, *Alternative Approaches to Meeting Basic Health Needs in Developing Countries*. In this report, the case study touts China's emphasis on improving rural healthcare systems and concludes by saying that "the greatest lesson that China offers is that it can be done – that a nation can within one generation move from a starving, sickness-riddled, illiterate, elitist semi-feudal society to a vigorous, healthy,

Despite these gains, population health suffered due to the famine associated with the Great Leap Forward and the violence of the Cultural Revolution. Moreover, the repeated turmoil of the Maoist years left villages to maintain their own health facilities with little support from the central government. University closures due to the Cultural Revolution deprived the country of a generation of trained, professional physicians. Throughout the Maoist period, the Ministry of Health's emphasis on a scientific approach to medical education clashed with Mao's belief that ideological correctness and enthusiasm were more powerful than technical knowledge.[4]

The rhetoric of Mao-era China suggested that there was universal national healthcare: according to official documents, over 90 percent of villages were covered by the Cooperative Medical System in 1976.[5] The reality, however, was far more complicated. Maoist healthcare prioritized urban areas and the elite. To maintain cadre[6] loyalty, Mao and the central leadership offered a more generous social safety net to cadres and SOE employees, which led to regressive allocation of healthcare funds. Cadres accounted for less than 2 percent of the population, yet 19–25 percent of the national budget for healthcare was allocated to providing for their medical care in the 1950s.[7]

By contrast, rural communities were expected to fund their own health services through the principle of "self-reliance" (*zili gengsheng* 自力更生). Most communities were too poor to provide enough funds for healthcare, however. Historical accounts and my interviews with older villagers and village officials indicate that the original CMS did not provide villagers with meaningful healthcare. A district-level bureaucrat in Gansu province explained that the CMS began in Gansu in 1957, but it "existed in name only" (*mingcunshiwang* 名存实亡) after 1966 due to the Cultural Revolution and the absence of resources.[8] Healthcare infrastructure

productive, highly literate, mass participation society. If China can accomplish it, other nations can too" (p. 49).

4 Mao Zedong, *Chairman Mao Talks to the People: Talks and Letters, 1956–1971*, ed. Stuart R. Schram (New York: Pantheon Books, 1975), 232–233.

5 Chak Kwan Chan, King Lun Ngok, and David Phillips, *Social Policy in China: Development and Well-Being* (Bristol, UK: Policy Press, 2008), 116.

6 In this chapter, I use the term "cadre" (*ganbu* 干部) rather than "leader" or "official" to distinguish those who had a formal position within the state apparatus and therefore received significant benefits, such as healthcare, housing, education, and pensions. Since cadres played an important role during this time period in terms of both ideology and governance, I use this term throughout the chapter. Elsewhere in this book, I use the term "local official" or "leader" to refer to individuals who serve on the village committee or who have a post working for the state.

7 Zhen, *Population and Health Policy in the People's Republic of China*, 24.

8 Interview GS W58, June 29, 2010.

deteriorated across the nation throughout the 1960s and 1970s. In one account, Edward Friedman and his coauthors vividly describe the deterioration of a typical county hospital in a village in northern China: "Crowded and overworked, it became shabbier and ever less hygienic. Patients who were largely immobile were told to defecate on the floors of their rooms, after which the site was swept up but not sanitized. There was no disinfectant to scrub the floor."[9] Without proper funding or personnel, facilities established in the 1950s could not be maintained by local communities. With closed markets and rampant poverty, villages did not have the resources to obtain medical supplies or hire trained personnel. Despite communist rule, rural health systems were underdeveloped and underfunded even as China was on the cusp of its transition to a market economy.

## Market Reforms and State Retrenchment: 1979–1990s

*Crossing the river by feeling for the stones.*

Deng Xiaoping on using gradual experimentalism to guide economic reforms[10]

As China moved from the planned economy of the Mao era to a mixed state-capitalist economic system, state attention to healthcare and social policy waned. The central leadership concentrated almost exclusively on economic growth and championed a market-oriented approach to social policy. The central government reduced its relative contribution to healthcare even further, and local governments were incentivized to prioritize economic growth over social policy.[11] Coupled with reduced state financing and growing demand, perverse incentives led public hospitals to overprescribe new drugs and high-tech treatments with high profit margins. Meanwhile, societal response to these shifts was minimal. While workers engaged in "rightful resistance"[12] to pressure the state to fulfill its commitments regarding pensions, similar acts of protest against

[9] Edward Friedman, Paul G. Pickowicz, and Mark Selden, *Revolution, Resistance, and Reform in Village China* (New Haven, CT: Yale University Press, 2005), 135.

[10] This quote is a traditional folk saying that was first used by Chen Yun in policy discussions and later popularized by Deng Xiaoping to emphasize experimentation as a guiding principle of economic reforms, in contrast to Mao's ideological vision. See Henry Yuhuai He, *Dictionary of the Political Thought of the People's Republic of China* (Armonk, NY: M. E. Sharpe, 2001), 287.

[11] In addition, state funding for healthcare was still allocated regressively: in the 1990s, a former vice-minister estimated that 80 percent of the government healthcare budget was used for medical coverage for cadres, who comprised less than 1 percent of the population. See Yanzhong Huang, *Governing Health in Contemporary China* (New York: Routledge, 2013), 67.

[12] Kevin J. O'Brien and Lianjiang Li, *Rightful Resistance in Rural China* (New York: Cambridge University Press, 2006).

the lack of access to affordable healthcare did not materialize. The lack of protest could be intrinsic to healthcare: it is unusual for social movements to mobilize around health policy unless it has already been put on the agenda by political elites.[13] Moreover, population health had improved overall in China in the previous decades due to economic growth, and there would be a lag in the societal effects of retrenchment (Figures 2.1 and 2.2). Finally, for rural areas, the so-called socialized system privileging those in the state sector had been gravely flawed. Satisfaction with the old system was therefore not high, which reduced expectations for state healthcare provision.[14]

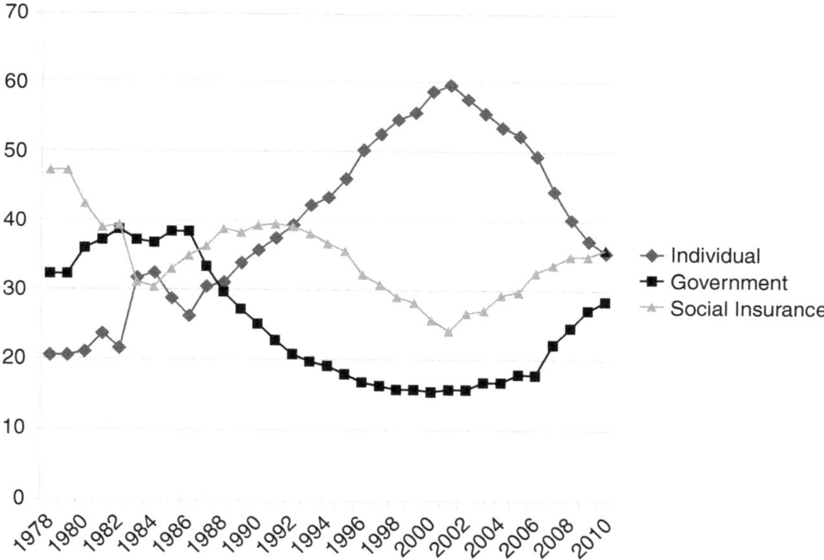


Figure 2.1 Individual, government, and social insurance contributions as a proportion of total health expenditures, 1978–2010.
Source: *Ministry of Health Statistical Yearbook*, 2010.

[13] Robert R. Kaufman and Joan M. Nelson, *Crucial Needs, Weak Incentives: Social Sector Reform, Democratization, and Globalization in Latin America* (Baltimore, MD: Johns Hopkins University Press, 2004).

[14] Kerry Ratigan, "Riding the Tiger of Performance Legitimacy? Chinese Villagers' Satisfaction with State Healthcare Provision," *International Political Science Review*, August 6, 2020, https://doi.org/10.1177/0192512120927482.

After Mao Zedong's death in 1976 and a brief power struggle among elites, Deng Xiaoping assumed control and initiated economic reforms. In the early 1980s, he began the process of opening the economy to foreign markets and investment, dismantling and reforming some SOEs, and further reducing the state's role in healthcare provision. This market-oriented approach to social policy was espoused by top leadership: according to Premier Zhao Ziyang, "the major reason why service industry and public institutions failed to develop well in the past was that we failed to treat them as enterprises, instead they were treated as a welfare undertaking, even charities; [therefore] whoever runs them will lose money, and there is no vitality at all."[15] In addition, the central government further reduced its contributions to health services in keeping with its new emphasis on economic development and a reduction in revenue until the 1994 tax reforms. Figure 2.1 depicts the change in health funding from the government, social insurance, and individuals as a proportion of total health expenditures from 1978 to 2010.

The 1994 tax reform and the fiscal structure of the Chinese state merit discussion, as the shift in resources from local government to central government impacted healthcare provision. From the start of economic reforms in 1978 until 1993, the share of revenue reaching the central government declined precipitously, and as a result the center found itself lacking resources for crucial functions. In response, the center instituted a major tax reform in 1994 that entailed four significant changes: the simplification and standardization of the tax system; the prohibition of local government-granted tax breaks; enhanced enforcement mechanisms; and a new system for allocating revenue to the central government or local government. To ensure more funds for the central government, the tax reform mandated specific tax revenue allocation strategies. Figure 2.2 shows the proportion of government revenue that was retained by the central government as compared to subnational governments, including provinces, cities, counties, and below. After 1994, the center kept a greater share of revenue, while local government was responsible for a greater share of expenditures (see Figure 2.3). Overall, the new system was relatively rule-based and institutionalized compared to the previous system, which often entailed bargaining between the center and local governments.[16] Local governments typically compensated for revenue shortfalls through "extra-budgetary" fees,

[15] Quoted in Huang, *Governing Health in Contemporary China*, 56.
[16] Shaoguang Wang, "China's 1994 Fiscal Reform: An Initial Assessment," *Asian Survey* 37, no. 9 (1997): 801–817, https://doi.org/10.2307/2645698.

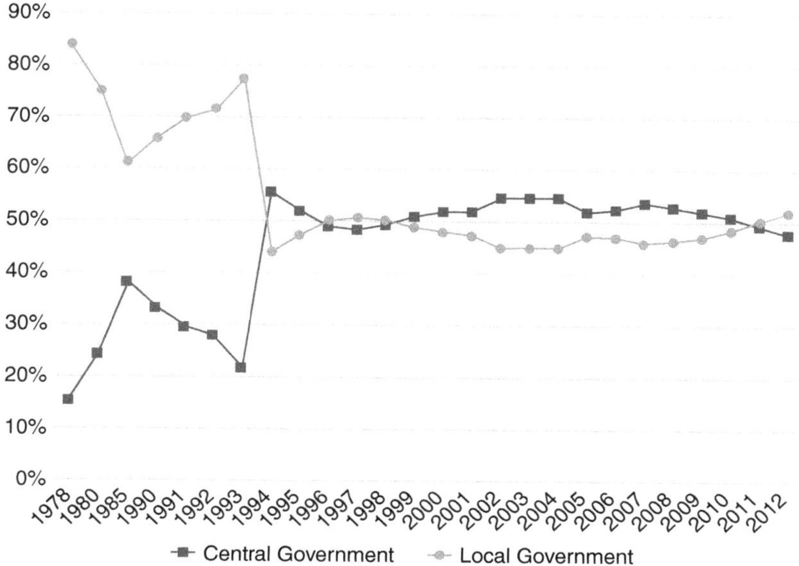


Figure 2.2 Proportion of revenue retained by central and subnational governments.
Source: *China Statistical Yearbook*, 2012 and 2013.

such as road maintenance fees, school fees, ad hoc fees for local projects, and the like.[17]

Nonetheless, the 1994 tax reform exacerbated the fiscal squeeze faced by local government. Figure 2.3 shows how the relative burden of expenditures shifted toward local government in the 1990s and throughout the early 2000s. Although revenue was split roughly equally between the center and local governments from the mid-1990s onward (Figure 2.2), local government took on an increasing share of the expenses of governing. The resulting tight local government budgets forced local officials to make difficult decisions regarding which programs would be funded and which would be neglected.

As the central government devolved social policy funding and implementation to local government in the 1990s, it also established economic growth as the top policy priority. Because the center evaluated local officials for promotion based on local economic growth rather than social

[17] Zhang, "Chinese Central–Provincial Fiscal Relationships, Budgetary Decline and the Impact of the 1994 Fiscal Reform."

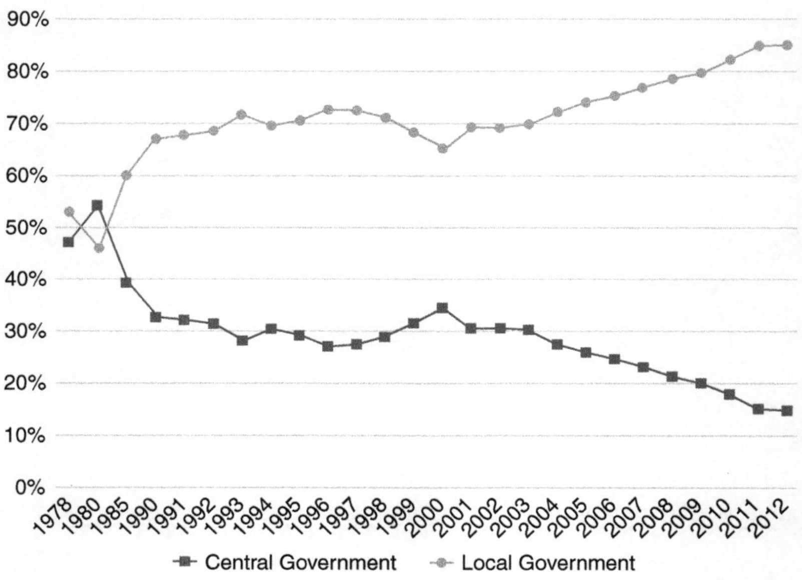


Figure 2.3 Proportion of expenditures by central and subnational governments.
Source: *China Statistical Yearbook*, 2012 and 2013.

welfare targets, many local officials focused on attracting foreign investment and promoting economic development.[18] As a result, local officials' emphasis on economic growth often occurred to the detriment of social policy, environmental protection, healthcare, and other public goods that were not directly linked to economic growth.

The 1994 tax system, coupled with the decentralization of social policy, exacerbated poor provinces' dependence on fiscal transfers from the central government, while wealthier provinces with ample locally generated revenue developed relative fiscal autonomy from the center. Throughout the 1990s and 2000s, the central government sought to alleviate poverty in poor provinces through earmarked fiscal transfers. While these transfers could be lifelines to struggling regions, they also tied the hands of the provincial government regarding policy priorities. Thus,

[18] Edin, "Remaking the Communist Party-State"; Hongbin Li and Li-An Zhou, "Political Turnover and Economic Performance: The Incentive Role of Personnel Control in China," *Journal of Public Economics* 89, no. 9–10 (2005): 1743–1762; Tony Saich, "Social Policy Development in the Era of Economic Reform," in *AIDS and Social Policy in China*, edited by Joan Kaufman, Arthur Kleinman, and Tony Saich (Cambridge, MA: Harvard University Asia Center, 2006), 15–46.

provinces that depended more heavily on these fiscal transfers were more likely to follow the letter of the law regarding central policy implementation. By contrast, wealthier provinces generated their own revenue but benefited from far fewer transfers for social policy – and thus enjoyed relative fiscal autonomy from the central government regarding social policy implementation. As a result, provincial leaders were more likely to encourage local innovation and local funding of social policy, and they sometimes dragged their feet in implementing policies that did not align with provincial interests, such as affordable housing.

Concurrently with economic reforms, the central government established fiscal decentralization in most policy areas, including health. As part of this initiative, the Ministry of Health reduced hospital budgets and began to allow market mechanisms to determine the prices of some medical treatments. Hospitals could no longer rely on government support but, rather, were required to be more fiscally independent and to increase economic efficiency. To increase revenue, healthcare providers began to inflate user fees and overprescribe expensive pharmaceuticals or high-end treatments. By the 1990s, most public hospitals received less than 10 percent of their revenue from the government and 60 percent from selling pharmaceuticals.[19] Health workers often relied on bribes to support their income, leading to the common practice of providing a "red envelope" (*hongbao* 红包) of cash to the doctor prior to procedures to ensure a good outcome.[20]

Due to these budgetary constraints, public hospitals began to function like profit-maximizing firms.[21] Hospitals were now held accountable to higher levels of government for their expenses. However, the government took some steps to ensure the accessibility of fundamental healthcare, including regulating the prices of some basic medicines.[22] Public hospitals faced price restrictions on what they could charge for routine visits, standard diagnostic tests, and common pharmaceuticals. By contrast, hospitals were permitted to profit from specialized treatments, new

19 Vivian Lin and David Legge, *Health Policy in and for China* (Beijing: Peking University Press, 2010), 304.

20 Yimin (申毅敏) Shen and Huiqin (侯慧琴) Hou, "医生收红包'潜规则'探秘 [Probing the 'Hidden Rule' That Doctors Accept Red Envelopes]," *Procuratorial Daily*, 2004, http://review.jcrb.com/zyw/n273/ca258338.htm; "南京医生自曝送红包经历 医患关系岂能为交易 [Nanjing Doctors Expose Their Experiences of Accepting Red Envelopes; How Can the Doctor–Patient Relationship Be Based on Under-the-Table Deals?]," *Xinhua Net*, 2006, http://news.xinhuanet.com/politics/2006-03/22/content_4332282.htm.

21 Private hospitals were introduced gradually and still constitute a small proportion of providers. Smaller private clinics are relatively common, but large hospitals are still generally public.

22 Some localities, especially wealthier provinces, provided subsidies to the poorest patients through the Ministry of Civil Affairs (Interviews with villagers and county officials in Counties A, B, C, H, and I, in Jiangsu).

drugs, and state-of-the-art interventions, particularly as new drugs lacked a price history from which to determine appropriate pricing. Profit margins for specialty treatments could reach as high as 15 percent.[23]

Meanwhile, the government adjusted the salary structure for physicians, including a bonus structure based on the income created for their hospitals.[24] Prior to market reforms, physicians were compensated by stable salaries, but now their remuneration was tied to the hospital's revenue. Furthermore, in comparison to other professional careers, physicians' salaries in China were (and still are) well below that of their peers abroad, making it difficult to attract talent to the profession and incentivizing corruption.[25] Thus, to generate revenue for the hospitals and themselves, physicians began to favor new, expensive, high-tech tests and treatments. This salary structure persisted into the 2000s, and overprescription of pharmaceuticals and expensive tests continues to be a source of concern. In February 2013, the State Council issued a guideline to reform this remuneration system, but successful implementation of this aspect of health reform has stalled. At the time of writing, doctors still endure difficult work conditions, long hours, and far less pay than their counterparts abroad or their peers in other professions in China.[26] Perverse incentives have encouraged irresponsible medical practices – such as the overprescription of antibiotics – that could threaten public health as well as lead to increases in the cost of those treatments that are not state-regulated.[27]

The economic reform period is often associated with a reduction in benefits for employees of urban SOEs, but rural areas also experienced repercussions from the shift in policy toward market-oriented economic reforms. Throughout the 1990s, villages lost both medical personnel and the Cooperative Medical System (CMS) without any concerted effort to build a new rural healthcare system. First, barefoot doctors – laypeople who received a few months of medical training and were only qualified to provide minimal care – no longer received state funding and could only practice medicine as private providers. Moreover, a lack of regulation, a lack of patients due to public mistrust in uneducated rural health

[23] David Blumenthal and William Hsiao, "Privatization and Its Discontents – The Evolving Chinese Health Care System," *New England Journal of Medicine* 353, no. 11 (2005): 1167.

[24] Ibid. [25] Cao, "The Chinese Medical Doctor Association," 74–97.

[26] Xiangchen (潇湘晨) Xiao, "我国严禁医生收入与药品收入挂钩 [China Prohibits Linking Doctors' Salaries to Prescriptions]," *Xinhua News*, 2013, http://news.xinhuanet.com/fortune/2013-02/21/c_124371680.htm.

[27] Karen Eggleston et al., "Health Service Delivery in China: A Literature Review," *World Bank Policy Research Working Paper* 3978 (Washington, DC: World Bank, 2006), http://hdl.handle.net/10986/8373.

workers, and the desire to increase profit margins led many barefoot doctors to abandon their previous mandate of preventive and basic medicine. Rather, like their urban peers, former barefoot doctors found that pharmaceuticals could produce a substantial profit and sought to offer more high-tech treatments and expensive pharmaceuticals that would increase revenue. However, few had adequate training to practice this type of care.[28] As a result, prices of medical care continued to rise, and quality of care was further compromised. Trained doctors were no longer obligated to practice in the countryside and, thus, chose to practice in more affluent areas where the quality of life and working conditions were better, leaving rural areas with fewer and fewer adequately trained medical personnel and further undermining rural health systems.

Second, the CMS was also dismantled during this period. A crucial aspect of the economic reforms was decollectivization through the Household Responsibility System, which mandated that villagers could now profit from the land that they worked rather than working in communes under a centrally planned economy. The goal was to enable agriculture to rebound and food production to stabilize. However, since the communes had funded the rural CMS, it subsequently lacked stable funding. Thus, with the adoption of the Household Responsibility System and the elimination of commune welfare funds, the CMS lost its funding structure. In addition, the CMS was eroded politically as well as financially. In 1982, a new cohort with political rather than medical credentials assumed the leadership of the Ministry of Health.[29] Shortly thereafter, the ministry sought to curry favor with the politburo by opposing the CMS due to its association with the Maoist period.[30] The repudiation of programs associated with the Maoist period was a common way for post-Mao elites to demonstrate their support for market reforms and recent policy shifts away from central planning and the Maoist style of governance.

Because of both political and economic factors, the inadequate health systems that had persisted in rural areas collapsed by the early 1990s. The CMS was eliminated in all but a few counties that maintained the system independently through the 1990s or, in some cases, until the present day.[31] Remaining village health stations were no longer supported

[28] Ibid. [29] Huang, *Governing Health in Contemporary China*, 56.

[30] Jane Duckett, "Challenging the Economic Reform Paradigm: Policy and Politics in the Early 1980s' Collapse of the Rural Co-operative Medical System," *China Quarterly* 205 (March 2011): 80–95.

[31] For the most part, counties that maintained the CMS also benefited from strong economic growth during the 1980s and 1990s. Reports of counties that maintained the CMS throughout the reform period generally focus on counties in wealthy regions, particularly around Shanghai. A few examples of localities that maintained the CMS are Jiao County

by local communities and had difficulty generating sufficient revenue to operate. Even city and county hospitals struggled to earn enough revenue to keep their doors open. The proportion of villages with health stations, which were often rudimentary, declined from 71 percent in 1979 to 55 percent by 1993.[32] Meanwhile, the number of tertiary hospitals in urban areas increased by over 55 percent from 1980 to 1995.[33]

Lack of funding and decentralization also affected public health. Local authorities across the country were now responsible for sanitation, regulation, and other public health affairs, but they often neglected these duties. The cadre evaluation system gave primacy to economic growth rather than social metrics (excepting population control); therefore, cadres would prioritize economic development over social policy.[34] Corruption, coupled with incentives to prioritize economic development, led to general disregard for social policy issues among local officials. In the context of this general vacuum in public health, it is not surprising that SARS severely affected China in 2003.

Decentralization was a boon for economic development, resulting in local governments competing to maximize economic growth and creating dramatic improvements in living standards for millions of urban Chinese. However, strategies that were so effective in fostering economic development created perverse incentives that further undermined the quality, access, and cost-effectiveness of healthcare.[35] Entrepreneurialism and new opportunities to create revenue, coupled with limited government support and hard budgetary constraints, created a highly dysfunctional healthcare system. In my interviews, hospital directors referred to this system as the "hospital as a firm" model.[36] Rural hospitals have had particular difficulty competing in a profit-driven system. Many of these hospitals are public People's Hospitals, but their government funding remains dismally low; they are still required to generate substantial

(郊县) in Shanghai; Zhaoyuan County (招远) in Shandong; Wu (吴县), Wuxi (无锡), and Changshu (常熟) in Jiangsu; and Wuxue (武穴) in Hubei (Xufeng Zhu, 政策变迁中的专家参与 [*The Participation of Experts in Policy Change*] [Beijing: China Remin University Publishing, 2012]). All but Wuxue in Hubei are located in wealthy provinces that prospered during the economic reforms. These counties provided part of the inspiration for a revival of the CMS in the late 1990s. By following these models, policymakers sought to reinvent the system as a risk-pooling, insurance-style program.

32 Lin and Legge, *Health Policy in and for China*, 305.

33 Ibid.

34 Edin, "Remaking the Communist Party-State"; Li and Zhou, "Political Turnover and Economic Performance"; Saich, "Social Policy Development in the Era of Economic Reform."

35 Barry R Weingast, Yingyi Qian, and Gabriella Montinola, "Federalism, Chinese Style: The Political Basis for Economic Success in China," *World Politics* 48, no. 1 (October 1995): 50.

36 Interview HNFH24, December 17, 2009.

revenue. Hospital directors in the hinterlands are frustrated with the system and often request more funds from the central government.[37]

In some ways, China's healthcare reform process was strikingly similar to neoliberal approaches to healthcare and structural adjustment in other developing countries. However, in other countries, structural adjustment programs were typically implemented because the World Bank and donor countries compelled borrowing governments through loan conditionalities.[38] By contrast, the CCP adopted fiscal discipline independently but retained a strong role for the state in the economy through regulation, public financing, and SOEs. The resulting health system no longer resembled state socialism except insofar as the Communist Party maintained control over the appointment of key personnel, such as hospital directors. In addition, the party-state has not permitted an autonomous professional association for doctors to emerge.[39] Rather, the profession of medicine is regulated by the state.

The incentive system for hospital revenue coupled with hard budget constraints that were established in the early 1980s remains largely in place today; as a result, overprescription of expensive treatments and pharmaceuticals continues to plague the system. In February 2013, the State Council issued additional reforms to hospitals and doctor remuneration, although the success of these policies remains to be seen at the time of writing. Chinese medical professionals continue to overprescribe antibiotics, creating a serious public health concern. Furthermore, inequality between urban and rural areas due to market reforms persists.[40] Overall, market-oriented reforms resulted in a healthcare system plagued with inequities, inefficiencies, and ballooning costs.

## Reengagement and Incomplete Reform: Late 1990s to 2013

*The "hospital as a firm" model is not working; we need more investment from the central government.*

Hospital director of a People's Hospital in rural Hunan Province, 2010[41]

[37] Interview HNFH24, December 17, 2009; Interview GSH56, June 24, 2010.

[38] One exception to this trend was Chile under the military regime of Augusto Pinochet.

[39] In 2002, the Chinese Medical Doctor Association (*zhongguo yishi xiehui* 中国医师协会) was founded under the Ministry of Civil Affairs, but it does not operate autonomously from the state.

[40] Winnie Yip, "Disparities in Healthcare and Health Status: The Rural–Urban Gap and Beyond," in *One Country, Two Societies: Rural–Urban Inequality in Contemporary China*, edited by Martin King Whyte (Cambridge, MA: Harvard University Asia Center, Harvard University Press, 2010), 147–165.

[41] Interview HNFH24, December 17, 2009.

Since the late 1990s, the central government has gradually intensified its emphasis on social policy, both rhetorically and fiscally. During the early 2000s, changes in China's political climate, an increasing institutionalization of the policymaking process, and augmented central government revenue coincided with a shift in the international community's stance on state involvement in social policy to facilitate the central government's reengagement with healthcare. The increased domestic involvement of think tanks and research organizations in the policy process provided information to relevant authorities about the dire situation in healthcare. The universe of conceivable policy options at the beginning of the twenty-first century expanded due to a shift in views on best practices and governance in international organizations such as the World Bank and the United Nations. While central government leaders had already been exploring options for alleviating the burden of healthcare, the SARS crisis served as a catalyst to government action and placed healthcare at the forefront of the national policy agenda.

Healthcare reform in China has thus far taken place in two waves: 1997 and 2009. The 1997 reform period emphasized competition among service institutions, market institutions, and the creation of state regulatory mechanisms. This first wave emerged largely as a response to former state-sector employees who were left without benefits after marketization. These workers constituted a politically threatening group, as they had benefited under the planned economy and were now losing out under market reforms. During this period, SOE workers challenged the state to uphold its end of the social contract. They would sometimes protest in the streets or outside government offices, using state slogans to emphasize their political loyalty under the condition that they receive the benefits they were promised.[42] The primary goal of the 1997 reform was to pacify these former state-sector employees, who were relative losers during the restructuring of many SOEs.

The government began to address the problem of healthcare and government spending by the late 1990s. Then, in 2003, President Hu Jintao and Prime Minister Wen Jiabao took office. Notably, their government adopted slogans such as "harmonious society" (*hexie shehui* 和谐社会) and "scientific development" (*kexue fazhan* 科学发展) as a way to indicate that equity would now be a priority as well as growth, suggesting that the central government would promote policies to reduce income inequality and improve the social safety net.

Another popular phrase used by CCP elites in the early 2000s was "moderately well-off society" (*xiaokang shehui* 小康社会). This phrase

[42] O'Brien and Li, *Rightful Resistance in Rural China*.

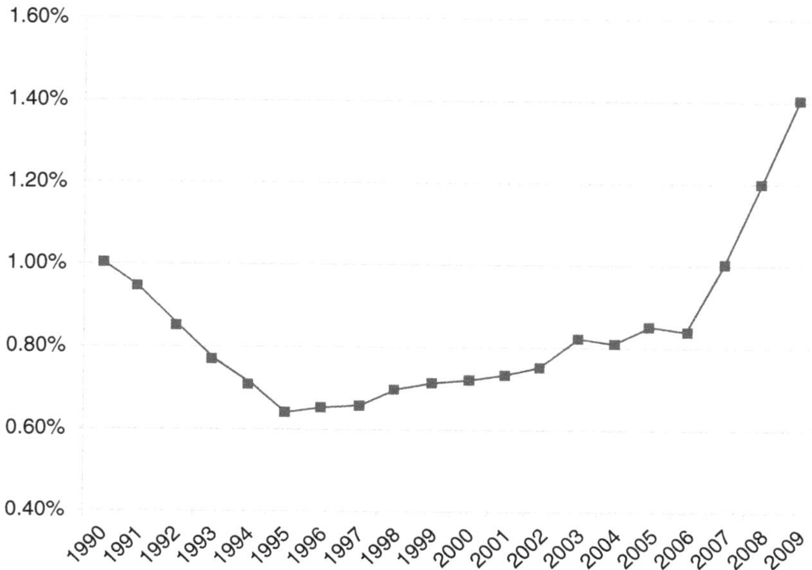


Figure 2.4 Government health spending as a percent of GDP in China, 1990–2009.
Source: *Ministry of Health Statistical Yearbook*, 2010.

originates in Confucian classics, but it reemerged at this time to indicate an emphasis on health and general well-being. By examining government health spending as a proportion of GDP between 1990 and 2009, we can see that the Hu-Wen administration backed up its rhetoric by increasing spending on healthcare (Figure 2.4) – although health spending as a percentage of GDP was still low even in 2009.

Changes in domestic politics, including increased revenue and a diversification of actors in the policymaking process, enabled government reengagement with healthcare provision in the late 1990s and early 2000s. First, the central government benefited from an increase in revenue due to the 1994 tax reform. Although China experienced unprecedented economic growth during the 1990s, the central state's extractive capabilities were severely reduced by decentralization in the 1980s. Since the central state was still suffering from the policies of the 1980s, Beijing had little capacity to subsidize healthcare until the 1994 tax reform, which increased the relative share of government revenue taken by the central government as compared to subnational levels of government. As a result of tax reform, the central government had more than doubled its share of tax revenue by the mid-1990s, facilitating funding for social policy provision.

Second, the government began to recognize the severity of the healthcare problem. By the late 1990s, the effects of state retrenchment were palpable, particularly among rural residents and the poor. As state support for healthcare had diminished over the previous decade, the cost of medical care became an increasing concern for many Chinese. Nationwide, the state had reduced its financial support for healthcare, and most health expenditures were paid by individuals. Figure 2.1 illustrates the relative decline in state spending on healthcare and the rise in out-of-pocket expenditures as a proportion of total healthcare expenditures during this period. There was a marked increase in state spending in 2003. As a result of economic reforms, about 90 percent of rural residents were left uninsured through 2003.[43] Rural residents were often unable to afford medical treatment, and catastrophic medical expenditures became a significant cause of poverty. These circumstances led to the development of two new idioms: "poverty due to illness" (*yinbingzhipin* 因病致贫); and "poverty due to catastrophic illness" (*dabingzhipin* 大病致贫).[44] One survey from 2003 indicated that 25 percent of respondents did not visit a doctor because of prohibitively high costs.[45] The Ministry of Health reported in the early 2000s that 22 percent of the rural poor identified "unmet medical needs" as the cause of their poverty.[46] Many lower-income Chinese were faced with the choice of impoverishment from medical expenditures or foregoing treatment. In response to this growing problem, the Ministry of Health began to encourage pilot projects in which risk-pooling health insurance programs were offered to villagers.

A third change in Chinese domestic politics contributed to the nature of healthcare reform: the gradual inclusion of research organizations in policymaking. Previous research on policymaking in China has examined the impact of think tanks on policy design, finding that think tanks impacted the policy process in areas such as foreign policy,[47] economic policy,[48]

[43] Saich, "Social Policy Development in the Era of Economic Reform," 22.

[44] Hongman Wang, 大国卫生之论 [*Arguments about Our Country's Health*] (Beijing: Peking University Press, 2006).

[45] Saich, "Social Policy Development in the Era of Economic Reform," 22.

[46] Ibid.

[47] Bonnie S. Glaser and Phillip C. Saunders, "Chinese Civilian Foreign Policy Research Institutes: Evolving Roles and Increasing Influence," *China Quarterly* 171 (September 2002): 597–616, https://doi.org/10.1017/S0009443902000372.

[48] Barry Naughton, "China's Economic Think Tanks: Their Changing Role in the 1990s," *China Quarterly* 171 (September 2002): 625–635, https://doi.org/10.1017/S0009443902000396; Michel Oksenberg, "Economic Policy-Making in China: Summer 1981," *China Quarterly* 90 (June 1982): 165–194, https://doi.org/10.1017/S0305741000000308.

international relations,[49] and police and public security.[50] Throughout the 1990s, the role of research and think tanks on policymaking increased dramatically, and elites emphasized the importance of research in policymaking.[51] A more pluralistic policy process with the meaningful involvement of nonstate researchers reached a peak during the Hu Jintao years, but it then became more restrictive under Xi Jinping's leadership.

In health policy, innovation originated from relatively independent actors: domestic and international NGOs, academics, research centers, and international organizations such as the World Bank or World Health Organization (WHO). Various groups within both the political elite and the scholarly community debated the role that the state should take in healthcare provision. In the proposals submitted to the government to be considered for inclusion in the 2009 healthcare reform, various Chinese universities advocated divergent paths to health reform. Some scholars and politicians recommended a health sector dominated by the state (including Li Ling of Peking University), while others advocated greater marketization (including Liu Guoen of Peking University). A mixed state–market approach prevailed, drawing heavily on recommendations made by this process. Many important aspects of reform are still incomplete, however, such as hospital reform.

Meanwhile, as domestic policymaking became more open within China, a significant paradigm shift in response to global inequities led international organizations to advocate for greater state involvement with healthcare provision worldwide. Many developing countries across the world had implemented austerity programs such as structural adjustment throughout the 1980s and 1990s, resulting in the absence of a social safety net (including provisions for basic education and healthcare). In the 1990s, however, the idea of state reengagement with social policy provision began to gain currency. As concerns about inequality mounted in some regions of the world, international organizations began to increase their emphasis on social policy provision, including advocating for state actors to provide funding or implement new programs. Although the Chinese government is not compelled to follow international trends, Chinese elites often consider empirical evidence and outside research in

[49] David Shambaugh, "China's International Relations Think Tanks: Evolving Structure and Process," *China Quarterly* 171 (September 2002): 575–596, https://doi.org/10.1017/S0009443902000360.

[50] Murray Scot Tanner, "Changing Windows on a Changing China: The Evolving 'Think Tank' System and the Case of the Public Security Sector," *China Quarterly*, no. 171 (September 2002): 559–574.

[51] State Council Development Research Center, "李克强在国务院发展研究中心调研时强调 [Li Keqiang Emphasizes Research at the State Council Development Research Center]," November 10, 2011.

policymaking. Some leading Chinese scholars feel that the most effective way to influence policy in China is to demonstrate empirically the deficiencies with current approaches.[52] Jane Duckett shows, for example, how ideas from international organizations likely shaped central leaders' choice of the New Cooperative Medical System to alleviate the financial burden of catastrophic illness in rural China.[53] Thus, as international organizations began to promote different alternatives for health policy, researchers at top universities in China marshaled evidence to advocate for increased government funding of healthcare. In this way, international trends affected policymaking in China through the involvement of domestic research organizations. The health reforms of 2009 also included greater public debate and deliberation than did previous policymaking processes in China. The 2009 proposal was posted online for public comment, receiving comments from over 30,000 citizens.[54]

Finally, the SARS crisis of 2003 provided a catalyst to place healthcare at the top of the government agenda, enabling Hu Jintao to assert his leadership in social policy and differentiate himself from his predecessor. In early 2003, an outbreak of SARS, a viral respiratory disease that is carried by animals, appeared in southern China, nearly resulting in a pandemic and provoking an international response. The disease spread rapidly from Guangdong Province and Hong Kong to twenty-seven other countries around the world, including Singapore, Vietnam, Germany, the United States, and Canada. The epidemic resulted in 8,096 probable cases of SARS and 774 deaths (a death rate of 9.6 percent).[55] The SARS crisis focused international attention on healthcare in China, attracting particularly harsh criticism of general hygiene and the public health system.

This public health crisis impelled the central government to begin improving public health and infectious disease monitoring by creating an electronic disease reporting system at the district level and establishing infectious disease hospitals in every district. However, as a district often comprises hundreds of thousands of people, this system still may not be

[52] Informal communication from academic advisors to the health reform process at a top university in Beijing in 2011.

[53] Jane Duckett, "International Influences on Policymaking in China: Network Authoritarianism from Jiang Zemin to Hu Jintao," *China Quarterly* 237 (March 2019): 15–37, https://doi.org/10.1017/S0305741018001212.

[54] Yoel Kornreich, Ilan Vertinsky, and Pitman B. Potter, "Consultation and Deliberation in China: The Making of China's Health-Care Reform," *China Journal* 68 (July 2012): 176–203.

[55] World Health Organization, "Summary of probable SARS cases with onset of illness from 1 November 2002 to 31 July 2003," www.who.int/csr/sars/country/table2004_04_21/en/index.html, accessed June 9, 2013.

sufficient for timely notification of an outbreak. Moreover, local governments are still neglecting to emphasize health education such as personal hygiene, sanitation, and preventive measures that could reduce the occurrence of epidemics in the future.[56] In 2020, the outbreak of COVID-19, a similar type of respiratory virus as SARS, revealed several persistent weaknesses in the healthcare system: local officials are incentivized to cover up possible problems when reporting to higher levels of government; a general lack of transparency plagues all levels of government; and health services are often overburdened even during a normal cold-and-flu season and are thus ill-equipped for epidemics. That said, strict quarantine, testing, and surveillance measures that the CCP implemented to respond to COVID-19 were highly effective in slowing the transmission of the virus within China throughout 2019 and 2020.[57] Nonetheless, by early 2022, many observers had noted concerns about draconian implementation of lock-downs and unregulated collection of personal data.[58]

While the 1997 reform focused mainly on regulating providers and expanding urban medical insurance, the 2009 Health Reform Plan specified five major goals: developing universal insurance; promoting equal public health; setting a state essential drug policy; improving community-based facilities; and conducting public hospital reform. While the party-state achieved universal insurance and made progress on the essential drug policy, community-based facilities and public hospital reform lagged behind well into the 2010s, in part because of the ambiguity of the initial reform and the lack of consensus regarding how to move forward with implementation.

The early 2000s reform process that culminated in the 2009 Health Reform Plan differed from that of 1997 in both procedure and substance. Recognizing that rising healthcare costs and access were severe problems that affected the nation as a whole rather than just a small community of former state-sector employees, the government began to experiment with pilot projects for risk-pooling health insurance plans. For these efforts, the government enlisted proposals from local and foreign academics. The government solicited expert advice from scholars at the Harvard School of Public Health for designing an effective New Cooperative Medical System, for example. Throughout the process, a variety of universities,

[56] Blumenthal and Hsiao, "Privatization and Its Discontents," 1169.
[57] Alex Jingwei He, Yuda Shi, and Hongdou Liu, "Crisis Governance, Chinese Style: Distinctive Features of China's Response to the Covid-19 Pandemic," *Policy Design and Practice* (July 2020): 1–17.
[58] Sheena Chestnut Greitens, "Surveillance, Security, and Liberal Democracy in the Post-COVID World," *International Organization* 74, no. S1 (December 2020): E169–190, https://doi.org/10.1017/S0020818320000417.

research centers, and private consultancies, as well as the World Bank and the WHO, submitted proposals for healthcare reform, advocating various plans. Some promoted a program with universal coverage similar to the United Kingdom's National Health System. Others advocated for market-oriented solutions. When compared to previous policy decisions, this relative transparency and inclusion of foreign academics suggested a notable shift in Chinese governance, which has since been reversed under Xi Jinping.

As a result of this process, the government mandated private firms and SOEs to provide workers medical savings accounts and catastrophic insurance, a policy largely inspired by the Singaporean model.[59] However, this policy has not entirely resolved the healthcare issue for workers because many do not work for formally organized employers, and some employers refuse to follow state mandates. Private health insurance has also emerged for the wealthy. In addition, the government began to allow public hospitals to enter into public–private partnerships. Some public hospitals contract out management to private companies. Private investment has been used for hospital construction, particularly in coastal provinces like Jiangsu and Zhejiang. Private medical facilities now represent an emerging market of interest for foreign investors.[60] Foreign investors, however, continue to face barriers to entry insofar as wholly foreign-owned hospitals are still prohibited in China; foreign companies must enter into joint ventures.

As evident from Figures 2.1 and 2.4, health reforms in the early 2000s resulted in a significant increase in government expenditure as well as reductions in out-of-pocket expenses for individuals. Yet a comprehensive, cohesive approach to healthcare reform has, thus far, been elusive. This is in part because diverse government agencies with divergent views have complicated both policy design and implementation. Agreement among agencies involved in the 2009 reform was difficult, and the Ministry of Health has been criticized for its reluctance to take a strong stance on the direction of health reform. A lack of leadership in the Health Reform Leading Small Group, which was tasked with coordinating the health reform, resulted in an incomplete and vague reform document.[61] Various government departments also jockeyed for

[59] Ibid.

[60] Lucy Hornby, "What's up, doc? Investors knock at China hospitals," Reuters News, September 11, 2011, https://www.reuters.com/article/idINIndia-59106920110902.

[61] The head of the Health Reform Leading Small Group, Li Keqiang, waited until 2011 to take a stance on reform. Some observers speculate that, as Executive Vice Premier, his equivocation was politically motivated because he was in line to become Premier, which he did in March 2013. As posited by Huang, Li may have been concerned that his public

healthcare tasks, further impeding the smooth implementation of health reforms. In the early 2000s, there were three forms of state-subsidized insurance in China: Urban Employees Basic Medical Insurance (UEBMI), for employees of the state or large formal entities; Urban Residents Basic Medical Insurance (URBMI), for other urban residents; and the New Cooperative Medical System (NCMS), for rural residents. The two urban insurance programs were run by the Ministry of Human Resources and Social Security (MHRSS), while the NCMS was run by the Ministry of Health. In 2016, the State Council merged the URBMI and the NCMS to improve equity.[62] Some observers suggest that the merger should improve reimbursement rates for rural residents, but it could require premiums that are too costly for villagers. Evaluations suggest that an urban–rural gap persists post-merger, with the NCMS providing lower reimbursement rates.[63]

One of the major goals of the 2009 reform was to expand and improve health insurance, particularly in rural areas. Initiated in 2003 as pilot projects, the New Cooperative Medical System achieved basic insurance coverage nationwide in rural areas. As part of this initiative to increase access to healthcare, the NCMS combined small household contributions with subsidies from the central and local government in a risk-pooling insurance program. Participation was voluntary, although there were accusations of coercion from village cadres.[64]

Because the responsibility for NCMS administration and program design was explicitly left to local governments, reimbursement rates and the specifics of the plan varied significantly, even among counties within the same province. Funding for the NCMS included fiscal transfers from the central government for each pilot program participant in central and western provinces. Meanwhile, wealthy coastal provinces were wholly responsible for funding the NCMS. In this way, the program represented a somewhat progressive attempt at redistribution. The NCMS seemed to have increased access to healthcare, even a few years

endorsement of an unsuccessful reform would have compromised his chances at the position. See Huang, *Governing Health in Contemporary China*, 79.

62 State Council of China, "Opinions of the State Council on the Integration of the Basic Medical Insurance for Urban and Rural Residents [国务院关于整合城乡居民基本医疗保险制度的意见]," Pub. L. No. CLI.2.262352 (2016).

63 Yang Li et al., "Differences Exist across Insurance Schemes in China Post-Consolidation," *PLoS ONE* 12, no. 11 (November 2017): 1–13, https://doi.org/10.1371/journal.pone.0187100.

64 Philip H. Brown, Alan de Brauw, and Du Yang, "Understanding Variation in the Design of China's New Co-operative Medical System," *China Quarterly* 198 (June 2009): 304–329.

after implementation. Hospital directors reported a large increase in patients, and villagers were somewhat satisfied after several years of the program. But concerns remained.[65] According to villagers and some local officials, several problems persisted: reimbursement rates varied significantly across localities; reimbursement rates were lower at higher levels of facilities, which disproportionately affected villagers in localities with less-developed health facilities; reimbursement rates were lower for out-of-area facilities, which was a serious problem for migrant workers; and drugs that were not on the essential drug list were often excluded from reimbursement, although patients were generally unaware of these limitations until they were at the pharmacy counter.[66] Moreover, there were scattered reports of the NCMS attracting corruption and cases of fraudulent illnesses to extract subsidies from the government (*jia bingli* 假病历).[67] Some policy evaluations of the NCMS found that the program increased the use of preventive care but did not decrease out-of-pocket expenditures, most likely due to rising costs.[68]

Despite further incremental reform since 2009, challenges remain. For example, health outcomes are still highly contingent on local conditions. In 2010, the life expectancy for residents of different provinces ranged from seventy-eight years (Shanghai) to sixty-four years (Tibet).[69] In addition, provinces have demonstrated an uneven commitment to healthcare. In wealthy provinces and national-level metropolises such as Beijing and Shanghai, government spending on rural healthcare as of 2010 was more than six times that of Guizhou, the poorest province in China.[70]

Further reform will also need to focus on the professionalism of physicians and perhaps empowering doctors to have their own autonomous, professional association,[71] although this is unlikely under Xi Jinping's leadership. The current practice of medicine suffers from generations of Chinese physicians whose professional careers have been contingent

[65] Interviews with hospital personnel in Hunan and Gansu, 2010.
[66] Interviews with villagers in Hunan, 2010.
[67] Interviews with hospital personnel and media reports in Hunan, 2010.
[68] Xiaoyan Lei and Wanchuan Lin, "The New Cooperative Medical Scheme in Rural China: Does More Coverage Mean More Service and Better Health?" *Health Economics* 18, suppl. 2 (July 2009): S25–S46.
[69] See *Ministry of Health Statistics Yearbook*, 2010. On average, life expectancy has vastly improved since the 1950s, when it was estimated to be forty-five years.
[70] Ministry of Health of the People's Republic of China, *China Public Health Statistical Yearbook* [中国卫生统计年鉴] (Beijing: Peking Union Medical College Publishing House, 2010).
[71] Cao, "The Chinese Medical Doctor Association."

on demonstrating loyalty to the state and communist ideology.[72] A new culture of professionalism will need to be fostered among physicians to support concurrent institutional efforts to create incentives to improve quality, increase access, and reduce cost.

Perhaps the most significant challenge for healthcare reform and social policy going forward is that, in general, local governments continue to prioritize economic growth. However, the party-state is beginning to include health policy targets in rural cadre evaluation systems in some provinces. For example, participation rates and average reimbursement rates for the rural health insurance program are now included. Targets are set by higher levels of government, which the county aims to reach.[73] Nonetheless, these targets are typically insufficient incentives to dramatically alter the behavior of local cadres, as they are still perceived as a lower priority than economic growth.[74]

The most recent wave of healthcare reforms in China has been focused on improving access through cost reduction and some investment in improving basic health systems in villages and urban districts. Additional reforms targeting hospital management and doctor remuneration are underway. However, further reforms will need to address rising costs and lack of regulation, as well. Despite an increase in government investment in healthcare, health inequality between urban and rural areas has not abated. Moreover, healthcare spending is focused on hospital care and urban areas; many rural areas still need investment in basic infrastructure.

A combination of domestic and international factors that developed in the late 1990s and early 2000s created the political environment necessary for the SARS disaster to catalyze reform. After 1978, revenue constraints caused Chinese state retrenchment in social policy, while healthcare costs began to rise. This confluence left the healthcare system in crisis, with challenges such as a spike in out-of-pocket expenditures and the withering of community clinics. By the early 1990s, tax reforms alleviated the central government's revenue crisis, and the increasing influence of outside research in policymaking created new potential pathways for the state's role in social policy. Concurrently, international organizations began to advocate state reengagement with social policy provision. As a result of pressure from below, shifts in governance style,

[72] Meng-Kin Lim et al., "China's Evolving Health Care Market: How Doctors Feel and What They Think," *Health Policy* 69, no. 3 (September 2004): 329–337, https://doi.org/10.1016/j.healthpol.2004.01.001.

[73] Interviews with county officials in Hunan and Gansu, 2010.

[74] James Kung, Yongshun Cai, and Xiulin Sun, "Rural Cadres and Governance in China: Incentive, Institution and Accountability," *China Journal* 62 (July 2009): 61–77.

and encouragement from at home and abroad, the Chinese government initiated a dialogue on healthcare reform that culminated in the 2009 plan to overhaul the system. However, the central government continues to engage in incremental reforms at the national level, while local governments have varied in their implementation of current guidelines.

# 3 Disaggregating Authoritarian Governance

## Provincial Policy Styles

Throughout the economic reforms of the past four decades, China's central government has devolved responsibility for social policy to local government. While Beijing continues to set broad policy priorities, the localities have been responsible for much of the funding and specific design of social policy within their jurisdictions. After state retrenchment in the 1990s, the central government began to reengage with social policy provision in the 2000s in response to growing discontent (see Chapter 2). Nonetheless, despite increased involvement and funding from Beijing, local government is still largely responsible for funding social policy and has significant control over the specifics of program design and implementation. Therefore, the same policy can look quite different across provinces and even across counties within the same province. What accounts for local variation in social policy provision? Is the variation that we observe idiosyncratic or does it exhibit a discernable pattern? Do local approaches to governance impact social policy provision? And, if so, how?

I contend that the observed variation in social policy provision is not idiosyncratic but rather reflects provincial approaches to governance. In this chapter, I provide a framework of specific provincial policy styles and demonstrate how distinct ways of governing impact social policy implementation. In the subsequent chapters, I will illustrate these provincial styles with in-depth case studies of three provinces. Using these case studies – with illustrative references to other, similar provinces – I show the implications of these policy styles for health policy and provide additional illustrative examples from education, poverty alleviation, and housing.

China's economic reforms began in a piecemeal fashion. In the early 1980s, as a strategy to experiment with elements of a market economy, the central government designated a few localities as special economic zones (SEZs), which were given greater latitude in economic affairs. SEZs could, for example, experiment with manufacturing for export and attract foreign direct investment (FDI). While market forces were gradually permitted in some regions, much of the country continued to function as a planned economy. The coastal provinces that were permitted to open up to the global economy earlier through policies such as SEZs benefited in both wealth and institutional improvements. Emboldened by newfound sources of wealth that gave them leverage vis-à-vis the central government, coastal provinces began to advocate for their interests by requesting modifications to policies that infringed on their interests or special transfers from the central government to meet the demands of foreign investors for infrastructure improvements.[1] Poorer inland provinces, forced to rely solely on the goodwill of the central government for fiscal transfers, did not enjoy this type of bargaining power.

In addition to getting a head start on economic growth, early coastal reformers' exposure to FDI and market forces enabled them to develop local institutions. Several studies have found that the presence of foreign firms shaped local governmental and legal institutions in China in important ways. Mary Elizabeth Gallagher found that foreign investors encouraged firms and workers to use legal channels to resolve disputes, thereby supporting relatively stronger legal institutions in these localities.[2] Cheryl Long and her coauthors also found that FDI had a positive effect on the host locality's governing and legal institutions, as foreign firms favor institutions that support contract enforcement, predictability in the institutional environment, and, of course, low taxes.[3] Denise van der Kamp and her coauthors found that FDI was associated with expeditious adoption of environmental transparency procedures, although they posit a different causal mechanism. Rather than argue that foreign firms advocate for environmental transparency, they propose that localities that generate their own revenue have greater latitude to respond to popular demands for environmental transparency, which are happily aligned with central-government goals in this case. Meanwhile, cash-strapped localities have little choice but to focus on generating revenue, often by sacrificing environmental or other social policies.[4] Van der Kamp's study of environmental transparency provides an example of how localities that generate their own revenue gain greater autonomy to pursue their

[1] Li, *Centre and Provinces*.

[2] Mary Elizabeth Gallagher, *Contagious Capitalism: Globalization and the Politics of Labor in China* (Princeton, NJ: Princeton University Press, 2007).

[3] Cheryl Long, Jin Yang, and Jing Zhang, "Institutional Impact of Foreign Direct Investment in China," *World Development* 66 (February 2015): 31–48, https://doi.org/10.1016/j.worlddev.2014.08.001.

[4] Denise van der Kamp, Peter Lorentzen, and Daniel Mattingly, "Racing to the Bottom or to the Top? Decentralization, Revenue Pressures, and Governance Reform in China," *World Development* 95 (July 2017): 164–176, https://doi.org/10.1016/j.worlddev.2017.02.021.

perceived local interests, and, in the Chinese case, locally generated revenue usually entails a healthy dose of FDI. Scholars have found similar patterns regarding the impact of FDI on institutions beyond China. Edmund J. Malesky found that FDI was associated with more economic reforms in eastern Europe, as firms may lobby local officials to reform, inform officials of practices in other countries, or simply threaten to leave if local practices do not change.[5] These dynamics are likely to have occurred in China as well.

In China, early economic reformers developed greater fiscal capacity and, therefore, increased political leverage vis-à-vis the central government. Concurrently, new foreign investors and domestic entrepreneurs demanded some predictability and consistency regarding contract law and legal institutions. The resulting economic development, political autonomy, and improved institutions produced a pragmatic approach to policymaking that prized innovation, experimentation, and decentralization. Meanwhile, provinces that were not selected for early reforms continued a paternalistic policy style fostered by the hierarchical *nomenklatura* system and a reliance on central transfers to fund mandated policies.

The dominance of pragmatism or paternalism in local policy implementation has had implications for social policy provision. Pragmatic provinces tend to emphasize social policies that support economic growth, especially education and healthcare. By contrast, paternalist provinces tend to prioritize social policies that prevent societal unrest, such as poverty alleviation and housing. Social policy outcomes, in turn, may have feedback effects that impact provincial governance. Figure 3.1 depicts this interaction. This chapter will examine these patterns through regression analysis of social policy spending at the provincial level in China.

## Previous Research: Explaining Variation in Social Policy Provision

Scholars studying the welfare state are increasingly including the developing world in their research and seeking new theories to explain the outcomes in these contexts.[6] Meanwhile, China scholars are beginning to employ these approaches to explain the wide variation in social policy

[5] Edmund J. Malesky, "Foreign Direct Investors as Agents of Economic Transition: An Instrumental Variables Analysis," *Quarterly Journal of Political Science* 4, no. 1 (March 2009): 59–85, https://doi.org/10.1561/100.00008068.

[6] Haggard and Kaufman, *Development, Democracy, and Welfare States*; Rudra, *Globalization and the Race to the Bottom in Developing Countries*.

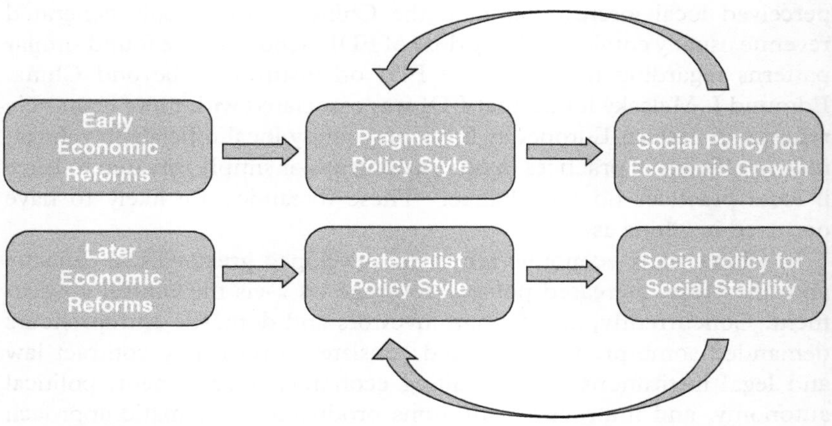


Figure 3.1 Emergence of policy styles and social policy provision.

provision found across Chinese localities. Recent scholarship focuses on structural and agentic explanations. Structural approaches tend to focus on either local wealth or needs, or both. For example, Jay Pan and Gordon G. Liu found that wealth and needs are associated with provincial general health expenditures. Specifically, they found associations between per capita provincial general budget revenue, the proportion of provincial population under age fifteen, urban employee basic health insurance coverage, and proportion of urban population.[7] Also studying healthcare, Xian Huang finds that fiscal resources and social risk are factors that incentivize local officials to adopt distinct regional approaches to health policy.[8]

Agentic approaches to explaining local variation in social policy tend to focus on the cadre evaluation system, which determines the promotion criteria for local officials. Tingjin Lin argues that promotion criteria for local officials have led to local variation in education financing.[9] Cai Zuo argues that local officials respond to the criteria set in the cadre evaluation system. She found that localities in which social policy is included in targets are more likely to prioritize social policy issues. Moreover, localities that already have higher welfare outcomes are more likely to set higher targets for these areas, perhaps resulting in a virtuous cycle for

[7] Jay Pan and Gordon G. Liu, "The Determinants of Chinese Provincial Government Health Expenditures: Evidence from 2002–2006 Data," *Health Economics* 21, no. 7 (July 2012): 757–777, https://doi.org/10.1002/hec.1742.
[8] Huang, "Four Worlds of Welfare."
[9] Lin, *The Politics of Financing Education in China.*

social policy provision.[10] In the vein of promotion-minded officials, Derek Tai-Wei Liu argues that local leaders with a longer time horizon and who are more likely to seek promotion are also more likely to allocate funds to social policy to reduce unrest.[11]

Dorothy Solinger and her coauthors explain local variation in the implementation of China's primary poverty-alleviation policy, the Minimum Livelihood Guarantee (MLG), through the interactions between structure and agency. The MLG is a means-tested cash transfer program available to the poorest citizens. Solinger and Yiyang Hu argue that wealthy cities are more generous with per capita MLG spending to keep unseemly individuals off the streets, whereas poorer cities allow MLG recipients to work in public view to reduce the burden on the city budget.[12] This suggests, as we might expect, that officials in poorer localities are more budget-sensitive than their counterparts in wealthy areas. Solinger and Ting Jiang argue that local officials in wealthier cities use the MLG to quell dissent, thereby undermining the primary goal of the MLG as poverty reduction.[13]

Despite these recent advances, the research on variation in social policy in China at the local level suffers from several shortcomings. First, the structural and agentic approaches sometimes conflict in their accounts. Are local differences due mainly to regional factors, such as wealth or needs, or to the initiative of local officials? Second, previous research tends to focus on one policy area. However, different types of social policy – health, education, poverty alleviation – play distinct roles in Chinese politics and society. This book focuses on healthcare, but I also draw examples from policies in other areas to illustrate similar patterns. Social policies serve distinct purposes in Chinese society, and officials face different incentives depending on the policy in question. Therefore, an exclusive analysis of one policy may be limited in its applications to another policy area. Third, previous research tends to focus on policy outcomes, such as total spending or benefits offered to recipients. These outcomes are important, but I also examine how regional politics can affect the policy process, focusing on implementation. I seek to advance our understanding of local politics' impact on social policy through

[10] Cai (Vera) Zuo, "Promoting City Leaders: The Structure of Political Incentives in China," *China Quarterly* 224 (December 2015): 955–984, https://doi.org/10.1017/S0305741015001289.

[11] Derek Tai-wei Liu, "Top-Down Accountability and the Politics of Social Spending in China." APSA 2010 Annual Meeting Paper (2010).

[12] Solinger and Hu, "Welfare, Wealth, and Poverty in Urban China."

[13] Dorothy J. Solinger and Ting Jiang, "When Chinese Central Orders and Promotion Criteria Conflict," *Modern China* 42, no. 6 (March 2016): 571–606, https://doi.org/10.1177/0097700416635507.

a policy-style framework that examines how structural factors shape incentives for local officials.

## Conceptualizing Provincial Policy Styles

What explains policy variation in an authoritarian regime? Scholars have observed the decentralized nature of policy implementation in China and the resulting regional variation in policy outcomes, but what explains these divergent approaches to policy? In a decentralized (or federal) electoral democracy, we could examine how different political parties at the local level impact policymaking,[14] but the CCP has a monopoly on political power in China. Moreover, due to the CCP's adherence to Leninist principles, such as democratic centralism, party members are not permitted to publicly express dissent from CCP decisions, which obscures the ways in which regional policy preferences may deviate from central directives. Thus, to uncover differences in regional approaches to governance in an authoritarian party-state, I examine policy style at the provincial level. Since one measure cannot capture the differences in provincial politics, I triangulate using a variety of metrics as indicators of distinct political tendencies.[15]

I examine the variation in political openness and economic development strategy in Chinese provinces by creating an index for each of these variables. The economic development strategy index measures the degree to which the province engages in export-oriented industrialization (EOI) to promote growth relative to other provinces. I created this index from four different economic indicators: exports; foreign direct investment; reliance on primary industry; and the number of patents filed. Exports and FDI are intended to provide an indication of the degree to which the province engages with the global economy. Provinces that have had more engagement with the global economy are also more likely to experience the institutional effects of these interactions. Foreign investors, for

[14] Simon F. Haeder and David L. Weimer, "You Can't Make Me Do It: State Implementation of Insurance Exchanges under the Affordable Care Act," *Public Administration Review* 73, no. s1 (September 2013): S34–S47, https://doi.org/10.1111/puar.12065.

[15] Several provinces have been accused of falsifying data, especially Liaoning, Jilin, and Inner Mongolia. See "Liaoning Government Admits False Growth Data from 2011–14," *Caixin Global*, January 18, 2018, www.caixinglobal.com/2017-01-18/101046468.html, accessed April 26, 2017; "Two Chinese Provinces Faked Economic Data, Inspectors Say," Bloomberg.com, June 12, 2017, www.bloomberg.com/news/articles/2017-06-12/two-chinese-provinces-falsified-economic-data-inspectors-say. However, the metrics that are most susceptible to falsification (such as gross regional product and jobless rates) are not included in my indices. In fact, by compiling various political and economic metrics, my index is more likely to reduce the impact of data falsification.

example, are likely to advocate for relatively predictable and stable legal institutions to ensure contract enforcement. By contrast, a province that relies on resource extraction (a primary industry) to generate revenue will not have experienced the institutional effects of engaging with the global economy. It may, by contrast, have developed a version of a subnational resource curse.[16]

I also include the number of patents filed per 10,000 people, as this is a possible observable implication of economic development strategy. First, the number of patents suggests greater economic activity related to developing innovative products that could potentially be globally competitive. Second, a larger number of patents suggests more innovation, which may reflect an overall climate of experimentalism within the province. Third, filing patents reflects a desire to protect intellectual property using the legal system, which necessitates a minimal degree of trust in legal channels. If firms are filing patents, they are also likely to advocate for relatively functional legal institutions.

The political openness index measures how "open" the political climate is relative to other provinces. I created this index from seven different indicators: public security spending; independent media organizations; presence of nongovernmental organizations; proportion of population identifying as an ethnic minority; anti-corruption; government innovation awards; and fiscal transparency. Although these indices are associated with wealth, I did not include wealth in the index because I seek to capture the observable actions of provincial leadership rather than outcomes. I will turn to outcomes in the next section. Moreover, although wealth plays a role in the policy process, my results suggest that it is not deterministic. Both indices are z-scores to normalize quantitative measures that would be on different scales. I describe in detail how I constructed each index in Appendix A.

Figure 3.2 shows provincial variation through a plot of policy style on the y-axis and economic development strategy on the x-axis. The scatterplot and summary statistics reveal several insights about Chinese provinces. First, export-oriented industrialization (EOI) is associated with political openness, making these factors difficult to disentangle in quantitative analysis with a small number of observations.[17] Second, there is more variation along economic development strategy than political openness (see Table 3.1). Since the CCP has encouraged a decentralized approach to economic growth but retained significant

[16] Qian Zhang and Roy Brouwer, "Is China Affected by the Resource Curse? A Critical Review of the Chinese Literature," *Journal of Policy Modeling* 4, no. 1 (January–February 2020): 133–152, https://doi.org/10.1016/j.jpolmod.2019.06.005.

[17] The correlation coefficient between the two indices is 0.43.

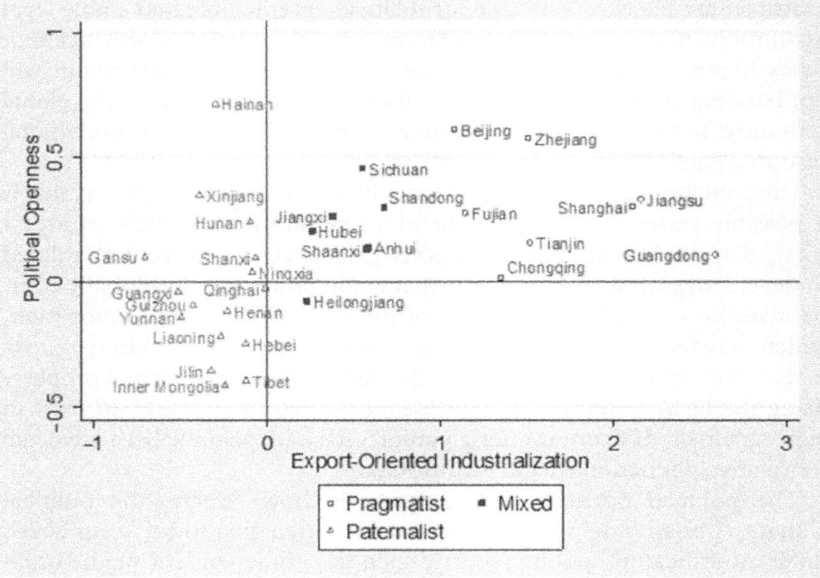


Figure 3.2 Scatterplot of economic and political indices.
Note: The indices are intended as estimates of the observable implications of different policy styles. The measurements vary in how well they perform in capturing the political climate. Notably, political openness is vastly overestimated in Xinjiang, likely due to a higher number of newspapers in ethnic minority languages, a high score for fiscal transparency, an average score for the number of NGOs, and average spending on public security. The 2010 *China Statistical Yearbook* indicates that Xinjiang spent less than half as much on public security (per capita) as did Tibet, although observers of the region would certainly note highly repressive policies in both provinces during this period.

control over political expression, it is not surprising to observe a smaller range for political openness. And yet, provinces do vary in their degree of political openness despite the potentially homogenizing effect of the Communist Party.

In addition to revealing differences in policy style, I am interested in whether different tendencies in governing are associated with social policy provision. To this end, I used the policy styles index to group provinces based on their dominant policy style. I performed a partition cluster analysis to group provinces into three clusters. I used k-means clustering, which is an iterative process that creates *k* groups by assigning each

Table 3.1 *Summary statistics of economic and political indices by group*

| | All Provinces | Pragmatist Group | Mixed Group | Paternalist Group |
|---|---|---|---|---|
| Export-Oriented Industrialization | | | | |
| Mean | 0.40 | 1.68 | 0.46 | −0.28 |
| Standard Deviation | 0.88 | 0.54 | 0.17 | 0.19 |
| Maximum | 2.59 | 2.59 | 0.68 | −0.01 |
| Minimum | −0.71 | 1.08 | 0.23 | −0.71 |
| Political Openness | | | | |
| Mean | 0.11 | 0.30 | 0.20 | −0.03 |
| Standard Deviation | 0.28 | 0.21 | 0.16 | 0.29 |
| Maximum | 0.71 | 0.61 | 0.46 | 0.71 |
| Minimum | −0.41 | 0.02 | −0.08 | −0.41 |

observation to the group with the closest mean.[18] Because of the small number of observations, I specify that provinces should be classified into three groups, which I label as pragmatist, paternalist, and mixed. The scatterplot in Figure 3.2 identifies each province's policy style by shape. Figure 3.3 depicts the geographic distribution of provincial policy styles.

The map in Figure 3.3 reveals that pragmatist provinces tend to be the wealthier, coastal provinces that industrialized first, as per central policies. The metropolis of Chongqing in central China is the one exception in this group, but it is also the least politically open of the pragmatist group. The paternalist group comprises provinces that are generally located inland, tend to be among the poorest (although not exclusively), and tend to be targeted for repressive policies in part due to discontented ethnic minority populations. Finally, some provinces exhibit neither unusually pragmatist nor extremely paternalist approaches to governance, producing a mixed policy style. In the following section, I examine how these distinct policy styles shape the policy process.

### *Pragmatist Provinces*

Pragmatist provinces embody Deng Xiaoping's maxim from the early stages of Chinese economic reforms: "It doesn't matter if a cat is black or white, as long as it catches mice."[19] Contained within this maxim is

[18] See STATA Manual, www.stata.com/manuals13/mvcluster.pdf#mvcluster.
[19] Deng, *Selected Works of Deng Xiaoping (1938–1965)*, 293.

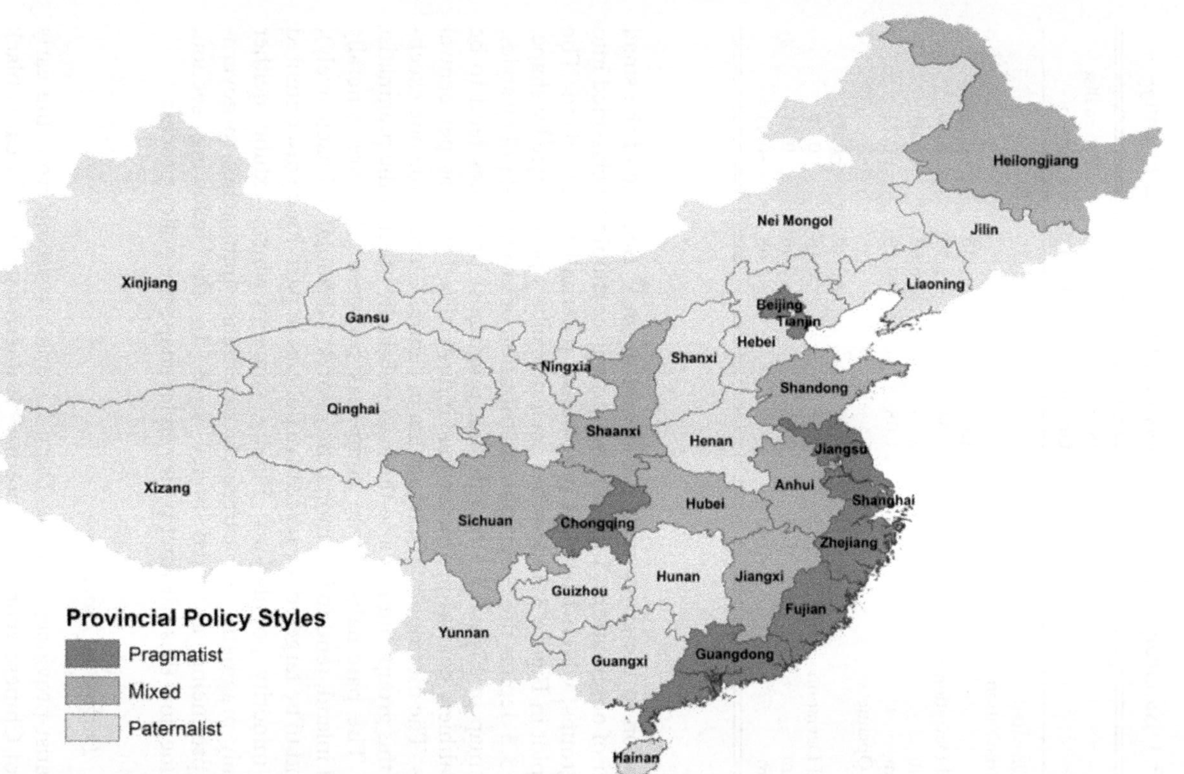


Figure 3.3 Map of provincial policy styles.

a signal regarding a fundamental change in central government policy: to get along and ahead, local officials should do whatever works to promote economic growth and not worry about ideology. Loosening the ideological reins on local officials enabled entrepreneurialism to flourish and contributed to the fantastic economic growth of the 1980s and 1990s. This shift toward pragmatism, coupled with opening up to world markets, enabled coastal provinces to surge ahead economically.

Provinces with a pragmatist policy style are, on average, wealthier than other provinces. They rely heavily on exports as an economic driver, and primary resources contribute little to economic development. These provinces are ethnically homogenous, with very small populations of ethnic minorities. Since these primarily coastal regions do not face destabilizing unrest and are influenced by foreign investors, they exhibit a more permissive political environment with higher levels of fiscal transparency and some commitment to anti-corruption. Pragmatist provinces also tend to have fewer restrictions on the media and telecommunications as compared to other provinces. In part because of firms' reliance on communication for commerce, these provinces do not regularly block all internet usage as do other regions of China.

Pragmatist provinces have developed a policy style that involves investing in human capital and encouraging policy innovation. To this end, they emphasize social policy as a strategy to support economic growth. These provinces develop human capital through social policy by prioritizing education, science, and technology over policies that seek to alleviate poverty, such as subsidized housing or pensions.[20] To encourage innovation, they further decentralize policy implementation to the county government, encourage early adoption of new policies and pilot projects, and support public–private partnerships. This approach has the potential to produce more effective social policy, as county officials have the flexibility to tailor implementation to local conditions. In addition, the involvement of nonstate actors can improve the efficiency and effectiveness of social policy by bringing distinct skill sets and additional capacity. Although these provinces can boast many policy successes, the decentralized approach of pragmatist provinces can also lead to greater within-province variation in social welfare provision as well as greater inequality, as will be discussed in the following chapter.

Because these provinces tend to be wealthier than other regions, the central government provides less direct support for social policy. As a result, they are relatively autonomous in funding and implementing many social policies. For example, the central government provides about

[20] Ratigan, "Disaggregating the Developing Welfare State."

one-third of the funding for rural health insurance for most provinces except the wealthy coastal ones. In these pragmatist provinces, the provincial government funds the bulk of the cost of rural health insurance, although it requires contributions from lower levels of government as well. Pragmatist provinces typically provide more autonomy to municipal and county governments to tailor policy to local conditions. As a result, local officials often need to learn how to design, implement, and sometimes innovate new policies by necessity.

Policy innovation is more common in pragmatist provinces. Following official notices from government ministries,[21] wealthier areas with better medical, human, and financial resources at their disposal are more likely to be chosen for pilot projects and the early implementation of new policies.[22] The logic for choosing these localities is that pilot projects are more likely to succeed under these propitious conditions.[23] For example, the rural health insurance program (initiated in 2003) was implemented two to three years earlier in Jiangsu as compared to Hunan and other interior provinces. This approach to pilot project selection reflects a broader strategy for governing a vast and diverse country: wealthier regions are afforded greater autonomy while less developed localities are more strictly monitored and regulated from above.[24]

New ideas in pragmatist provinces often emerge from the bottom up and may entail public–private partnerships. For example, Jiangsu's southern city of Suzhou was the first in the country to privatize a public hospital, sparking debate on hospital reform at the national level.[25] However, because of the greater autonomy afforded local government in pragmatist provinces, social policy is more uneven within the province. For example, reimbursement rates and individual premiums for rural health insurance can vary significantly from northern Jiangsu to southern Jiangsu.

21 Ministry of Health and Ministry of Finance, "关于做好新型农村合作医疗试点有关工作的通知 [Notice on Proper Implementation of the New Cooperative Medical System Pilot Projects]," 319 (2005).

22 Interviews JSAW01, HNGW30.

23 Of course, selecting favorable conditions for pilot projects is not an empirically rigorous approach to testing a new policy, but, however much the CCP may be considered experimentalist (see Heilmann and Perry, *Mao's Invisible Hand*), the party often does not adhere to the scientific method.

24 Yumin Sheng, *Economic Openness and Territorial Politics in China* (New York: Cambridge University Press, 2010).

25 Hua (辛华) Xing, "苏州允许设立私营医院 [Suzhou Allows Establishment of Private Hospitals]," 人民日报 [*People's Daily*], 华东新闻 [*Xinhua News*], 2002, www.people.com.cn/GB/paper40/5749/581937.html.

Although some measures suggest that there are lower rates of corruption in pragmatist provinces, these regions are not immune to graft and misuse of power. There can also be significant outcry when there is a highly publicized instance of abuse of power. However, these issues do not seem to be so intense as to threaten the stability of the regime in these provinces. Moreover, some argue that the nature of corruption in these provinces is such that it can complement, or at least not detract from, economic growth.[26]

### *Paternalist Provinces*

In sharp contrast to pragmatist provinces, paternalist provinces rely less on exports and more on natural resources. In some cases, these provinces exhibit a subnational variation of the "resource curse."[27] Resource-rich provinces tend to be home to large clusters of restive ethnic minorities and are the poorest regions of the country. The dependence on resource extraction, coupled with the prevalence of internal conflicts with the indigenous population in provinces such as Tibet and Xinjiang, has led to a restrictive political environment and a paternalist policy style. These provinces are the least open to innovation and take a top-down approach to social policy provision. Natural resource moguls misuse their power and undermine development through corruption. The approach to social policy is ad hoc, as these provinces tend to use social policy as a tactic to co-opt restless communities in order to put out political fires.

Because their approach to social policy is ad hoc and targeted, these provinces contain quite a bit of variation as to which types of social policy are emphasized and which are implemented effectively. Thus, selecting a suitable case study to represent the group is particularly difficult. Perhaps the most revealing case study would be Tibet or Xinjiang, but the political climates in these cases are so restrictive as to preclude meaningful research. Therefore, I utilize Yunnan, which is illustrative of many of the political dynamics found elsewhere but was somewhat more open to researchers than Tibet or Xinjiang.

Yunnan is an interesting case because, in some respects, the province has become less politically tolerant in the 2000s. For example, after working with a flourishing NGO sector in the 1990s, local government

[26] Andrew Hall Wedeman, *Double Paradox: Rapid Growth and Rising Corruption in China* (Ithaca, NY: Cornell University Press, 2012).

[27] Hong Yu and Yongnian Zheng, "The Resource Boom in China's Resource-Rich Provinces: The Role of the State-Owned Enterprises and Associated Problems," *Asian Survey* 56, no. 2 (April 2016): 270–300, https://doi.org/10.1525/as.2016.56.2.270; Zhang and Brouwer, "Is China Affected by the Resource Curse?"

enacted additional restrictions on NGOs despite recognizing their usefulness with respect to social service delivery.[28] Concerns about the potential of NGOs to foment political instability, particularly in the wake of the Color Revolutions in central and eastern Europe in the early 2000s, created skepticism about their aims and concern over their potential to challenge the current political order. Thus, Yunnan has become relatively politically restrictive regarding NGOs and researchers, both foreign and domestic. Subsequently, under Xi Jinping, the central government further restricted NGO and scholarly activity through nationwide regulations. However, this book focuses on the Hu Jintao years (2002–12).

Paternalist provinces often implement social policy in a top-down fashion. They adopt province-wide standards sooner than their pragmatist counterparts. They sometimes even micromanage policy implementation in ways that encourage coercion by local officials, as will be discussed in Chapter 5. Paternalist provinces are prone to corrupt practices that undermine economic and social development. As they receive significant subsidies from the distant central government, local actors are more likely to devise schemes to siphon off funds for themselves. For example, in Hunan, there have been reports of hospitals and medical workers fabricating cases of illness to extract subsidies from the government (*jiabingli* 假病历).[29] While this phenomenon was acknowledged to be a common problem by nearly all the local officials and hospital personnel with whom I spoke in Hunan, my interviewees in Jiangsu – a pragmatist province – appeared to be sincerely unaware of this problem within their own province even when prompted.

### *Mixed Provinces*

Mixed provinces exhibit elements of pragmatism in addition to elements of paternalism. They tend to be more politically open than paternalist provinces but more restrictive than pragmatist provinces. This combination produces a policy style in which provincial leaders take a top-down approach to policymaking and standardize new policies across the province, but they also exhibit some elements of pragmatism. These provinces also tend to be much more frugal in their social policy allocations (see Figure 3.4).

In mixed regions, the central government provides some subsidies for social policy, and the province tends to institute regulations to

[28] Jessica C. Teets, *Civil Society under Authoritarianism: The China Model* (New York: Cambridge University Press, 2014).

[29] Interviews with hospital personnel and media reports in Hunan, 2010.

standardize social policy at the provincial level. As a result, there is less within-province variation than occurs in pragmatic provinces. For example, in Hubei, the funding structure from rural health insurance – including per capita contributions from the province, county, and individual – was standardized at the provincial level early in the implementation process.[30] Of course, some variation remains, and local governments do not immediately comply with provincial-level regulations, but this effort from the provincial government does tend to reduce within-province variability. Due to the greater involvement of the provincial government, these provinces are generally later adopters of new policy and tend to exhibit less innovation at the local level. Provinces with a mixed policy style tend to take a top-down approach to policymaking but may not micromanage like a paternalist province – an approach that often results in pro forma implementation by local government.

On the one hand, top-down implementation and province-wide standardization reduce within-province variation and inequality, mitigating the effects of a "postcode lottery,"[31] in which one's benefits vary based on residence. However, reduced autonomy for local government below the provincial level also limits the opportunity to develop the capacity and capabilities of local officials in the interest of good governance. The rural health insurance program provides an illustrative example of the implications of top-down implementation. In a pragmatist province, counties had the autonomy to set up new offices and committees to determine reimbursement percentages, thereby requiring local officials to determine the specifics of the policy (such as reimbursement percentages) at the county level. Thus, in theory, local officials were required to learn about the policy and consider the most appropriate course of action for their locality, further developing human capital within local government. By contrast, in a mixed province, counties generally followed provincial-level guidelines with little opportunity for local officials to shape policy implementation, thereby widening the gap in local government capacity and the quality of local governance between the provinces. In this way, officials in pragmatist provinces have had additional opportunities for leadership and capacity building, while local

[30] Hubei Provincial Government Bulletin, "湖北省人民政府关于全面推进新型农村合作医疗制度建设的指导意见 [Hubei Province People's Government Instructive Opinion on the Full Promotion of the Construction of the New Cooperative Medical System]," May 2008.

[31] Patrick Butler, "Q&A: Postcode Lottery," *The Guardian*, November 9, 2000, www.theguardian.com/society/2000/nov/09/NHS; Kate Devlin, "Healthcare Postcode Lottery Means Patients Losing out on Cancer Treatments," *The Telegraph*, September 8, 2008, www.telegraph.co.uk/news/health/2700686/Healthcare-postcode-lottery-means-patients-losing-out-on-cancer-treatments.html.

officials elsewhere are beholden to provincial (and central) authority, both financially and in terms of decision-making. While policies such as rural health insurance afford the opportunity for pragmatist provinces to continue to build local state capacity, other provinces are left waiting for government transfers and do not have the autonomy or resources to shape policy implementation.

This is not to say that mixed provinces never innovate or exceed expectations for social policy provision. For example, Shenmu County in Shaanxi Province has gained notoriety for using the revenue generated by coal mining to establish an extensive social welfare system for county residents, including universal healthcare, free education through secondary school,[32] housing subsidies, and poverty relief programs.[33] Anhui, also in the mixed group, served as a model for the national policy on essential drugs, although implementation was problematic.[34] While there are certainly anomalies, provinces in the mixed group are less likely to be policy innovators than pragmatist provinces.

Table 3.2 summarizes the main features of the dominant policy styles that I find in China: pragmatist, paternalist, and mixed. As stated in the introductory chapter, I examine four dimensions of policy styles in Chinese provinces: provincial policy priorities; local state capacity; institutions; and patterns of behavior. Table 3.2 summarizes the central tendencies of these dimensions for each of the three policy styles. I turn to the question of the impact of policy style on social policy provision in the next section.

## Policy Styles and Social Policy Provision

In this section, I examine how the three groups of provinces diverge in their social policy priorities. I use provincial social policy spending as the outcome variable to measure social policy priorities. Following previous research, I use social policy spending to capture the observable implications of the provincial governments' priorities.[35] Measures of social welfare that focus on the well-being of the population (e.g., life expectancy,

32 Typically, nine years of compulsory education beginning at age six are virtually free in public schools. Public secondary schools, however, increasingly charge various operating fees that can be a significant burden on lower-income families.

33 The county has received some coverage from the state media for its efforts. See "Public welfare programs in Shenmu County, Shaanxi Province," *China.org.cn*, December 27, 2009, www.china.org.cn/photos/2009-12/27/content_19138418.htm.

34 Huang, *Governing Health in Contemporary China*, 75.

35 Research on welfare regimes commonly examines differences in social policy spending. Cross-national research often focuses on education, health, and social security. See Gough and Wood, *Insecurity and Welfare Regimes in Asia, Africa and Latin America*; Rudra, *Globalization and the Race to the Bottom in Developing Countries*. I also include spending on subsidized housing, as spending on the Minimum Livelihood Guarantee

Table 3.2 *Provincial policy styles and social policy (SP) in China*

| | Pragmatist | Paternalist | Mixed |
|---|---|---|---|
| Local State Resources | Large provincial budget<br>Little central support for SP<br>Professionalized local state | Small provincial budget<br>Dependent on central transfers for SP<br>Low-capacity local state | Medium provincial budget<br>Some central transfers for SP<br>Medium-capacity local state |
| Institutional Approaches | Decentralized<br>Attentive to corruption<br>Higher transparency | Provincial standards<br>Less attentive to corruption<br>Lower transparency | Provincial standards<br>Less attentive to corruption<br>Lower transparency |
| Patterns of Policymaking | Bottom-up approach<br>Innovative<br>Inclusive of nonstate actors | Top-down approach<br>Less innovation<br>Selective inclusion of nonstate actors | Top-down approach<br>Less innovation<br>Exclusive of nonstate actors |
| Social Policy Strategy | Human-capital promotion<br>Broad eligibility<br>Shallow benefits | Social control<br>Targeted benefits with conditionality | Social control<br>Broad eligibility<br>Minimalist benefits |
| Social Policy Priorities | Education | Targeted poverty alleviation | Social security<br>Subsidized housing |

infant/maternal mortality) often reflect overall levels of socioeconomic development rather than government priorities. Moreover, the way in which allocated funds translate into the provision of specific services (e.g., number of hospital beds per capita, number of teachers per capita) is often impacted by other factors and may be confounded by corruption. Thus, I focus on social policy spending as an indication of provincial priorities.

I find that provinces with a more pragmatist policy style tend to prioritize education and health while spending less on the social safety net, poverty alleviation, and housing. Spending can reveal divergence in provincial priorities, but it is limited in capturing qualitative differences in how local officials implement policies. After the quantitative analysis of provinces, I use in-depth case studies in the following chapters to examine how the policy process differs across provinces.

programs became an increasingly important part of China's efforts to alleviate poverty in the 2000s.

To examine variation in social policy spending, I use provincial spending on four different types of social policy as the dependent variables: education, health, social safety net, and housing. Education includes all levels of educational spending, from early childhood education through tertiary and professional education. As reported by the National Bureau of Statistics, the overall category of healthcare does not differentiate between different types of state health spending and includes funding for state hospitals, subsidized government insurance programs, and public health programs. According to the 2010 *China Statistical Yearbook*, "social safety net and employment" includes spending on a variety of poverty-alleviation programs and structures, including "civil affairs administration; national social safety net subsidy fund; retirement from administrative departments; subsidies for enterprise closures or bankruptcies; employment subsidies; pensions; retiree resettlement; social welfare; services for people with disabilities; urban minimum living allowance; other urban social relief; rural social relief; natural disaster relief; Red Cross services; other social safety nets and employment expenses."[36] Housing refers to government-subsidized housing, which is provided to low-income residents as per central-government directives to provide affordable housing. The central government increased its emphasis on low-income housing beginning in 2010, resulting in improved local compliance with central policy. As a result, data on local housing expenditures begin in 2010. Nonetheless, provinces with high-value real estate markets have continued to resist affordable housing policies, as will be discussed in Chapter 4 on pragmatist provinces.[37]

Figure 3.4 provides an overview of per capita social policy spending by policy-style group. Pragmatist and paternalist provinces spend about the same amount per capita. This similarity may be surprising at first glance, as pragmatic provinces are wealthier due to locally generated revenue. However, paternalist provinces enjoy significant amounts of fiscal transfers from the central government, which are typically earmarked for various types of social policy, resulting in budgets for social welfare that are comparable to those of pragmatist provinces. By contrast, mixed provinces are often caught in a middle-income trap: they are too wealthy to be eligible for some central transfers and too poor to generate their own revenue for social policy. Thus, the mixed group tends to face the most stringent budgetary constraints, which leads to frugality in social welfare.

[36] State Statistical Bureau of the People's Republic of China, *China Statistical Yearbook* (Beijing: China Statistical Publishing, 2011).

[37] Huang, "Low-Income Housing in Chinese Cities."

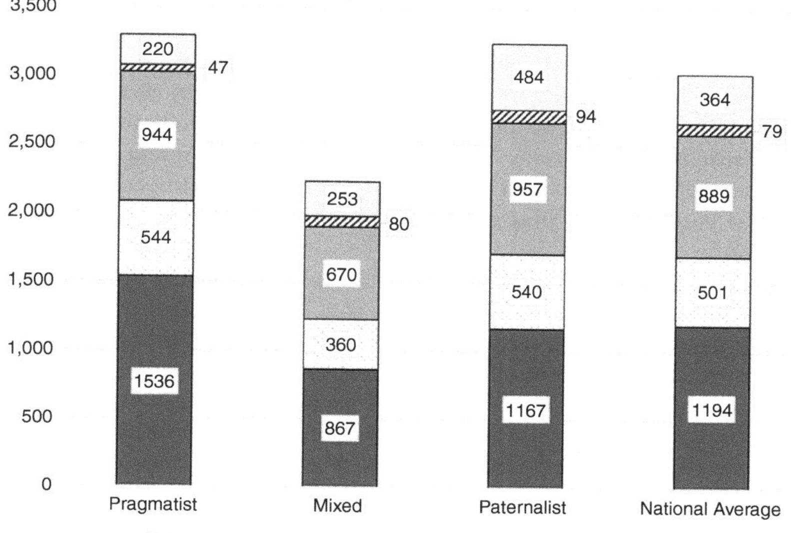


Figure 3.4 Per capita spending on social policy by policy-style group in RMB.

Each policy style also exhibits differences in social policy priorities. Paternalist provinces spend more than double what their pragmatist counterparts do on housing and the MLG. This distinction is notable because housing and the MLG are policies that are explicitly means-tested and, therefore, more easily targeted to areas of discontent. One could argue that paternalist provinces, with their poorer populations, have a greater need for the MLG. However, the need for affordable housing should not be as acute in paternalist provinces as their pragmatist counterparts. Rising real estate prices in coastal provinces, where pragmatism dominates, have created a housing crisis for so many residents that the central government pushed for affordable housing policy in the 2000s. But coastal provinces resisted, as will be discussed in Chapter 4.

Pragmatist provinces spend somewhat more on education than paternalist provinces and 1.77 times more than mixed provinces. Although the difference in education spending between pragmatist and paternalist provinces is small, their populations' educational needs must be contextualized. On the one hand, the overall cost of living is higher in pragmatist provinces. However, paternalist provinces have needy populations that are expensive to educate. Paternalist provinces, with larger rural populations, have high per-student education costs due to their dispersed populations. Boarding schools for secondary school are more common. Students are likely to need more educational resources, as they may not speak Mandarin at home and their families are less likely to have access to private enrichment programs. Thus, although overall spending is similar, it is reasonable to expect that paternalist provinces might need to spend more per student than pragmatist provinces to provide a comparable education.

While we can observe differences in social policy spending between the various provincial styles, some may argue that local differences are attributable to needs or wealth rather than policy style. The first hypothesis is that provincial policy could be responding to distinct local needs. Provinces that have dire needs in specific social policy areas may choose to allocate their resources accordingly and, therefore, would lack funds for policies that might be perceived as less necessary. If this were the case, we would expect to see a greater proportion of spending on poverty alleviation in provinces with a lower per capita income. While there is, indeed, an inverse association between the proportion of poverty-alleviation spending and per capita income, the relationship is weak, leaving much of the variation unexplained.[38] Also, we might expect greater proportions of education spending in provinces that have greater educational needs, such as those with high rates of illiteracy or those that need additional resources to provide multilingual education programs to ethnic minorities.

To test these propositions, I examined the association between education spending several years after the data on illiteracy and ethnic minority populations were collected.[39] The logic is that, if the needs hypothesis were supported, provincial leaders would have identified a need and responded accordingly by prioritizing education over other types of social policy. Contrary to this hypothesis, gross education spending is inversely, but weakly, associated with illiteracy.[40] The association between the *proportion* of education spending and illiteracy is somewhat stronger,

[38] The correlation coefficient between the proportion of social safety net spending and per capita income is –0.31.

[39] I took data on illiteracy from 2009 and spending from 2011. This is not a perfect measure, but the lag time between the identification of a problem and a policy response could be short in an authoritarian regime if there were political will to address the problem. The lag is not necessary for the proportion of ethnic minorities, as we can presume that provincial authorities are aware of whether or not there are significant proportions of ethnic minorities in the province. The proportion of ethnic minorities is most reliable from the 2010 census data, so I use the data from that year.

[40] Correlation coefficient of –0.35.

though still weak, and it is still an inverse association, which undermines the needs hypothesis.[41] The association between the proportion of ethnic minorities in the population and education spending is somewhat stronger than illiteracy, but it is still inversely correlated.[42] Therefore, the direction of these associations suggests that the needs hypothesis does little to explain subnational variation in social policy priorities. It is worth noting, in fact, that the inverse relationship between illiteracy and education spending suggests that the causal arrow goes in the other direction – underfunded schools may contribute to higher illiteracy rates. However, a close examination of this hypothesis is beyond the scope of this book. What the data do suggest is that provinces are not solely responding to their local needs.

The second alternative hypothesis is that provincial priorities could be dictated by wealth. Wealthier provinces may be more likely to prioritize education over poverty alleviation merely because they have the luxury to do so. Indeed, education spending and poverty alleviation are both highly and positively correlated with wealth as measured by gross regional product (GRP).[43] In other words, wealthier provinces spend more on all types of social policy, on average. However, looking at the *proportion* of spending on different types of social policy, the data suggest a more complicated story. Wealth can explain some of the variation in the proportion of spending on education, but the strength of the association drops by half.[44] Wealth offers even less explanatory power with the proportion of spending on social safety net spending, which is weakly and inversely correlated with GRP.[45] Thus, the wealth hypothesis is also insufficient to explain variation in social policy provision.

To be clear, I do not claim that wealth and needs are irrelevant to social policy allocations. Rather, I contend that, even after accounting for wealth and needs, there remains significant variation in provincial social policy spending that can only be explained by considering provincial politics. I test whether policy style is associated with social policy spending when controlling for wealth and needs through a series of

[41] Correlation coefficient of –0.43.

[42] The correlation coefficient for education spending and ethnic population is –0.54; between proportion of education spending and ethnic population, it is –0.46. The magnitude of the latter estimate is likely overestimated due to an influential outlier.

[43] Education spending and GRP have a correlation coefficient of 0.96. Social safety net spending (poverty alleviation and pensions) and GRP have a correlation coefficient of 0.63.

[44] The correlation coefficients between the proportion of education spending and GRP and the log of GRP are 0.43 and 0.48, respectively.

[45] The correlation coefficient between the proportion of social safety net spending and GRP is –0.33. The magnitude of this estimate is likely overestimated due to several outliers, as apparent in a scatterplot. The author can make scatterplots available upon request.

between-effects regression models with provincial social policy spending as the outcome variable.[46] Tables 3.3 and 3.4 report the results of these

[46] Since panel data present numerous challenges (see Sven E. Wilson and Daniel M. Butler, "A Lot More to Do: The Sensitivity of Time-Series Cross-Section Analyses to Simple Alternative Specifications," *Political Analysis* 15, no. 2 [March 2007]: 101–123, https://doi.org/10.1093/pan/mpl012), I considered several alternate specifications of the model and concluded that the between-effects model (BEM) was the most appropriate for these data. The BEM regresses the mean of the dependent variable on the mean of the independent variables, but it does not take into consideration dynamic effects over time, as such: $\overline{Y_l} = \beta\overline{X_l} + u_i$.

Since the dependent variable for these models, social policy spending, does not change dramatically over the period under consideration, it is reasonable to exclude time from the model. My analysis is focused on the cross-sectional variation of provinces rather than dynamic variation. Rather than providing variation over time, the benefit of panel data in this analysis lies in capturing general tendencies for provincial social policy spending, thereby ensuring that the data are not merely a snapshot of spending in a single anomalous year. Moreover, the BEM prevents an artificial inflation of the sample size, as may occur when utilizing multiple observations (e.g., multiple years) of the same unit (e.g., provinces). Because of the resulting smaller sample size, the BEM also provides a relatively conservative estimation (see Sven E. Wilson and Daniel M. Butler, "A Lot More to Do: The Promise and Peril of Panel Data in Political Science," [Unpublished manuscript, Brigham Young University Department of Political Science, 2004], 9), thereby reducing the likelihood of a Type I error, or false positive. I conducted several robustness checks on these models. They yield similar results when using random effects and panel-corrected standard errors (see Nathaniel Beck and Jonathan N. Katz, "What to Do (and Not to Do) with Time-Series Cross-Section Data," *American Political Science Review* 89, no. 3 [September 1995]: 634). The variables of interest are statistically significant, and the sign and magnitude of the coefficients is similar in these two alternate specifications. I prefer the between-effects model, as it provides a conservative estimate without resorting to an atheoretical model. I also ran the models using a weighted version of the policy styles index computed by principal component analysis (PCA). The results were consistent.

As another robustness check, I ran the models with the dependent variable lagged by one year as a control variable. Including the lagged dependent variable does absorb much of the variation of the dependent variable. However, this does not necessarily demonstrate that the independent variables are not related to the outcome. Plümper and his coauthors show that the coefficient for the lagged dependent variable can be biased upwards (see Thomas Plümper, Vera E. Troeger, and Philip Manow, "Panel Data Analysis in Comparative Politics: Linking Method to Theory," *European Journal of Political Research* 4, no. 2 [March 2005]: 327–354). I would expect that social spending in Chinese provinces is closely related to spending in the previous year, as is the case with government spending cross-nationally. Moreover, for each province, social policy spending changes little over this time period, reducing the need to capture dynamic effects. In other words, the variation of interest is cross-sectional, not over time. Thus, a model with a lagged dependent variable would not be appropriate for this analysis because it would obscure the cross-sectional variation between provinces in social spending.

In short, since the BEM provides the most conservative estimates without resorting to an atheoretical model and is appropriate for an analysis that focuses on cross-sectional (rather than dynamic) variation, I report the results of these models. That said, the nature of panel data and the small-n approach of the BEM warrant caution. Therefore, I triangulate to better understand this phenomenon by examining the results of the cluster analysis, the panel data, and qualitative evidence of how social policy varies across Chinese provinces. In this way, we can gain a better understanding of how China's provincial politics impact welfare provision. Taken together, the evidence suggests that the results of the analysis are not likely to be spurious.

Table 3.3 *Between-effects regression models of provincial social policy spending: education and health*

| Independent Variables | Dependent Variables | | | | | |
|---|---|---|---|---|---|---|
| | Education Spending | Education Spending | Education Spending as Proportion of Total Expenditures | Education Spending as Proportion of Total Expenditures | Health Spending | Health Spending as Proportion of Total Expenditures |
| | (1) | (2) | (3) | (4) | (5) | (6) |
| Policy Style | 58.69** | 47.76* | 0.38 | 0.35 | 18.65$^{\dagger}$ | 0.02 |
| Education Transfers | 1.14E-05 | | 1.21E-07 | | | |
| Key Universities | | 7.03* | | −0.03 | | |
| Health Transfers | | | | | 9.54E-04* | −4.86E-07 |
| Population | 0.04** | 0.04** | −2.59E-04 | −2.70E-04 | 0.01$^{\dagger}$ | 8.68E-07 |
| Log of GRP | 81.67$^{\dagger}$ | 104.16* | 1.95* | 2.23* | 22.30 | 0.01 |
| Dependency Ratio | −1.45 | 1.02 | 0.06 | 0.07 | 0.40 | 0.03 |
| Inequality (20:20) | 35.36$^{\dagger}$ | 47.84* | −0.09 | −0.17 | 6.95 | −0.37 |
| Percent Urban | −1.13 | −1.54 | −0.09$^{\dagger}$ | −0.07 | 0.28 | −0.04 |
| Observations | 122 | 131 | 122 | 131 | 131 | 131 |
| R-Squared (Overall) | 0.63 | 0.71 | 0.32 | 0.39 | 0.63 | 0.21 |

*Significance Codes:* ***$p<0.01$, ** $p<0.05$, * $p<0.10$, $^{\dagger}$ $p<0.15$

*Data Sources:* Policy style is an original measure. For data sources and calculation of this index, see Appendix A. Key universities data are from China Education On-line, 2005. Inequality measure calculated based on data from provincial yearbooks, 2003–13. All others from National Bureau of Statistics, 2003–13.

*Note:* Xinjiang excluded due to data anomalies.

Table 3.4 *Between-effects regression models of provincial social policy spending: poverty alleviation and housing*

| | Dependent Variables | | | | | |
|---|---|---|---|---|---|---|
| | Social Safety Net Spending | Social Safety Net Spending as Proportion of Total Expenditures | MLG Spending | MLG Spending as Proportion of Total Expenditures | Housing Spending | Housing Spending as Proportion of Total Expenditures |
| Independent Variables | (7) | (8) | (9) | (10) | (11) | (12) |
| Policy Style | 0.70 | −1.34* | 1.32E+08 | −0.11 | 1.12 | −0.26 |
| Social Safety Net Transfers | 5.27E-04*** | 1.43E-05*** | | | | |
| MLG Transfers | | | 8016.71*** | 2.42E-06*** | | |
| Fiscal Transfers | | | | | 0.08*** | 2.58E-03** |
| Population | 0.02 | −7.53E-04† | 20116.69 | −1.52E-04* | −0.01 | −6.04E-04** |
| Log of GRP | 21.37 | 1.23 | 4.59E+08 | 0.36† | 7.30 | 0.02 |
| Dependency Ratio | −0.22 | 0.13 | −5172138 | 0.01 | 1.68 | 0.15** |
| Inequality (20:20) | 45.63** | 2.04** | 3.24+E07 | −0.01 | 8.78† | 1.03*** |
| Percent Urban | 5.34** | 0.13† | −1.69+E07 | −0.02 | 0.76 | 0.03 |
| Observations | 125 | 125 | 125 | 125 | 54 | 54 |
| R-Squared (Overall) | 0.79 | 0.24 | 0.82 | 0.36 | 0.69 | 0.73 |

*Significance Codes*: *** $p<0.01$, ** $p<0.05$, * $p<0.10$, † $p<0.15$

*Data Sources:* Policy style is an original measure. For data sources for this index, see Appendix A. Minimum Livelihood Guarantee spending from the *Ministry of Civil Affairs Statistical Yearbook*, 2003–13. Fiscal transfers compiled from the *Finance Yearbook of China*. Inequality measure (20:20 ratio) calculated based on data from provincial yearbooks, 2003–13.[47] Social safety net transfers are central government transfers earmarked for pensions and poverty alleviation, calculated from *China Civil Affairs Yearbooks*, 2003–13. All others from National Bureau of Statistics, 2003–13.
*Note:* Xinjiang excluded due to data anomalies.

[47] The 20:20 ratio was calculated by dividing the mean per capita disposable income for the wealthiest 20 percent of urban households by the bottom 20 percent of the same. For Guangdong, Hainan, and Liaoning, mean household income was used in lieu of per capita income because the latter was not reported. Data on rural household income by quintile (or similar) is not available in most provinces for these years. I prefer this measure to other measures of inequality, such as the Gini, because it is resistant to outliers. This measure is used by the United Nations

models. Descriptive statistics for all variables in Tables 3.3 and 3.4 are presented in Appendix A, specifically Table A.1.

I estimated models with two versions of the outcome variable: total spending in a designated policy area; and spending in a policy area as a proportion of the provincial budget. In addition to education, health, social safety net, and housing, I also included spending on the MLG. The MLG is the primary poverty-alleviation program in China, although it consumes a small proportion of the budget. Social safety net, on the other hand, comprises a variety of poverty-alleviation and pension programs, as previously discussed.

The provinces generally do not report the proportion of social policy expenditures that come from provincial revenue as opposed to transfers from the central government. To control for the effect of central transfers, I included earmarked transfers for the corresponding type of social policy as an independent variable. For education, however, the meaning of earmarked education spending as reported in the *Educational Finance Statistical Yearbooks* is ambiguous.[48] Therefore, I also include the number of "key" universities in the province. Significant central-government fiscal transfers are destined for key universities that are targeted as part of a national strategy to improve elite higher education. Earmarked spending on housing is not available for these years, so I use the total amount of fiscal transfers from the center to the province as a proxy.

The models reveal a consistent pattern. Provinces with a more pragmatist policy style (higher score for policy style) are more likely to prioritize education and healthcare, but, all else being equal, they are less likely to allocate funds for social safety net, poverty alleviation, and housing. This tendency reflects trends observed at the cross-national level by scholars of welfare regimes.[49] The models of education spending have positive, statistically significant coefficients for policy style, suggesting that pragmatist provinces are more likely to spend more on education – even when controlling for wealth, needs (dependency ratio), and central transfers. The coefficient for policy style for health spending is also positive, but it narrowly misses the threshold for statistical significance at the $p<0.10$ level.

[48] The *Educational Finance Statistical Yearbooks* provide data on fiscal transfers, but the yearbook is ambiguous regarding the nature of those transfers. In addition, dramatic year-to-year fluctuations in the data suggest that the yearbooks may have changed their methods over time, but the publishers do not include documentation explaining any changes in measurement. The publisher did not respond to requests for clarification regarding the meaning of the data. Moreover, there is no association between provincial education spending and earmarked education transfers (correlation coefficient of 0.00), leading me to suspect problems with the education transfer data.

[49] Rudra, *Globalization and the Race to the Bottom in Developing Countries*.

Conversely, while the results from models 7 through 12 are more mixed, models 8, 10, and 12 suggest that provinces with a more pragmatist policy style tend to allocate *less* to social safety net, poverty alleviation (MLG), and housing. Put another way, provinces with a more paternalist policy style allocate more to these types of social policy. However, the policy-style variable in this set of models is only statistically significant in model 8, where the outcome variable is spending on social safety net as a proportion of provincial expenditures.

Overall, the models support a consistent relationship: more pragmatist provinces tend to prioritize health and education, whereas more paternalist provinces tend to prioritize the social safety net, poverty alleviation, and housing. However, the models are less successful at explaining variation in spending on the social safety net and poverty alleviation. That said, I expect these results to be conservative, taking into consideration that the type of model and collinearity between several independent variables is likely to depress the statistical significance of the estimated coefficients. Moreover, due to data limitations, the sample size is small. In sum, these models suggest that policy style has a relationship with social policy spending even when controlling for wealth, needs, and earmarked fiscal transfers from the central government.

Although analyzing spending can illuminate some patterns in the relationship between policy style and social policy implementation, spending cannot capture the nuanced differences in social policy provision. To analyze this variation across provinces with different policy styles, the following chapters examine case studies of health policy with additional examples from education, poverty alleviation, and housing policy.

## Causal Mechanism

Political and economic factors set the conditions for provinces to take different approaches to governing. But is there a causal mechanism that suggests whether provincial leaders take a more pragmatist or paternalist approach? Previous research has established that central leaders exert control differently over different regions of the country. Yumin Sheng, for example, convincingly shows that the center faces a dilemma. Beijing needs to collect revenue from wealthier provinces and distribute funds to poorer provinces. Subsidies to poorer provinces will buy their allegiance to the center, but central leaders also need to ensure that wealthy provinces comply with tax policies and do not rebel. Sheng argues that

Beijing appoints regime loyalists to lead wealthier provinces, thereby ensuring greater compliance with revenue sharing.[50]

Sheng's argument implies that loyalists leading wealthy provinces may be more compliant in policy areas beyond revenue extraction. However, in other policy areas, regime loyalists leading wealthy provinces – such as those in the pragmatist group – often deviate from central directives and sometimes resist central policy without apparent repercussions from Beijing. Thus, in practice, the regime loyalists leading wealthier provinces tend to enjoy more autonomy in policy implementation and, in turn, offer greater autonomy to local government within the province. By contrast, poorer provinces tend to follow central policy more closely, sticking to the letter of the law.

After the 1994 tax reform, the central government established distinct fiscal relationships with provinces based on their reliance on the center for fiscal transfers (see Chapter 2). Throughout the 1990s and 2000s, earmarked central transfers became an important part of funding for social policy in poorer provinces, while wealthier provinces were able (and forced) to use their locally generated revenue to fund similar programs. By the 2000s, Wanlong Lin and Christine Wong found that most subsidies for rural areas were entirely locally financed in the eastern region, while the central and western regions received between 50 to 100 percent of the funds needed for these policies through fiscal transfers from the central government.[51] Earmarked transfers for social programs, sometimes referred to as "conditional grants," "should be monitored by higher-level governments to insure proper compliance ... [and may] compromise local government budget autonomy."[52] As a result, the center has tolerated greater autonomy for wealthier provinces in social policy but kept a tighter rein on poorer provinces. I show the greater autonomy of pragmatist provinces in the following chapters through case studies. I also test the relationship between central control and policy style by examining fiscal transfers from the center to the provinces.

Provinces that receive more fiscal transfers are more likely to exhibit a paternalist policy style. I tested this proposition through a regression model with policy style as the dependent variable and fiscal transfers as the independent variable of interest (Table 3.5). I included the following

[50] Sheng, *Economic Openness and Territorial Politics in China*.

[51] Wanlong Lin and Christine Wong, "Are Beijing's Equalization Policies Reaching the Poor? An Analysis of Direct Subsidies Under the 'Three Rurals' (Sannong)," *China Journal* 67 (January 2012): 35. Wong and Lin's study included subsidies for compulsory education, the NCMS, the Medical Care Relief Fund, the Minimum Living Guarantee, and the Livestock Insurance Subsidy.

[52] World Bank and the Development Research Center of the State Council, the People's Republic of China, *Urban China*, 599.

Table 3.5 *Between-effects regression model of provincial policy style*

| Independent Variables | Policy Style |
|---|---|
| Fiscal Transfers | −0.0008* |
| | (0.00) |
| Population | 0.0002** |
| | (0.00) |
| Income Per Capita | 0.0000 |
| | (0.00) |
| Dependency Ratio | 0.0650** |
| | (0.03) |
| Percent Ethnic Minority | −0.0059 |
| | (0.01) |
| Percent Urban | 0.0285 |
| | (0.03) |
| Observations | 124 |
| R-Squared (Overall) | 0.70 |

*Significance Codes:* *** $p<0.001$, ** $p<0.05$, * $p<0.10$
*Data Sources:* Policy style is an original measure. For data sources and calculation of the policy style index, see Appendix A. For descriptive statistics of the independent variables in this table, see Appendix A, specifically Table A.1. All others from National Bureau of Statistics, 2003–2013.

control variables: population, wealth (income per capita), dependency ratio, percent ethnic minority, and percent urban. Fiscal transfers are negatively associated with policy style, and the coefficient is statistically significant, suggesting that receiving more fiscal transfers from the center is associated with paternalism.

The case studies in the following chapters demonstrate how provincial leaders manifest their autonomy. Although pragmatist provinces may be led by regime loyalists who comply with tax policy, officials in these provinces feel empowered to shape and sometimes resist central directives regarding social policy. Paternalist provinces, by contrast, tend to implement policy by closely following guidelines from the center. Even when local government, such as the city or county, issues their own guidelines for the implementation of a new policy, localities from paternalist provinces tend to echo the central and provincial directives on that policy. In this way, the center's tolerance of autonomy within some provinces contributes to distinct local approaches to the policymaking process.

### Alternative Explanations

Two alternative explanations have been posited that could explain the observed local variation in social policy provision: the cadre promotion hypothesis and the industrial policy hypothesis. First, scholars suspect that cadre promotion criteria impact local officials' behavior. This also may be true in social policy, as Tingjin Lin argues when examining education.[53] Others have also found that, as Beijing has adjusted its priorities to include social welfare, local government may have adjusted cadre evaluation to include social policy targets.[54] This shift in cadre evaluation targets had not yet become prevalent during the Hu Jintao government, however.

Second, the economic development strategy employed by each province impacts the types of social policy that the local government emphasizes. Economic strategy helps explain monetary allocations, Rudra's research shows, such as which provinces spend more on education as compared to poverty alleviation.[55] However, economic development strategy does not explain the *qualitative* differences in how the provinces approach the policy process, from adoption to implementation. There is no reason to assume that export-oriented provinces would necessarily take a more decentralized approach to policymaking and be more willing to rely on nonstate actors in social policy provision. Certainly, economic policy is an important part of the story, but we also need to consider the differences in political openness across provinces to get a complete picture of local variation in the policy process.

Moreover, if economics were the sole factor, then we would not see so much variation in terms of political openness among provinces with similar exposure to the global economy. For example, Zhejiang and Tianjin rank similarly in terms of their economic orientation, but Zhejiang is far more politically open than Tianjin. On the other end of the spectrum, Hunan and Tibet are ranked similarly economically, but Hunan is far more politically open than Tibet (see Figure 3.2). Thus, my framework of policy styles includes both economic and political factors to provide a more nuanced picture of provincial variation in policymaking.

## Caveats

As an analytical model, the policy-style framework helps us understand and explain important regional variation in policymaking in China. This

[53] Lin, *The Politics of Financing Education in China.*
[54] Zuo, "Promoting City Leaders."
[55] Rudra, *Globalization and the Race to the Bottom in Developing Countries.*

book focuses on the implications for social policy, but the framework could be extended and applied to other policy areas as well. However, the usual caveats apply. While these policy styles may be present in any province, I posit that each province has a dominant policy style. Furthermore, the degree to which a province fits neatly into each group varies as well; some provinces may exhibit elements of more than one policy style. Nonetheless, I contend that conceptualizing regional policy styles helps us understand and explain social policy outcomes as well as the durability of the Chinese party-state more broadly.

When talking about these policy styles in this book, I will be referring to a spectrum of possibilities within the Chinese context. That is, even relatively "permissive" provinces are still embedded in a single-party authoritarian regime. For example, as further restrictions on speech have been enacted by Xi Jinping, all provinces have been subject to new regulations and additional restrictions. Similarly, all provinces will be subject to new national laws, such as those on internet security, national security,[56] and management of foreign NGOs,[57] as well as the 2020 National Security Law focusing on Hong Kong,[58] all of which suggest an increasingly restrictive political environment nationwide. Nonetheless, I posit that, within the national context, localities will continue to vary in the openness of their political climate.

## Conclusions

The policy-style framework cannot perfectly explain every case: Chinese provinces certainly vary in how they govern over time and across different policy areas. Nonetheless, I posit that policy style provides a useful analytical tool to help us understand and explain regional variation in social policy provision. In the following chapters, I demonstrate how these regional tendencies produce divergent social policy priorities and distinct approaches to implementation.

In the pages to come, I conduct a detailed examination of each policy style, drawing on in-depth analysis of three provinces as case studies: Jiangsu,

[56] Elizabeth M. Lynch, "China Passes National Security Law," *China Law & Policy* (blog), July 1, 2015, http://chinalawandpolicy.com/2015/07/01/china-passes-national-security-law/; "National Security Law," China Law Translate | 国家安全法 (blog), July 1, 2015, http://chinalawtranslate.com/2015nsl/?lang=en.

[57] Sophie Beach, "Proposed Internet Security Law Raises Concerns," *China Digital Times (CDT)*, July 8, 2015, https://chinadigitaltimes.net/2015/07/proposed-internet-security-law-raises-concerns/.

[58] Donald Clarke, "Hong Kong's National Security Law: a first look," *The China Collection*, June 30, 2020, https://thechinacollection.org/hong-kongs-national-security-law-first-look/.

Yunnan, and Hubei. These three provinces were selected to provide variation in their policy styles. In each case, I will discuss the dominant policy style in the province and how it impacts health policy, with some additional examples from education, poverty alleviation, and housing. Each chapter will also reference other provinces with the same prevailing policy style.

# 4 The Pragmatist Policy Style

In the previous chapter, I show that Chinese provinces diverge in their social policy priorities. This divergence cannot be fully explained by economic factors alone, such as needs or wealth. Instead, I posit that economic and political factors have led to the development of provincial policy styles that, in turn, structure how subnational officials approach social policy implementation. My analysis of all thirty-one provinces in Chapter 3 suggests that greater central intervention, captured by fiscal transfers, is associated with a more paternalistic policy style even when controlling for economic factors. Fiscal transfers reflect both a province's economic reliance on the central government as well as the center's concerns about regional unrest.

In this chapter, I show how pragmatist provinces shape social policy provision through the devolution of responsibility to local government. Pragmatist provinces have followed Deng Xiaoping's "do what works" approach to the policy process. Despite the risks within an authoritarian system, officials in pragmatist provinces are more likely to experiment and innovate. These provinces devolve more responsibility to their localities, which provides opportunities for local officials to learn new skills and develop capacity in new areas. However, as they are generally wealthier, pragmatist provinces receive fewer fiscal transfers from the center for social policy. Therefore, they sometimes drag their feet in implementing unfunded mandates that do not coincide with their provincial priorities.

## The Emergence of Pragmatism

What conditions enable local officials to deviate from the norm in an authoritarian context? While there may be some palpable rewards – promotion, revenue, popular support – forging a new path also carries the risk of failure. If a new plan goes awry, local officials will face the consequences, which could be career-ending or worse. Nonetheless, some Chinese provinces allow much more discretion to local officials in the policy process than is afforded to their counterparts elsewhere. As a result, local government innovates, works with nonstate actors, and takes different approaches to solving problems. This approach to policymaking can produce more effective policy solutions but can also lead to greater within-province variation in service provision. A constellation of factors creates an environment in which this type of policymaking can occur, even in a one-party state. One group of provinces exhibits more autonomy than is typical for China and certainly much more autonomy in policymaking than we would generally expect from authoritarian regimes. I refer to this group as the pragmatist provinces.

Although most closely associated with Deng, pragmatism has resonated with leaders of the Communist Party since at least the early twentieth century. From 1919 to 1921, John Dewey held a lecture tour in China that heavily influenced Mao and other Chinese elites.[1] In China, Dewey emphasized the importance of the scientific method and empiricism. He advocated for a pragmatic approach to philosophy and living in which one ought to carefully consider context when solving problems. He was opposed to "isms" and grandiose ideology disconnected from experience or context.[2] Deweyan pragmatism resonated with traditional Chinese approaches to education and learning and was easily incorporated by Mao.[3]

During the Maoist period, the CCP leadership – dominated by Mao – alternated between a highly ideological approach to governing in a quest to achieve a communist utopia and periods of pragmatism to stabilize the country. In the wake of the famine caused by the Great Leap Forward, Deng advocated for pragmatism in his 1962 speech "Restore Agricultural Production." Deng justified his pragmatic approach by referring to the CCP's success in the civil war:

> The reason we defeated Chiang Kai-shek is that we did not always fight in the conventional way. Our sole aim is to win by taking advantage of given conditions. If we want to restore agricultural production, we must also take advantage of actual conditions. That is to say, we should not stick to a fixed mode of relations of production but *adopt whatever mode that can help mobilize the masses' initiative*. . . . In some cases, instead of giving full consideration to the different conditions and particular circumstances of different areas, we jumped to conclusions and made everyone do the same thing. As I have mentioned on other occasions, we have had

1 Heilmann, "Policy-Making through Experimentation: The Formation of a Distinctive Policy Process."

2 John Dewey, *Lectures in China, 1919–1920* (Honolulu: University Press of Hawaii, 1973); Gregory Pappas, "The Centrality of Dewey's Lectures in China to His Socio-political Philosophy," *Transactions of the Charles S. Peirce Society: A Quarterly Journal in American Philosophy* 53, no. 1 (Winter 2017): 7–28.

3 Heilmann, "Policy-Making through Experimentation," 79.

too many movements . . . and all of them were nationwide in scope. It seems that they have not worked out successfully.[4]

He advocated against mass campaigns and top-down mobilization in favor of allowing localities to try different approaches to stimulate agricultural production. After Mao's death, Deng further promoted pragmatism, adopting "seeking truth through facts" as the party's "work style" and repudiating the ideological approach of the Gang of Four.[5] He continued to refer to the success of the CCP in winning the civil war and emphasized that "seeking truth through facts" was a core element of Mao Zedong thought. He maintained that Mao's pragmatic approach of taking context into consideration when solving problems was crucial to the party's success.[6]

Marx and Engels propounded the ideological line of dialectical and historical materialism, a line which Comrade Mao Zedong summarized in the four Chinese characters "Seek truth from facts." To seek truth from facts, we must proceed from reality in all things, link theory with practice and hold practice to be the touchstone of truth – that is the ideological line of our Party. When we say this line has been reaffirmed, we mean it has been restored. It was abandoned for a period to the great detriment of the Party's cause, the country and the image of the Party and the state. But still, it must be remembered that this ideological line was laid down by Comrade Mao Zedong.[7]

Thus, in the reform period, Deng emphasized the importance of pragmatism as well as the links between Mao Zedong and the idea of "seek[ing] truth from facts."

To understand how this approach to governance emerged in contemporary politics, we need to examine China's distinctive process of economic development and internationalization. China's coast internationalized ahead of the rest of the country through export-led industrialization.[8] These provinces were the early beneficiaries of the economic reform period, largely due to the accident of geography. Their proximity to Taiwan, Hong Kong, and maritime trade routes facilitated early economic development based on

[4] Emphasis added. Deng Xiaoping, *Selected Works of Deng Xiaoping, 1938–1965* (Beijing: Intercultural Publishing, 2011), 293–294.

[5] 1980 speech, "Adhere to the Party Line and Improve Methods of Work," in Deng Xiaoping, *Selected Works of Deng Xiaoping, 1975–1982* (Beijing: Foreign Languages Press, 1984).

[6] See, for example, Deng's 1978 speeches "Hold High the Banner of Mao Zedong Thought and Adhere to the Principle of Seeking Truth from Facts" and "Emancipate the Mind, Seek Truth from Facts and Unite as One in Looking to the Future," in Deng, *Selected Works of Deng Xiaoping, 1975–1982*.

[7] From Deng's 1980 speech, "Adhere to the Party Line and Improve Methods of Work," in Deng, *Selected Works of Deng Xiaoping, 1975–1982*.

[8] David Zweig, *Internationalizing China: Domestic Interests and Global Linkages* (Ithaca, NY: Cornell University Press, 2002).

exports. To take advantage of their proximity to trade routes, the central government bestowed select preferential policies on coastal localities, first choosing a few cities and towns as special economic zones (SEZs) and then offering preferential policies to increasingly more towns in several waves of reform.[9] These preferential policies enabled coastal towns to pursue economic development and export-oriented industrialization, while the rest of the country still had to operate within the constraints of the planned economy. SEZs had greater control and flexibility over their own economies, capital, and labor markets. They offered lower tax rates to attract investors from other regions and abroad. Foreign investment would later serve as a bargaining chip for these provinces to elicit concessions from the central government.[10] With their liberalized economies, SEZs benefited from the rising price of land, a key source of revenue for local government in China. As a result, SEZs internationalized rapidly and their economies took off, while inland China lagged behind.[11]

Shenzhen, in Guangdong Province, demonstrates the effect of these preferential policies nicely. In 1980, Shenzhen was a humble collection of small towns and fishing villages with one important advantage: location. Shenzhen borders Hong Kong, one of the trade centers of Asia. Taking advantage of a natural trade relationship with the nearby capitalist port, the central government designated Shenzhen as the first SEZ. By 2010, Shenzhen had grown from a population of about 300,000 to a bustling, modern city of over 10 million, the majority of whom were migrant workers.[12] Other early SEZs had a similar experience.

In addition to unprecedented economic dynamism, provinces with early SEZs became more integrated in the global economy with waves of foreign investment lapping at their shores. Foreign firms wanted things like a predictable political environment, reliable contracts, and courts that would uphold previous agreements. Of course, when conflicts arose, many firms were disappointed with Chinese legal institutions and continue to be so. Nonetheless, businesses generally thought it was worth the risk to try to grab a slice of the growing Chinese pie, and so they put mounting pressure on local officials to create a more predictable commercial environment through functioning institutions. Slowly but surely, firms' desires for predictability and stability molded local institutions, shifted how local officials governed, and shaped how officials saw their role as agents of the state.

9 Ibid.
10 Li, *Centre and Provinces*.
11 Zweig, *Internationalizing China*, 60.
12 Ming Lu and Yiran Xia, "Migration in the People's Republic of China," ADBI Working Paper Series (Tokyo: Asian Development Bank Institute, September 2016), 14, www.adb.org/publications/migration-people-republic-china/.

These provinces were transformed. They subsequently developed a different style of governing, fully taking advantage of the pragmatism advanced by Deng Xiaoping and marking a sharp turn away from the ideology of the Maoist era. Local officials in pragmatist provinces became more willing to partner with nonstate actors so long as it would advance the overarching goal of economic growth. They were willing to strengthen institutions somewhat and to hold a relatively looser grip on telecommunications, including, eventually, the internet.[13]

Provincial leaders on the coast began to cultivate their autonomy vis-à-vis the central government during the early years of economic reform by bargaining with the center and flexibly interpreting central policies. Linda Chelan Li explains how Guangdong, a pragmatist province, lobbied for exceptional treatment from the center. Guangdong's implementation of several economic polices deviated from central policy, including allowing substantial domestic investment in SEZs, exceeding investment quotas, diverting state bank loans to investment projects, and increasing extra-budgetary income.[14] When Beijing placed limits on domestic investment in infrastructure, for example, Guangdong would negotiate exemptions on an ad hoc basis. Foreign investment could only be accepted as a joint venture, requiring significant domestic capital. Thus, as Guangdong attracted foreign investment, provincial authorities forced the center to exceed its limits and allow the domestic investment necessary to retain the foreign funds. In one year, the limits were raised by more than 40 percent for Guangdong, while the center had reduced infrastructure investment elsewhere.[15] Guangdong also sought to develop "international cities," as they argued that this was in line with the sentiments expressed on Deng's Southern Tour. First, the province would need autonomy and investment to build an international metropolis. Then, once established, the additional "Hong Kongs" would give the province even more power and, therefore, autonomy.[16] In other cases, provincial authorities explicitly ignored the center. Central policies were "filed away" and then disregarded.[17]

[13] That said, of course, relative openness in telecommunications and political expression tends to ebb and flow over time, including in pragmatist provinces. During the Hu Jintao years, for example, all provinces experienced relative political conservativism in the lead-up to the 2008 Olympics. With all eyes on China, we can presume that the central government was keen to reduce expressions of dissent. Overall, however, the early 2000s were a period of relative opening-up, which gave pragmatist provinces the opportunity to engage even more in the global economy.

[14] Li, *Centre and Provinces*, 150–217.

[15] Li, *Centre and Provinces*.

[16] Ibid., 192–201.

[17] Ibid., 173.

Guangdong's flexible implementation of central policies did not go unnoticed. But when Beijing began to criticize the province for its actions, provincial officials published an article in a provincial paper defending themselves and reasserting their autonomy:

> The Party Centre and the State Council previously instructed Guangdong and Fujian to go one step ahead of the rest of the country ... and allowed the two provinces to act according to the Special Policy [reform and opening], and "flexible measures." This means that the centre does not require the two provinces to follow strictly the policy documents which are meant for the use of the rest of the country, but rather to follow the Special Policy documents tailored specifically for these regions. ... Now that the centre has flashed a "special green light" to the two provinces, and we [in going in the direction of this special green light] are merely going around the "ordinary" red light [meant for the rest of the country], what is there to be criticized?[18]

In this article, provincial officials made clear that, in their view, reform and opening had offered Guangdong and other coastal provinces a privileged position in which they did not need to follow central policy to the letter. Rather, officials in these provinces felt strongly that they had the autonomy to decide whether and how to implement central policy. I argue that this approach to policy implementation continued into the 1990s and 2000s, evolving into a pragmatist policy style. Later, pragmatist provinces in the 2000s took a similar approach to social policy by choosing to emphasize some policies over others and allowing localities within the province to determine many of the details of social policy provision.

While pragmatist provinces pursued economic growth in the 1980s and early 1990s, fiscal realities in Beijing impacted local officials everywhere. Over the course of the economic reform era, the central government increased the share of revenue that the localities sent up to Beijing in a series of tax reforms, with the 1994 reform being the most significant. To offset the effect of these reforms, the central government instituted a system of rebates and subsidies to redistribute some of the country's wealth in a somewhat progressive fashion. The central government began to siphon off more revenue from the wealthier provinces, allowing them fewer subsidies. Early reformers, such as Guangdong, fought back to retain funds for infrastructure and economic development, but local government had fewer resources to provide social welfare and community services.[19]

To be sure, the regions that benefited most from economic reforms took different approaches to economic development. In the 1980s and 1990s, while some regions began with private enterprise development (like

[18] Quoted in Li, *Centre and Provinces*, 179.
[19] Li, *Centre and Provinces*.

Wenzhou), others – like southern Jiangsu – focused on town and village enterprises (TVEs), and some focused predominantly on FDI (like the Pearl River Delta).[20] Nonetheless, by the 2000s, there was a stark difference in governance style between those that had opened up earlier, particularly those with the geographic advantage of being coastal, and those that maintained a planned economy for longer. Indeed, the focus of this chapter – Jiangsu – had many TVEs in its southern regions and did not initially take an FDI-driven approach to development. Nonetheless, after thirty years of economic development and reforms, FDI as a proportion of gross regional product was somewhat higher in Jiangsu than in Guangdong, and both provinces were receiving far more FDI than a paternalist province such as Yunnan.

With gaping inequality threatening to cause instability in other parts of the country by the 1990s, the central government began to send more subsidies and earmarked transfers to poorer provinces. Wealthy provinces received significantly less funding from the central government, and in some cases local government was responsible for funding social policy without any central support. For example, the central government funded about one-third of the rural health insurance program for inland provinces – initiated as pilot projects in 2003 – but sent no subsidies to coastal provinces for the same program.

Since pragmatist provinces were saddled with funding and implementing social policy directives from the central government, these provincial governments began delegating some of the responsibility to lower levels of government by allowing even greater autonomy to municipalities, counties, and townships. The leadership in Guangdong, for example, saw the decentralization of many tasks to the localities as a core principle of the reforms. As early as 1983, one Guangdong leader stated: "To the outside, more open; to the inside, looser; to those below, more leeway."[21]

The increased autonomy encouraged innovation, as local governments sought cost-effective strategies to address social policy problems. Gradually, the policymaking environment became less restrictive and more pragmatic, all the while with a focus on export-led growth. By the beginning of the twenty-first century, after three decades of this gradual process, these provinces exhibited a pragmatist policy style distinct from their counterparts inland.

[20] Changdong Zhang, "Reexamine Regional Models of China's Economic Growth: Toward an Integrated Analytical Framework," *Sociology Compass* 14, no. 5 (May 2020): e12781, https://doi.org/10.1111/soc4.12781.

[21] Kevin P. Lane, "One Step Behind: Shaanxi in Reform," in *Provincial Strategies of Economic Reform in Post-Mao China: Leadership, Politics, and Implementation*, edited by Peter T. Y. Cheung, Chae-ho Chŏng, and Zhimin Lin, Studies on Contemporary China (Armonk, NY: M. E. Sharpe, 1998), 103.

## The Pragmatic Policy Style

The pragmatic policy style prioritizes economic growth as the end goal and is willing to "do what works" to achieve it. Putting aside ideology (relatively speaking), local officials in these provinces often partner with nonstate actors to promote economic development. Pragmatist provinces embody the spirit of Deng Xiaoping's famous metaphor about championing pragmatism over ideology ("It doesn't matter if a cat is black or white, as long as it catches mice"): they are going to do what works to grow the economy and not let ideology – or even central policy – get in the way.[22]

Sebastian Heilmann identifies this pragmatic strain in the CCP as an important source of the experimentalism that has enabled China to distinguish itself as more flexible in policymaking than other authoritarian regimes.[23] Building on his findings, I argue that this pragmatism is more prevalent in some regions of the country than others. Both pragmatism and paternalism are present in how CCP officials govern, but what determines when they do more of one than the other? If pragmatism is encouraged throughout China, why do we sometimes see greater innovation and more experiments in some regions than in others? Over time, as regions that benefited from economic reforms learned to be more pragmatic and more experimental, they shed some of their paternalist tendencies from earlier periods.

The pragmatist policy style impacts both *which* policies take priority and *how* social policy is implemented. Due to these provinces' general emphasis on economic growth and relatively low poverty rates, pragmatist provinces tend to emphasize social policies that will promote economic growth, such as education. The benefits afforded to residents tend to have broad eligibility rather than narrow targeting. For example, pragmatist provinces are some of those with the least restrictive residency requirements for taking the local university entrance examination. Table 4.1 summarizes the main characteristics of the pragmatist policy style and its implications for social policy.

## Economics, Politics, and Social Policy in the Pragmatist Provinces

The economic and political characteristics of Jiangsu and other pragmatist provinces reveal a group that has greater exposure to the global economy and is more politically open. This combination has led to a policy style that prioritizes social policies to support economic growth.

[22] Deng, *Selected Works of Deng Xiaoping (1938–1965)*, 293.
[23] Heilmann, "Policy-Making through Experimentation."

Table 4.1 *Characteristics of the pragmatist policy style*

| | |
|---|---|
| Local State Resources | Large provincial budget<br>Little central support for social policy<br>Professionalized local state |
| Institutional Approaches | Decentralized<br>Attentive to corruption<br>Higher transparency |
| Patterns of Policymaking | Bottom-up approach<br>Innovative<br>Inclusive of nonstate actors |
| Social Policy Strategy | Human-capital promotion<br>Broad eligibility<br>Shallow benefits |
| Social Policy Priorities | Education, some health |

Jiangsu is a populous, but ethnically homogenous, wealthy coastal province with a low dependency ratio. Jiangsu relies heavily on exports and FDI to generate economic growth. Although Jiangsu did not begin the economic reform era with an FDI-led strategy, FDI had become an important part of its development by the 2000s. Despite its wealth, Jiangsu is more unequal than other pragmatist provinces as well as compared to the national average. Jiangsu's heightened inequality illustrates one effect of the dynamics observed in pragmatist provinces due to their greater intraprovincial decentralization of many policies.

Metrics of the political environment suggest that Jiangsu and other pragmatist provinces are somewhat more politically open than their counterparts inland. Overall, the group exhibits more transparency, less corruption, and more space for nonstate actors. Pragmatist provinces, and Jiangsu in particular, are more fiscally transparent and may have less corruption than their inland peers. In 2010, Jiangsu had fewer individuals involved in corruption cases than the national average when adjusting for population.[24] My fiscal transparency index suggests that Jiangsu is more transparent than the national average, whereas the pragmatist group as a whole is lower than the national average in this metric. Pragmatist provinces tend to surpass the national average in government innovation, although Jiangsu lags behind this group and the average in this category.

[24] Since Xi Jinping's anti-corruption campaigns in 2013, high numbers of corruption cases could suggest enthusiastic compliance with central government policy. However, Hu Jintao did not prioritize an anti-corruption campaign in 2010. Therefore, we may interpret numbers of individuals involved in corruption cases as reflecting the prevalence of corruption within the province.

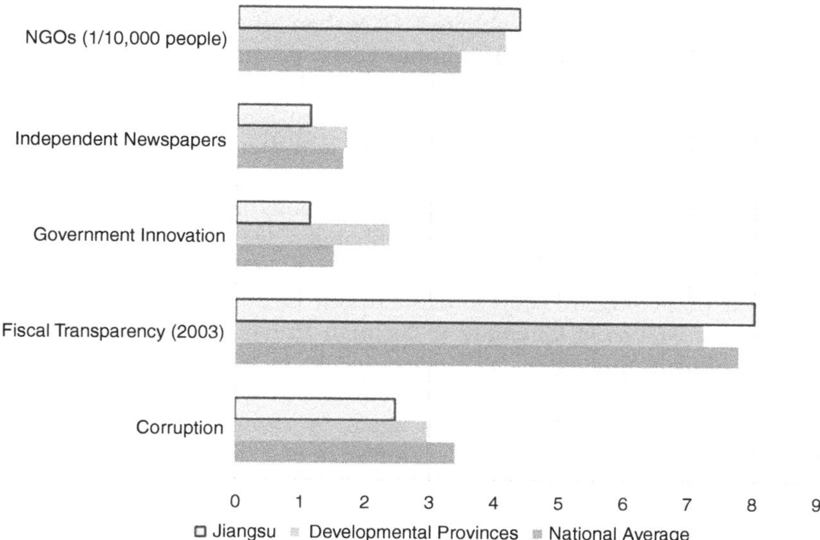


Figure 4.1 Political characteristics: Jiangsu and pragmatist provinces (2010, unless otherwise noted).
Note on measurement: Corruption is the number of people involved in corruption cases in the province in 2010 per 100,000 persons. Government innovation is the number of awards or finalists in national competitions for government innovation from 2003 to 2012, per 10 million persons. Independent newspapers is per 10 million persons. Fiscal transparency is an original index of transparency in publishing data on provincial revenue and expenditures. Data for this index is from 2003 (see Appendix A for details on calculation of fiscal transparency).

Pragmatist provinces tend to have a more open environment for public debate and more opportunities for nonstate actors to be involved in the policy process. On average, this group has more independent newspapers than the national average (per population) and more registered NGOs. Jiangsu has somewhat fewer independent newspapers than the group average and the national average, but it has more NGOs than the group average. Overall, Jiangsu and other pragmatist provinces have a somewhat more politically open environment as compared to other provinces (Figure 4.1).

The treatment of NGOs by pragmatist provinces underscores their relatively open political environment.[25] In addition to having more

[25] NGOs have been constrained by onerous regulations and limitations in their operations in China. Until the 2010s, some of these regulations included the "dual management

registered NGOs than their counterparts inland, pragmatist provinces were, in general, more amenable to NGOs than other provinces, qualitatively speaking. During the Hu Jintao years, pragmatist provinces pioneered reforms to facilitate the work of these nonstate actors.

Much like many new policies in China, innovations related to NGOs began first as pilot projects in a few cities and then spread nationwide. For example, Shenzhen, in coastal Guangdong Province, was the first to pilot the direct registration of social associations in 2006, followed by several cities and districts in Jiangsu.[26] Shanghai was the first to establish a Non-Profit Incubator (NPI). Similar nonprofit incubation policies then appeared in Beijing in 2008 and Shenzhen in 2010 (both pragmatist regions), as well as in Chengdu in Sichuan Province (mixed group) in 2009.[27] Shortly thereafter, NPI expanded to at least nine cities in six pragmatist provinces and two cities in a mixed province.[28]

In 2009, Shanghai led the way again by bringing nonprofits into community service through the development of a "venture philanthropy competition" in which nonprofits submitted bids to provide community service projects funded by the local Welfare Lottery Fund. NPI supported the competition with capacity building for participating organizations and by selecting the nonprofits that would receive funding.[29] Shanghai's innovative venture philanthropy competition spread to eight cities in three pragmatist provinces and to a city in Jiangxi, a mixed province.[30]

registration" system, in which NGOs had to register first with a government agency that would act as its sponsor and then with the Ministry of Civil Affairs. This requirement was gradually dismantled in many provinces by 2012, the end of the Hu Jintao government. By 2016, Xi Jinping had introduced new restrictions on NGOs, particularly those with foreign involvement, but this shift is beyond the scope of this book.

[26] Jun Li and Weiping Ye, "直接登记制下的社会组织行政监管研究 [Research on the Administrative Supervision of Social Organizations under the Direct Registration System]," 天府新论 [*Tianfu Xinlun/New Theory*] 2014, no. 5 (2014): 8–13; Mingmin Zhang 张明敏, "江苏 从太仓试点到全省推进 [Jiangsu: From the Pilot of Taicang to the Whole Province]," *China Philanthropy Times* [公益时报], October 28, 2013, www.gongyishibao.com/html/yaowen/2411.html.

[27] Jun Han, "The Emergence of Social Corporatism in China: Nonprofit Organizations, Private Foundations, and the State," *China Review* 16, no. 2 (June 2016): 39–40.

[28] Nanjing and Suzhou (Jiangsu), Dongguan and Zhuhai (Guangdong), Hangzhou and Jiaxing (Zhejiang), Xiamen (Fujian), Chongqing, and Tianjin. NPI also reached two other cities in a mixed province, Jinan (Shandong) and Hefei (Anhui). Han, "The Emergence of Social Corporatism in China," 40.

[29] Han, "The Emergence of Social Corporatism in China," 40–41.

[30] Shenzhen (Guangdong), Dongguan (Guangdong), Guangzhou (Guangdong), Shunde (Guangdong), Hangzhou (Zhejiang), Suzhou (Jiangsu), Wuxi (Jiangsu), Kunshan (Jiangsu), as well as Jiujiang in a mixed province (Jiangxi). Han, "The Emergence of Social Corporatism in China," 40–41.

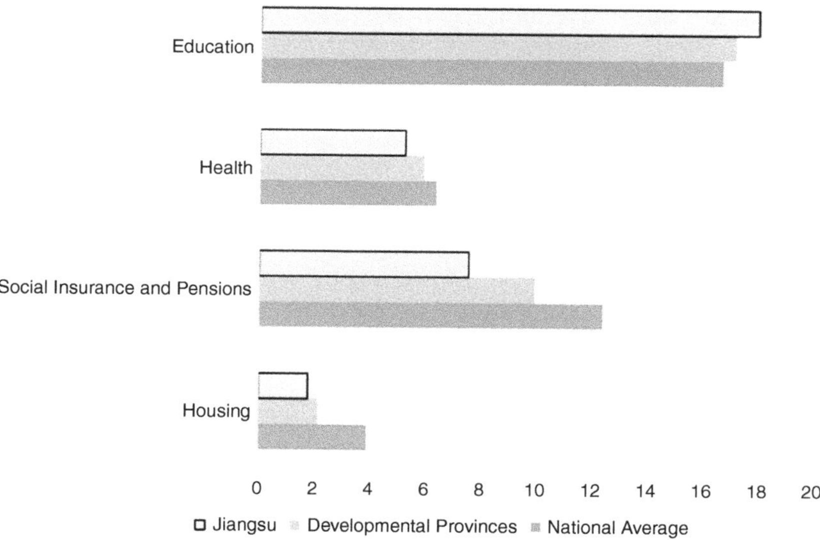


Figure 4.2 Proportion of provincial spending on social policy in Jiangsu and pragmatist provinces.
Sources: Data compiled from *China Statistical Yearbook*, 2009–13.
Note: Data is averaged over the years 2008–12, except for housing. Housing is averaged from 2010 to 2012 because data on housing prior to 2010 was not available.

If local needs could explain innovation in nonstate community service, we would expect to see these new policies for nonprofits in poorer provinces with greater social welfare needs, but this is not the case. Similarly, if wealth could explain variation in social policy provision, we might expect that coastal provinces would allocate more funds to social policy and provide a more robust social welfare system, therefore not needing to involve nonstate actors. Instead, however, pragmatist provinces are the most likely to encourage nonprofits and nonstate actors to provide social policy. This suggests that these provinces take a different approach to governance and the role of the state in social policy provision than we might expect in an authoritarian regime.

Jiangsu's allocations for social policy emphasize education as compared to those of other provinces. Figure 4.2 presents spending on different types of social policy as a proportion of total provincial spending in Jiangsu, pragmatist provinces, and the country as a whole. Like other pragmatist provinces, Jiangsu spends more on education than the

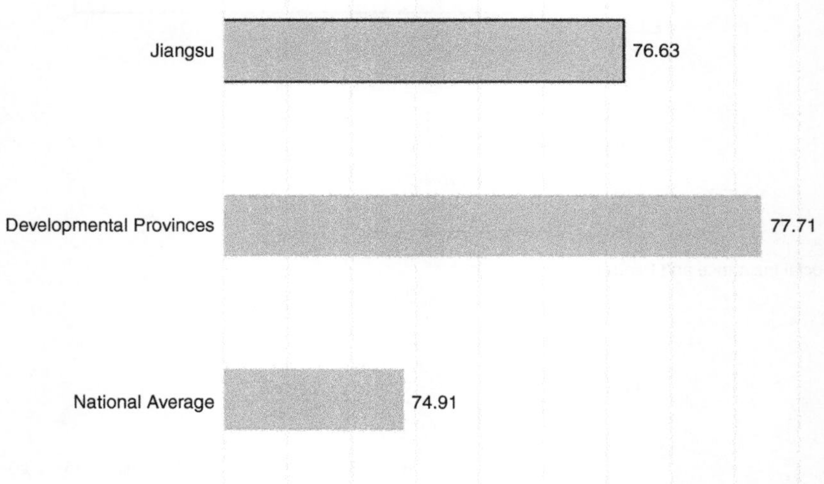


Figure 4.3 Life expectancy in Jiangsu and pragmatist provinces in 2010.
Source: Data compiled from *China Statistical Yearbook*, 2013.

national average. Pragmatist provinces tend to spend less on social insurance and pensions than the national average, and Jiangsu allocates even less to this area than other pragmatist provinces. Jiangsu and other pragmatist provinces allocate about half as much to subsidized housing as the national average. Jiangsu allocates somewhat less to healthcare than other pragmatist provinces, and the group as a whole prioritizes health less than the national average. However, the difference in health spending between pragmatist provinces and the national average is somewhat less than the gap in spending for other types of social policy.

Pragmatist provinces have achieved the most gains in social policy outcomes, even in areas that have received little attention from the local government. Figures 4.3 and 4.4 compare several social policy outcomes between Jiangsu, other pragmatist provinces, and the country as a whole. For example, even though pragmatist provinces tend to spend less on healthcare than their peers, they have achieved better population health outcomes since the economic reform period. In Jiangsu and other pragmatist provinces, life expectancy is higher on average, and maternal and infant mortality rates are lower. In some cases, these population health

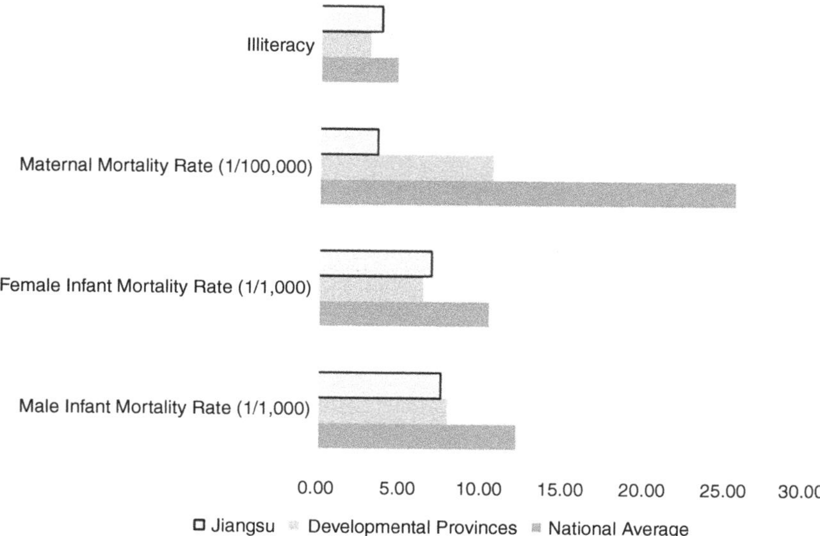


Figure 4.4 Social policy outcomes in Jiangsu and pragmatist provinces. Sources: Data compiled from *China Statistical Yearbook*, 2009–13. Infant mortality compiled from 2010 National Census. Infant mortality rates are estimates after adjustments for underreporting.

metrics from pragmatist provinces are comparable to countries in the Organization for Economic Co-operation and Development (OECD). Over the course of the economic reform period, the state reduced its role in healthcare until the early 2000s.[31] Nonetheless, pragmatist provinces achieved impressive gains in population health due to the benefits of economic development. Meanwhile, the provinces that lagged behind economically also continued to have significant challenges in health. In addition, pragmatist provinces have a lower rate of illiteracy than their counterparts, which is not surprising given their investment in education. In the context of state retrenchment, the relative success of a province like Jiangsu suggests that some of these societal gains ought to be attributed to overall economic growth and improved population well-being rather than to social policy interventions per se.

[31] Duckett, *The Chinese State's Retreat from Health*.

### Policy Adoption and Implementation in Pragmatist Provinces

Policy adoption and implementation in Jiangsu reveal how the pragmatist policy style impacts social policy provision. On the one hand, pragmatist provinces take a pragmatic approach to social policy, seeking innovative solutions to social policy challenges by involving local officials and nonstate actors. On the other hand, these provinces sometimes shirk their responsibilities, delegating social policy to lower levels of government. The greater degree of decentralization in pragmatist provinces leads to greater intra-province inequality in social policy provision.

### Health

Because pragmatist provinces receive little central support for social policy, including few fiscal transfers for healthcare, their provincial governments have further delegated implementation to local governments such as the city and county. Lower-level officials are tasked with implementing policy and, as a result, pragmatist provinces often exhibit greater intra-provincial inequality in social policy provision. In this context, local officials tend to experiment – and may involve nonstate actors where possible – to comply pro forma with current policy while reducing the impact on local budgets.

Although healthcare could support human capital development, as in Rudra's productivist states,[32] Chinese policymakers generally do not perceive healthcare as a means to economic growth. By the 1990s, after the dismantling of socialist-era health systems, medical expenses had become a significant source of poverty, particularly in rural areas where villagers were paying out-of-pocket for almost all services. Poverty due to catastrophic illness began to undermine the era's fantastic economic growth and pose potential problems for social stability. As a result, in both rhetoric and policy, policymakers in the 2000s focused on health reform as poverty reduction and as a measure to prevent families from falling back into poverty when faced with catastrophic health expenses. This nationwide approach to healthcare as poverty reduction deviates from cross-national research on developmental states that suggests that investment in health can be a tactic to support economic growth.[33]

The perception of healthcare as a form of poverty reduction in China trickles down to local state actors, impacting their priorities in the policy adoption and implementation processes even in pragmatist

[32] Rudra, *Globalization and the Race to the Bottom in Developing Countries.*
[33] Ibid.

provinces. When I spoke to local officials in Jiangsu, they claimed to be in favor of the expansion of health insurance because catastrophic health expenditures had become a significant economic burden on families. Prior to the rural health insurance program, villagers would be forced to borrow from friends and family. According to local officials, the most destitute patients could apply for aid from the local Civil Affairs Bureau, but this option was a last resort and used sparingly.[34] In my interviews, relatively few villagers were even aware of this subsidy, though some did remark that Civil Affairs subsidies would only be relevant for those who were extremely poor.[35] Overall, villagers and local officials alike were pleased that the new rural health insurance policy ameliorated the financial repercussions of healthcare costs. Neither local officials nor villagers suggested that healthcare costs were a source of social instability, even when prompted.

Funding structures shape which level of government implements health policy and how policies are implemented on the ground. When new policies are funded by earmarked transfers from the central government, the provincial government is more likely to standardize the implementation of the policy within some general parameters. However, when a new policy is largely funded by the province, as in a pragmatist province, the provincial government is more likely to further delegate responsibility for funding – along with other details of implementation – to lower levels of government, resulting in greater within-province variation.

When the central government began encouraging pilot projects and, subsequently, widespread adoption of a new rural health insurance program, the New Cooperative Medical System (NCMS), the 2003 regulation establishing it specified that county-level governments would be responsible for "carrying out the plan in its entirety."[36] Moreover, coastal provinces such as Jiangsu were explicitly afforded greater autonomy in the program's implementation. However, these provinces also received lower subsidies from the central government to pay for the new benefit because pragmatist provinces capture more revenue locally. Regarding coastal provinces, the erstwhile Ministry of Health merely stated: "The average per capita contribution level in localities in the eastern region should not be lower than the central and western regions." According to the same document, localities (provinces, districts, and municipalities are specifically mentioned) in the

[34] Interviews with local officials in Jiangsu, 2009–10.
[35] Interviews JSJP47, JSKP51.
[36] Notification of the Opinion of the State Council General Office published by the Health Bureau and other Departments Related to Establishing the New Cooperative Medical System, trans. by LawInfoChina, CLI.2.45115, January 16, 2003.

eastern region would also have more autonomy to determine their own funding structure.[37]

Village health services and the NCMS illustrate the decentralized approach to funding health in Jiangsu. Although villages occupy a liminal position vis-à-vis the party-state,[38] villages in Jiangsu tend to provide the bulk of healthcare funding at the village level, while their inland counterparts enjoy more support from higher levels of government. Of 146 villages sampled in my survey, 64 percent in Jiangsu reported that the bulk of local health spending (more than 60 percent) came from the village itself rather than from higher levels of government. By contrast, only 44 percent in Hubei and 48 percent in Yunnan – a mixed province and a paternalist province, respectively – reported the same proportion of health spending from the village. In these two provinces, villages were more likely to receive a greater proportion of funds for healthcare from higher levels of government.

Villages vary widely in their per capita health spending (see Figure 4.5). This gap in spending among villages is largely due to differences in what the village can contribute rather than what they receive from higher levels of government, including the central, provincial, municipal, and county governments. Village leaders reported that, on average, subsidies for health from higher levels of government were not substantially different across the three provinces in our survey. However, the lowest level of the state – the village in rural China – contributes much more to healthcare in wealthy as opposed to poorer provinces (again, see Figure 4.5). The differences in village wealth lead to a per capita gap in rural health spending across provinces and, in Jiangsu, to inequality in health spending within the province despite transfers from higher levels of government.

The rural health insurance program also demonstrates how Jiangsu decentralized healthcare more than other provinces did. In the early years of the NCMS, coastal provinces such as Jiangsu did not receive funding from the central government for the new policy, whereas inland provinces generally received about two-thirds of their funding from the central government. Some regions received as much as 80 percent from the center. Since Jiangsu had to fund the program without central support, the provincial government provided between 20 and 60 percent of

37 Ministry of Health, 卫生部办公厅关于做好2009年下半年新型农村合作医疗工作的通知 [Ministry of Health General Office notice on proper implementation of the New Cooperative Medical System in the second half of 2009], 卫生部, 卫办农卫发 [2009] 108号, 部门规范性文件, CLI.4.118483, June 29, 2009.

38 Village leaders are not technically government officials, although they are increasingly paid by the government. Unlike higher levels of government, the village does not have a parallel Communist Party structure. Village leaders are directly elected, although limitations on village elections began under Xi Jinping.

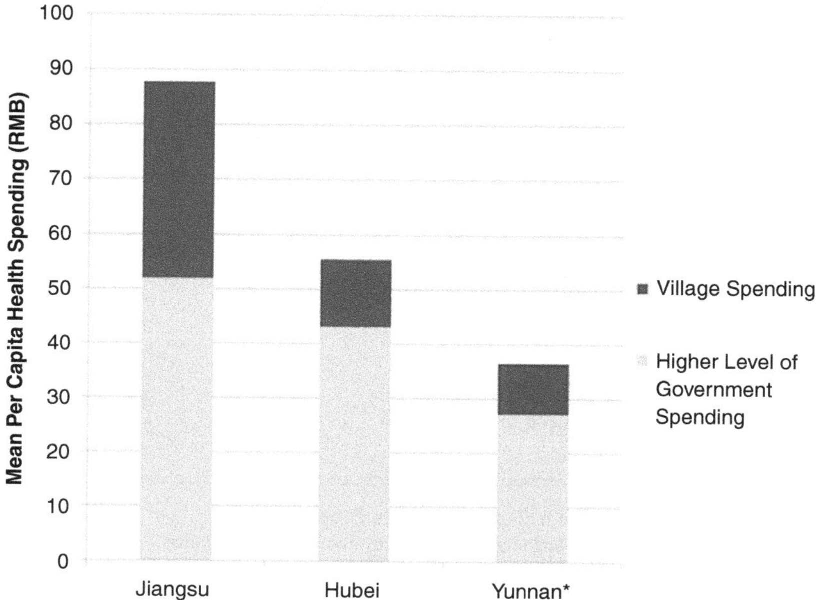


Figure 4.5 Average per capita spending on health in villages, disaggregated by province and source of funds, 2011.
Source: Author's survey of village leaders. Observations=146 villages.
Note: "Higher levels of government spending" includes spending from all levels of government higher than the village (i.e., township, county, municipal, provincial, and central levels).
* One village in Yunnan was omitted due to enumerator error.

the funding to the localities, depending on the area. In my fieldwork, I found that the remainder of the funding was split between the municipality, the county, and the individual, with the county and the individual each paying a larger portion than the municipality.[39]

A decentralized approach to funding and implementation leads to greater local variation in the quantity and quality of services provided within the province. This within-province inequality flourishes in pragmatist provinces. For example, in the first years of implementing the NCMS, county officials in Jiangsu determined reimbursement levels for patients incurring medical costs. Table 4.2 summarizes standard reimbursement levels for several counties in Jiangsu and Hunan. In Jiangsu,

[39] Author's fieldwork.

Table 4.2 *NCMS reimbursement levels for town- and village-level hospitals, 2009*

| County Code | Province | GRP Per Capita (2008 RMB) | First Year of NCMS | Inpatient Percent | Outpatient Percent |
|---|---|---|---|---|---|
| J | Jiangsu | 31,000 | 2004 | 55 | 20 |
| A | Jiangsu | 21,000 | 2004 | 55 | 25 |
| C | Jiangsu | 17,000 | 2004 | 60 | 30 |
| K | Jiangsu | 14,000 | 2003 | 65 | 20 |
| B | Jiangsu | 13,000 | 2004 | 60 | 40 |
| I | Jiangsu | 12,000 | 2004 | 80 | 20 |
| H | Jiangsu | 10,000 | 2003 | 60 | 55 |
| E | Hunan | 6,000 | 2007 | 70 | 30 |
| F | Hunan | 5,000 | 2006 | 70 | 40 |
| G | Hunan | 21,000 | 2006 | 70 | 30 |
| D | Hunan | 16,000 | 2007 | 70 | 30 |

*Source*: Author's interviews with county officials in 2009 and 2010.
*Note:* GRP per capita is rounded to preserve the anonymity of informants.

reimbursement for inpatient treatment could range from 55 to 80 percent and from 20 to 55 percent for outpatient treatment. By contrast, counties in Hunan were instructed to follow provincial guidelines to standardize reimbursement levels.

Since funding for healthcare is more localized in pragmatist provinces such as Jiangsu, local officials play a larger role in determining how – and how much – money will be spent on healthcare and other social policies. Greater responsibility for local officials also translates into greater autonomy and within-province variation. In my interviews, local officials in Jiangsu described how they had much greater autonomy in policy implementation than their counterparts in inland provinces.[40] As a result, local officials in pragmatist provinces tend to be more professionalized and see themselves as policymakers rather than bureaucratic automatons carrying out the will of higher levels of government.

Since local officials in pragmatist provinces play a greater role in shaping how policies are implemented, there are more opportunities for new policies to be customized in a bottom-up process. For example, in the implementation of the NCMS, counties in Jiangsu were tasked with determining the specifics of the funding structure, individual premiums, and reimbursement rates for patients. As a result, local health bureaus

[40] Interviews JSAW01, JSBW07, JSCW10.

had to hire or train officials with the skills necessary to make these judgments. Moreover, since Jiangsu, like most pragmatist provinces, was an early adopter (see Table 4.2), local officials had few guidelines for how to implement the new policy. In the early stages of the NCMS, the central government only provided vague recommendations for implementation.[41] Local officials, in accordance with central government directives, were encouraged to tailor new policies to local conditions.

As part of the first wave of counties to adopt the policy, officials in Jiangsu could not draw on past experiences from other provinces. They had to improvise. County officials realized that they would need additional expertise and that they might benefit by learning from the experiences of others in the region. To pool their resources in figuring out how to implement this new policy, several counties started regular meetings to discuss the policy and to decide on appropriate reimbursement levels. In northern Jiangsu, officials from six rural counties and one urban district set up regular meetings and decided to standardize their rural health insurance programs. They met monthly within the municipality and disseminated information among themselves to create a uniform program.[42] Notably, this collaboration was initiated by local actors rather than the provincial or central governments. By contrast, other provinces in the mixed and paternalist groups established provincial-level guidelines to standardize the new policy's implementation upon adoption.

Consistent with regulations from the central government,[43] wealthier areas are more likely to be chosen for pilot projects and the early implementation of new policies because they have conditions that are favorable for a new policy's success.[44] Of course, selecting favorable conditions for pilot projects is probably not a wise approach to testing new policies, but that issue is beyond the scope of this book. Thus, implementation in Jiangsu (and other coastal regions) occurred two to three years before implementation in Hunan (and other interior regions). This approach to pilot project selection reflects a broader strategy of decentralization: wealthier regions are often afforded greater autonomy, while less developed localities are more strictly monitored. In addition to the NCMS,

41 At the time of this writing, the central government had encouraged gradual standardization of the rural health insurance program, although rural–urban discrepancies remained.
42 Interviews JSAW01, JSBW07, JSCW10.
43 Ministry of Health, "Notification of the Opinion of the State Council General Office Published by the Health Bureau and Other Departments Related to Establishing the New Cooperative Medical System" CLI.2.45115, January 16, 2003; Ministry of Health and Ministry of Finance, "关于做好新型农村合作医疗试点有关工作的通知 [Notice on Proper Implementation of the New Cooperative Medical System Pilot Projects]."
44 Interviews JSAW01, HNGW30.

Jiangsu and other pragmatist provinces have piloted other policies in health. For example, Jiangsu also instituted direct billing for rural health insurance ahead of other provinces.[45] As previously mentioned, Suzhou and other coastal cities have permitted private hospitals to operate ahead of other regions. And Sanming City (Fujian) pioneered contentious reforms of their healthcare system.[46]

### Other Social Policies

Like other areas of social policy in China, much of the funding and management of education has been delegated to local government. However, the level of government taking primary responsibility for education varies depending on the level of education as well as the province. The central government provides transfers for elite higher education institutions (HEIs), which are mainly located in pragmatist provinces, as well as for K–12 education in poorer provinces.[47]

At the start of the twenty-first century, the Chinese economy was poised to make a transition from low-end manufacturing to high-tech innovation. Much as they had led the trend in opening up to foreign markets in the early reform period, pragmatist provinces were best situated to lead this shift as well. To this end, pragmatist provinces ramped up their spending in education to cultivate the human capital necessary for innovation.[48] On average, pragmatist provinces invest more than their inland counterparts on education, in both gross and relative terms. But spending aggregated at the provincial level fails to tell the whole story. Not only do pragmatist provinces spend more on education in both relative and absolute terms, but they also allocate their education funding differently.

45 Author's fieldwork, 2011.

46 Alex Jingwei He, "Maneuvering within Fragmented Bureaucracy and Vested Interests: Policy Entrepreneurship in China's Local Health Care Reform," *China Quarterly* 236 (December 2018): 1088–1110, doi:10.1017/S0305741018001261.

47 Across China, children are expected to attend nine years of compulsory schooling. Students can then continue to complete secondary school. Students who seek higher education can take the university entrance exam (*gaokao* 高考) to gain admission, or they can pursue technical training in vocational schools. As in many countries, China's public universities have greater prestige and a reputation for better research and teaching than newer private universities. Nonetheless, higher incomes have enabled families to pay higher tuitions for private higher education when their children fall below the state college admission exam cutoff. The rising upper-middle class increasingly chooses to send their college-age children abroad for their education, both to attain the prestige (and sometimes higher quality) of a foreign degree and (sometimes) to improve the prospects for youngsters who score poorly on the state college entrance exam.

48 Gang Guo, "Decentralized Education Spending and Regional Disparities: Evidence from Chinese Counties 1997–2001," *Journal of Chinese Political Science* 11, no. 2 (September 2006): 45–60.

The central government has supported elite higher education nationally as part of a strategy to modernize and industrialize the country. In this way, education deviates from other social policies in China. In general, the central government provides fiscal transfers for social policy in poorer provinces. In education, however, in addition to relatively progressive subsidies, the center transfers significant funds for elite universities, which are mainly located in pragmatist provinces. Thus, while the center typically takes a relatively progressive approach to fiscal transfers for social policy, education policy deviates from this trend because of the important role of elite education in cultivating new generations of leaders to innovate and foster economic growth. Particularly in the wake of the "lost generation" that was deprived of higher education during the Cultural Revolution, the CCP needed to provide opportunities to train new generations of professionals.

Significant central-government fiscal transfers are destined for "key" universities that are targeted as part of a national strategy to improve elite higher education.[49] Transfers to key universities belie efforts at progressive spending in social policy, as most of these institutions are in pragmatist provinces. Jiangsu has eleven key universities, for example, whereas the national average is under four. Pragmatist provinces have more than seven key universities each, on average.[50] Through these elite institutions, pragmatist provinces have a distinct advantage in attracting talented youth and building a thriving economy. Higher education institutions themselves continue to have strong links with the party-state, however, affording them little autonomy in operation.[51] Yet market forces and shifts in what the reform economy needs in terms of educational preparation has led them to converge in the type of majors that they offer and the structure of the institution.[52]

[49] "Project 211: A Brief Introduction (II)," *China Education and Research Network*, www.edu.cn/20010101/21852.shtml, accessed June 26, 2018; Kinglun Ngok and Weiqing Guo, "The Quest for World Class Universities in China: Critical Reflections," *Policy Futures in Education* 6, no. 5 (October 2008): 545–557, https://doi.org/10.2304/pfie.2008.6.5.545.

[50] "全国重点大学名单-中国教育在线 [List of National Key Universities]," *China Education On-line* [中国教育在线], June 29, 2005, http://www.eol.cn/article/20050629/3142081.shtml.

[51] Litao Zhao and Jinjing Zhu, "China's Higher Education Reform: What Has Not Been Changed?" *East Asian Policy* 2, no. 4 (December 2010): 115–125.

[52] Bin Wu, Aijuan Chen, and Hongfei Ji, "The Isomorphism of Chinese Universities: An Analysis of Higher Education Expansion and Consequences," Discussion Paper 55, China Policy Institute, University of Nottingham, December 2009, www.nottingham.ac.uk/cpi/documents/discussion-papers/discussion-paper-55-isomorphism-universities.pdf.

The stated goals of education in Jiangsu are to provide a foundation for economic development and modernization, reflecting the priorities of the pragmatist policy style.[53] Hu Jintao, followed by his successor, Xi Jinping, popularized the catchphrase "*xiaokang shehui*" (小康社会), which translates (inelegantly) as "moderately well-off society." Education in Jiangsu aims to achieve this goal of being a well-off, modern society. In other words, the provincial leadership views investing in education as an investment in economic development overall.

According to central government policy, the province's main task in education is to reduce inequality between school districts.[54] But compliance with this policy is highly uneven. Pragmatist provinces tend to devolve the responsibility of funding and implementation of K–12 schooling to lower levels of government and make little attempt to reduce inequalities within the province. Thus, local leaders (province and below) in pragmatist provinces are more likely to ignore central directives to reduce inequality across school districts.[55] First, these provinces have more autonomy related to economic and social policymaking and are, in general, less fiscally dependent on the central government. Second, local officials in these provinces have more latitude in terms of how to allocate resources. They may choose, for example, to allocate resources to areas that they think will be the most likely to stimulate economic growth and, therefore, increase the local revenue base.

Local officials benefit from prioritizing elite higher education in three ways. First, insofar as education stimulates economic growth and increases revenue, officials can siphon off funds for themselves, either through legal or extralegal means. Second, officials who have a track record of sending more revenue to the central government are more likely to be promoted.[56] Third, local officials may benefit from targeted funding to key universities in a personal way. Local officials' children often attend key universities, and, thus, they may have an interest as parents in ensuring that these schools are as well-funded as possible while allowing other schools to languish.[57] None of this would be possible, however, if local officials did not have the autonomy that is afforded to them in pragmatist provinces. Gang Guo finds that rural counties spend less on education, and "counties that raise more revenues are able to spend more on education."[58] This suggests that efforts at

[53] "江苏教育改革发展显著特点-徐州教研网 [Remarkable Features of Educational Reform and Development in Jiangsu]," http://jys.xze.cn/Item/32.aspx, accessed June 22, 2016.
[54] Lin, *The Politics of Financing Education in China.*
[55] Ibid.
[56] Ibid.
[57] Ibid., 29.
[58] Guo, "Decentralized Education Spending and Regional Disparities," 57.

progressive redistribution are dwarfed by vast differences in local spending, much like what I found with village spending on healthcare.

Poverty alleviation is another area of social policy in which pragmatist provinces are given greater autonomy to manage their own affairs. In response to growing inequality in the reform period, the central government tasked local government with implementing the Minimum Livelihood Guarantee (MLG). During the Hu Jintao government, the CCP substantially increased its commitment to the MLG by steadily increasing the number of recipients and the amount of the benefit.[59] However, the center's approach to poverty alleviation differed across China's provinces. For most pragmatist provinces, the center considered local economic growth sufficient to address poverty and allowed these provinces to manage MLG implementation with relative autonomy. By contrast, the National Poverty Reduction Conference mandated that provincial leaders of inland and impoverished regions be held accountable for the results of poverty alleviation in their jurisdictions through the "poverty reduction responsibility system."[60]

Due to the relative autonomy afforded to them in poverty alleviation, pragmatist provinces exhibit far more variance in the average disbursement per urban MLG recipient. Figure 4.6 displays the mean MLG spending for provinces with different policy styles. With the possible exception of Chongqing, pragmatist provinces would be likely to have greater autonomy in MLG implementation. And, indeed, pragmatist provinces exhibit far more variation in their disbursement levels for urban MLG beneficiaries. The average disbursement for pragmatist provinces ranges from RMB 1217 to RMB 3796, a range of over RMB 2500. By contrast, the average disbursement in paternalist provinces has a range of RMB 917, and mixed provinces display the tightest range at RMB 524.[61] The standard deviation of disbursement for the pragmatist group is 4.5 times that of the mixed group, further underscoring the greater variation within this group.[62]

Variation in MLG disbursement might be partially explained by variation in the cost of living and, therefore, the poverty line for different localities. However, even provinces with a similar per capita income vary significantly in their disbursements, such as Beijing, Shanghai, and

[59] Jiwei Qian, "Anti-Poverty in China: Minimum Livelihood Guarantee Scheme," *East Asian Policy* 5, no. 4 (January 2014), https://doi.org/10.1142/S1793930513000366.

[60] Sangui Wang, Zhou Li, and Yanshun Ren, "The 8–7 National Poverty Reduction Program in China – The National Strategy and Its Impact" (Washington, DC: International Bank for Reconstruction and Development/World Bank, 2004), 10.

[61] Mixed provinces have a minimum average disbursement of RMB 1,323 and a maximum of RMB 1,847. Paternalist provinces have a minimum average disbursement of RMB 1,027 and a maximum of RMB 1944.

[62] The standard deviation is RMB 877 for the pragmatist group, RMB 195 for the mixed group, and RMB 256 for the paternalist group.

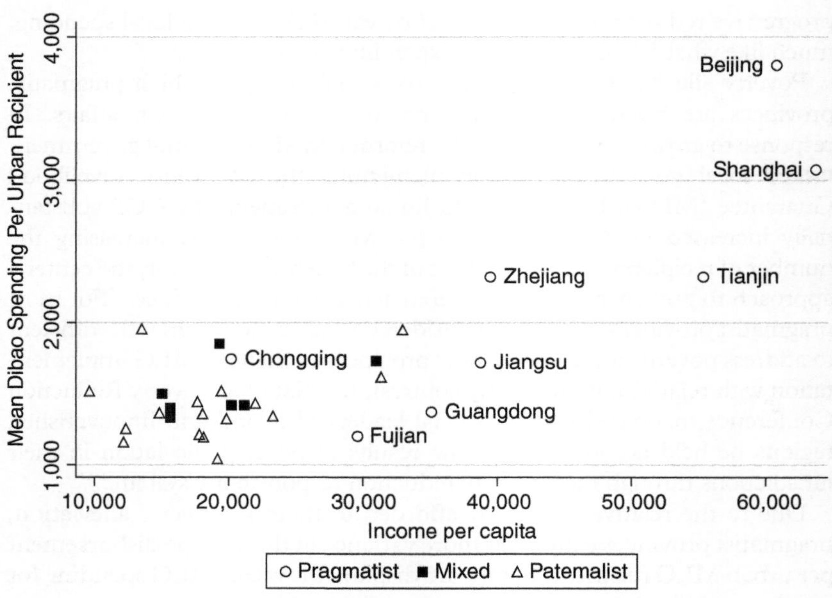


Figure 4.6 Mean MLG spending per urban recipient, 2010.

Tianjin (all of which are also cities with the administrative status of a province). This variation suggests that local officials are implementing the MLG program differently across localities.

Using a city-level analysis, Dorothy Solinger and Yiyang Hu argue that wealthier cities are willing to be more generous with the *dibao* to reduce unsightly street vendors, whereas cities with smaller budgets tolerate this type of informal work in the hopes that fewer people will need to rely on government assistance.[63] Similar to Solinger and Hu's findings, the variation in disbursements at the provincial level suggests that pragmatist provinces utilize their relative autonomy to implement the policy as they see fit.

Provinces with a pragmatist policy style have been resistant to providing affordable housing, despite having the most acute challenges in this area and the resources to address the problem. They also tend to emphasize the role of private actors in supplying this benefit, whereas their counterparts inland tend to take a more state-led approach to housing policy. By the 2000s, the cost of housing was one of the top concerns of urban residents across the country. In a nationwide survey, including

[63] Solinger and Hu, "Welfare, Wealth, and Poverty in Urban China."

both urban and rural respondents, nearly 40 percent of Chinese agreed that "housing conditions are poor [and they] can't afford to build/ purchase housing." Another 24 percent thought that the high cost of housing was the most pressing problem facing the country.[64] Housing costs are a far more severe problem in urban areas, and we can assume that the proportion of respondents concerned about this issue would be much higher if rural respondents were omitted.

During the Maoist period, many urban residents were employed by state-owned enterprises (SOEs) that provided housing. With the advent of economic reforms in 1978, housing was gradually marketized. Housing prices rose, particularly as the central government incentivized real estate development as a driver of economic growth in the late 1990s in the wake of the Asian Financial Crisis.[65] In addition, migrants increasingly populated the coastal cities, leading to additional demand for affordable housing – something that the government was continuing to address at the time of writing.[66] In the early twenty-first century, the central government oscillated between encouraging real estate growth and dampening the market because of concerns that housing prices could incite instability. Due to concerns about overheating in the real estate market, central and local governments began to experiment with cooling mechanisms, such as instituting a property tax (piloted in Chongqing and Shanghai in 2011).[67] The central government subsequently required property taxes to be used for affordable housing projects.[68] Amid popular concerns over the price of housing, the Hu Jintao government instituted news policies to expand the availability of affordable housing.

In the early 2000s, the central government instituted several waves of new policies to encourage local government to expand the provision of affordable housing. However, initial efforts stalled as there were no performance targets for local officials to provide low-income housing prior to 2010.[69] Not only did local governments therefore vary immensely in their compliance with central government policy, but they also

[64] Chinese Academy of Social Sciences, "2011 General Survey of Chinese Society [2011 年度中国社会状况综合调查]," 2012, www.sdccass.cn/pic/Upload/Files/baogao/201203/F6346722794823612054106.pdf.

[65] Ya Ping Wang et al., "The Maturation of the Neo-Liberal Housing Market in Urban China," *Housing Studies* 27, no. 3 (April 1, 2012): 347, https://doi.org/10.1080/02673037.2012.651106.

[66] Huang, "Low-Income Housing in Chinese Cities."

[67] Huang, "Low-Income Housing in Chinese Cities," 959; Wang et al., "The Maturation of the Neo-Liberal Housing Market in Urban China," 347–348.

[68] Yonghua Zou, "Contradictions in China's Affordable Housing Policy: Goals vs. Structure," *Habitat International* 41 (January 2014): 14, https://doi.org/10.1016/j.habitatint.2013.06.001.

[69] Huang, "Low-Income Housing in Chinese Cities," 952.

generally failed to meet the center's targets for affordable housing. Despite central policies mandating otherwise, Huang shows that only 1 percent of the revenue generated from land conveyance fees was used for affordable housing in coastal cities, and the wealthiest cities – who had benefited the most from rising real estate prices – used none of this revenue for affordable housing.[70] These cities included Beijing, Tianjin, Shanghai, and cities in Zhejiang and Fujian provinces. Furthermore, Huang notes that many local governments were still not in compliance with directives to use land fees for affordable housing, as only 1.5 percent of this revenue was used for housing nationwide.[71]

In the 2000s, coastal cities in pragmatist provinces had the greatest need nationally in terms of affordable housing, but they have also been the most reticent to subsidize housing. In the early 2000s, migrants flocked to eastern cities when real estate prices spiked, particularly along the coast.[72] And yet, even after the central government increased monitoring of housing policy in 2010, pragmatist provinces resisted affordable housing. On the one hand, wealthier cities in pragmatist provinces could raise much more funding for affordable housing than their poorer counterparts.[73] On the other hand, these provinces allocate a relatively small proportion of their provincial budget to housing (see Figure 4.2).[74] China's National Development and Reform Commission was providing progressive subsidies for housing by the end of the Hu Jintao era, at RMB 500, 400, and 300 per square meter for the western, central, and eastern regions respectively.[75] Nonetheless, despite progressive central subsidies, vast differences remained in the proportion of funding allocated to housing and how housing policies were implemented. In this case, conventional wisdom about local needs or wealth fail to explain pragmatist provinces' lack of attention to affordable housing, since they were the most resistant to central policies for allocating funds to housing while also having the deepest coffers.

The potential for revenue from real estate explains local governments' opposition to affordable housing policies. Land, as a finite resource controlled by the local government, provides ample opportunity for generating revenue. Local governments prefer to lease land to investors, preferably manufacturers or others with the potential to produce long-term tax revenue. As China did not begin to introduce a property tax until

[70] Ibid., 950–951.
[71] Ibid., 950–951.
[72] Wang et al., "The Maturation of the Neo-Liberal Housing Market in Urban China."
[73] Zou, "Contradictions in China's Affordable Housing Policy," 13.
[74] Based on figures from 2010, when the NBSC started reporting provincial spending on housing in the national yearbook.
[75] Huang, "Low-Income Housing in Chinese Cities," 958, fn76.

the end of the Hu Jintao era, leasing the land to residential developers would only produce a one-off gain.[76] Further complicating matters was the fact that land prices impact local government revenue. When land prices dip, it causes local revenue to contract, and local government tended to reduce funding to affordable housing as a result.[77] Prioritizing economic growth over poverty alleviation, pragmatist provinces during the Hu Jintao era focused on managing the real estate market for growth rather than social assistance.

Affordable housing programs consist of a mix of government subsidies and the provision of rent-controlled housing. These programs, which evolved substantially under the Hu Jintao government, target both low and middle-income households and sometimes even qualifying migrants.[78] Ostensibly, these policies were adopted across the country as per central government directives. Nonetheless, localities chose to implement them quite differently. Provinces with a pragmatist policy style tended to emphasize the role of private actors in supplying affordable housing, whereas their counterparts inland would to take a more state-led, top-down approach to housing policy. Jiangsu, for example, issued additional guidelines regarding housing policies in 2011 in response to the central government's heightened emphasis on low-income housing.[79] Taking a pragmatist approach to the policy, the provincial government emphasized the role of the private sector. The 2011 opinion states: "New commercial housing projects should be built with a proportion allocated to public rental housing, *as determined by the city and county government*" (emphasis added). The document also encourages industrial parks and corporations to build public rental housing for migrant workers, explicitly involving the private sector but allowing localities to determine the extent of public housing. Finally, the provincial government expressed

76 Zou, "Contradictions in China's Affordable Housing Policy," 12.

77 Ibid., 13.

78 Standard affordable housing programs initiated by the central government in the Hu Jintao era include: cheap rental housing (CRH), economic and comfortable housing (ECH), and public rental housing (PRH). CRH targets low-income households and makes rental housing accessible through rent control, rent subsidies, and rent reduction. CRH can be provided by public or private entities. ECH is usually a home-ownership program for low-income households (and middle-income households before 2007), which utilizes free or low-cost land from the municipal government and dwellings built by developers. PRH is a rental program for lower-middle-income households and some qualifying migrants in which the government may provide free land, regulated rents, or reduced fees and taxes. PRH may be provided by public or private entities. See Huang, "Low-Income Housing in Chinese Cities."

79 "江苏省政府办公厅关于加快保障性安居工程建设的意见 [Opinions of the General Office of the Jiangsu Provincial Government on Accelerating the Construction of Affordable Housing Projects]," www.law110.com/law/32/jiangsu/law1102006215260.html, accessed November 24, 2015.

the intention to work with the private sector to increase affordable housing through an innovative approach. Jiangsu began encouraging real estate developers to build smaller commercial units that the government could then rent through the Public Rental Housing (PRH) program, which provides subsidized housing for lower- and middle-income households. While the units were leased under PRH, the government would compensate the developer for any interest incurred on loans associated with the construction project. After a predetermined period, the housing units would be returned to the developer for sale on the commercial market.

By the end of the Hu Jintao era, some localities were beginning to experiment with new programs for subsidized housing for migrant workers. For example, migrants in Tianjin (a pragmatist province) and Chengdu (the capital of Sichuan, a mixed province) could benefit from low-income housing in exchange for relinquishing their rights to land in the countryside.[80] It is no coincidence, however, that these two cities are also among those pursuing *hukou* reform by eliminating the distinction between urban and rural residence permits for local residents.

## Conclusions

I began this chapter by describing how the distinct trajectory of coastal provinces led to the economic and political conditions that produce a pragmatist policy style. In these provinces, government officials tend to be more pragmatic and focus on economic growth. Thus, social policy serves as another tool to support economic growth, as with education policy. Moreover, because these provinces are wealthier and, therefore, receive less funding for social policy from the central government, provincial officials are more likely to further delegate social policy provision to lower levels of government. The higher degree of decentralization in these provinces means that local officials have greater responsibility, which can facilitate innovation and involvement of more actors. But this approach also leads to heightened intra-provincial inequality in social service provision, as in health policy implementation. Similarly, Jorge Martinez-Vazquez and his coauthors also find that wealthier provinces are more tolerant of inequality within the province, possibly because they are less reliant on central government transfers.[81]

Pragmatist provinces are reluctant to provide benefits that could interfere with revenue for local government, such as affordable housing policy.

80 Huang, "Low-Income Housing in Chinese Cities," 959.
81 Jorge Martinez-Vazquez, Baoyun Qiao, and Li Zhang, "The Role of Provincial Policies in Fiscal Equalization Outcomes in China," *China Review* 8, no. 2 (Fall 2008): 135–167.

In the case of housing, pragmatist provinces have encouraged the involvement of the private sector and other nonstate actors, but their contribution was minimal as of the 2010s.[82] Pragmatist provinces take disparate approaches to poverty alleviation, demonstrating their relative autonomy in policymaking vis-à-vis the central government. Overall, they spend relatively little on the MLG, but some pragmatist provinces do offer relatively generous benefits to recipients, perhaps reflecting a preoccupation with keeping the indigent off the streets.

The pragmatist policy style also appears in societal perceptions of the state's role in social policy provision. For example, in my survey, villagers in Jiangsu expressed greater expectations for healthcare provision by the state on average than did their counterparts in other provinces. Generally, these villagers were not necessarily more "statist" than others; rather, they maintained that the state should be responsible for healthcare because economic conditions are good. For example, one villager from Jiangsu, the most developed province in the sample, said: "The country is economically developed. [The state] should care more about the lives of the masses."[83] This sentiment suggests that the pragmatist policy style may permeate more than officialdom. Officials and villagers alike are aware of Jiangsu's relatively developed status and history of prioritizing economic growth. Now that residents consider themselves to be part of a relatively well-off province, they also have greater demands for state provision of social services. Moreover, Chinese citizens are likely to be sensitive to the political zeitgeist, both local and national, since a general awareness of the workings of the party-state is necessary to get along and ahead. Thus, Jiangsu residents are more likely to feel empowered to voice critical views of the government in addition to having higher demands and greater expectations.[84]

Finally, the pragmatist policy style has implications for the quality of governance. To implement the NCMS in Jiangsu, for example, counties had to set up new offices and committees to determine reimbursement percentages. In Hunan, by contrast, counties generally followed provincial-level guidelines with little opportunity for local officials to shape policy implementation. In some ways, this pattern widens the gap in

[82] Kerry Ratigan and Jessica C. Teets, "The Unfulfilled Promise of Collaborative Governance: The Case of Low-Income Housing in Jiangsu," in *The Palgrave Handbook of Local Governance in Contemporary China*, edited by Jianxing Yu and Sujian Guo (Singapore: Palgrave-Macmillan, 2019), 321–344.

[83] Survey respondent #1072 (*guojia jingji fazhanle, yinggai geng guanxin qunzhong shenghuo* 国家经济发展了，应该更关心群众生活).

[84] I argue elsewhere that villagers with greater knowledge of urban life and life beyond the village are more likely to have higher expectations for state healthcare provision. See Ratigan, "Riding the Tiger of Performance Legitimacy."

local government capacity and the quality of local governance between the provinces. Jiangsu has had additional opportunities for leadership and capacity building, while local officials in Hunan follow provincial (and central) authority both financially and in terms of decision-making. While policies such as the NCMS afford the opportunity for wealthier provinces to continue to build local state capacity, others are left waiting for government transfers and do not have the autonomy or resources to affect policy implementation.

# 5 The Paternalist Policy Style

In this chapter, I describe the paternalist policy style and show how it impacts social policy implementation at the provincial level and below. The top-down approach in paternalist provinces produces relatively standardized social policy but reduces opportunities for officials to innovate and tailor policies to local conditions. Fiscal transfers from the center often foster corruption and dependency in these provinces. Thus, many paternalist provinces have experienced rising inequality despite targeted policies and transfers. While focusing on health policy in paternalist provinces, this chapter also discusses the impact of paternalism on education, poverty alleviation, and housing. I use Yunnan as the primary case, but I also include examples from Hunan and Gansu. Despite their differences, examples from all three provinces reveal the many ways paternalism shapes the policy process.

## The Persistence of Paternalism

The story of economic development on China's coast is well known. The central government strategically selected geographically advantaged localities as "special economic zones," thereby permitting market forces to shape economic development and enable greater engagement with the global economy. This gradualist approach provided coastal regions with a first-mover advantage, which had economic and political implications. Meanwhile, however, the central government continued with a more tightly controlled approach to policymaking in the inland provinces. Thus, despite China's radical transformations throughout the economic reform period, noncoastal provinces continued to exhibit a paternalist policy style reminiscent of the prereform era.

Yunnan exemplifies how the interactions between the central and provincial government led to a paternalist policy style despite economic reforms. Since the Maoist period, the central government has been concerned about Yunnan due to its location bordering Vietnam, Laos, and Myanmar (Burma); its diverse population of twenty-five different ethnic minorities, which comprise 38 percent of the province's population; its abundant natural resources, such as aluminum, lead, zinc, and tin; its favorable climate for agriculture, including the lucrative, state-owned tobacco industry; and its history of reluctant compliance with central leadership. During the Vietnam War, the American military presence near Yunnan further worried central leaders.[1] Ethnic minorities periodically rebelled, and the province was slow to establish revolutionary and CCP committees during the Cultural Revolution.[2] After Mao's death, Deng Xiaoping appointed new leadership in Yunnan, seeking to maintain stability and quell dissent. Not only did the new leadership immediately demonstrate their loyalty by parroting Dengist slogans about modernization and economic growth, but it also emphasized organizational discipline.[3]

While all provinces received the message to prioritize economic growth, the paths available to achieve that growth differed across regions. Local officials (below the provincial level) in coastal regions were able to pursue industrialization – supported by preferential policies – thereby empowering them both fiscally and politically.[4] By contrast, Yunnan and other inland provinces relied on state-led initiatives that were dictated by higher levels of government and prioritized the development of natural resources. For example, the central government encouraged Yunnan to continue developing its state-owned tobacco industry, as well as mining and tourism, in part due to the revenue these industries raised for local and central government.[5] Rather than creating the conditions for market forces to flourish in Yunnan, in other words, the province continued to emphasize large-scale state-owned enterprises in natural resources and tourism.[6]

The top-down, state-led strategies for economic development employed in Yunnan received approval from central-level officials, which had the effect of encouraging path dependency.[7] John Donaldson characterizes Yunnan as a developmental state because the province oriented economic development around large-scale industries (tobacco, mining, and tourism). But since this process was directed by the central

[1] Dorothy J. Solinger, "Politics in Yunnan Province in the Decade of Disorder: Elite Factional Strategies and Central-Local Relations, 1967–1980," *China Quarterly* 92 (December 1982): 632.
[2] Ibid., 631–633.
[3] Ibid., 648.
[4] Jean C. Oi, "Fiscal Reform and the Economic Foundations of Local State Corporatism in China," *World Politics* 45, no. 1 (October 1992): 125, https://doi.org/10.2307/2010520.
[5] John A. Donaldson, "Why Do Similar Areas Adopt Different Development Strategies? A Study of Two Puzzling Chinese Provinces," *Journal of Contemporary China* 18, no. 60 (June 2009): 421–444.
[6] Ibid.
[7] Ibid.

government and reinforced the presence of state-owned enterprises (SOEs), Yunnan maintained a paternalist policy style. Unlike coastal provinces, it did not introduce market forces and new actors, such as foreign investors and entrepreneurs. In addition, Yunnan's overall development model relied on trickle-down economic growth that largely excluded the poor and contributed to a high level of provincial inequality.[8] Furthermore, by instituting and maintaining a large role for SOEs in the economy and a top-down approach to the economic development plan, Yunnan perpetuated a paternalist policy style that would impact social policy implementation in addition to economic policymaking.

Although many aspects of governing were decentralized in the reform era, paternalist provinces often failed to reap the benefits of decentralization. In remote rural regions of Yunnan, for example, elected local representatives are held accountable to higher levels of government rather than their local communities, and they lack the political power to influence decision-making as it pertains to their village.[9] Moreover, impoverished villages are typically financially dependent on higher levels of government, lacking sufficient resources to engage in policy experimentation of the sort that might be found in a wealthy locality.

As many inland provinces were not permitted to benefit from early economic reforms, these areas continue to be poorer and more reliant on fiscal transfers from the central government. While earmarked fiscal transfers can be a lifeline to ameliorate poverty, central assistance also ties the hands of local leaders. These provinces – and the localities under their jurisdiction – have therefore been more likely to follow central policies and guidelines closely rather than innovate and shape programs to meet local needs. Moreover, as some of these provinces have larger proportions of marginalized ethnic minorities, the CCP tends to take a politically conservative approach to governing due to concerns about potential unrest and instability. It is because the central government keeps these provinces under tighter rein that they developed a paternalist policy style, whose characteristics are summarized in Table 5.1.

Paternalism is nothing new in China. Paternalistic approaches to organizing society appear in China as early as the dynastic period and continued through the tumultuous twentieth century – even throughout economic reforms. Dorothy Solinger argues that, during both the

8 John A. Donaldson, *Small Works: Poverty and Economic Development in Southwestern China* (Ithaca, NY: Cornell University Press, 2011).

9 Jianchu Xu and Jesse Ribot, "Decentralisation and Accountability in Forest Management: A Case from Yunnan, Southwest China," *European Journal of Development Research* 16, no. 1 (March 2004): 170–171, https://doi.org/10.1080/09578810410001688789.

Table 5.1 *Characteristics of the paternalist provinces*

| | |
|---|---|
| Local State Resources | Small provincial budget<br>Dependent on central transfers for social policy<br>Less professionalized local state |
| Institutional Approaches | Province-wide standards for policy<br>Less attentive to corruption<br>Lower transparency |
| Patterns of Policymaking | Top-down approach<br>Less innovation<br>Selective inclusion of nonstate actors |
| Social Policy Strategy | Social control<br>Targeted benefits with conditionality |
| Social Policy Priorities | Targeted poverty alleviation |

imperial and the Maoist eras, the Chinese state cultivated legitimacy through paternalist functions that aimed "to provide and uphold a shared ideology, to appoint and discipline elites at all levels, and ultimately to guarantee economic security for the populace."[10] Solinger explains that this paternalist relationship has, historically, been uncertain because of the limitations of the planned economy and the difficulties that the center has had in reaching the periphery. As a result of this uncertainty, she argues, "skillful lower-level elites learn how to scrounge for themselves by barter, concealment, or hoarding whenever centrally run systems slacken."[11]

A top-down, campaign-style approach to educating and mobilizing the citizenry persisted even after the Maoist period. The CCP has used this approach for a wide variety of issues, ranging from public health to cultivating expertise in international trade law.[12] As the center funneled resources to the coast, inland provinces became increasingly uncertain of central paternalism and concerned that central fiscal support might

[10] Dorothy J. Solinger, "Uncertain Paternalism: Tensions in Recent Regional Restructuring in China," *International Regional Science Review* 11, no. 1 (1987): 24, https://doi.org/10.1177/016001768701100103.

[11] Solinger, "Uncertain Paternalism," 25.

[12] Yanzhong Huang, "The SARS Epidemic and Its Aftermath in China: A Political Perspective," in *Learning from SARS: Preparing for the Next Disease Outbreak: Workshop Summary*, edited by Stacey Knobler et al. (Washington, DC: National Academies Press, 2004), 116–136, www.ncbi.nlm.nih.gov/books/NBK92479/; Gregory Shaffer and Henry S. Gao, "China's Rise: How It Took on the US at the WTO," Legal Studies Research Paper Series No. 2017–15 (Rochester, NY: Social Science Research Network, March 20, 2017), 43, https://papers.ssrn.com/abstract=2937965.

diminish, thereby leading local officials to develop new tactics for coping with shifting realities.[13] In the early 2000s, the legacies of uncertain paternalism continued to persist and were particularly acute in some regions of the country.

Paternalism has continued to impact education through 2012. Gregory Fairbrother and Zhenzhou Zhao argue that the various Chinese states since the late Qing dynasty have used a paternalistic approach to inculcate nationalist values in the population as a strategy for state legitimation. While heavy-handed patriotic education might be more associated with the Maoist period, they show that ideology and "civic morality" persisted as core elements of the education system through the Hu Jintao years.[14] Several documents intended to guide curriculum development in primary and secondary schools, for example, emphasized morality to promote national unity and development. The guidelines link the persistence of "feudal superstition" with other societal problems, such as prostitution and gambling.[15] Fairbrother and Zhao argue that state legitimation in China has been based in "the overarching concept of paternalism, with its associated characteristics of faithfulness to an orthodoxy of good governance, concern for material and spiritual livelihood, attentiveness to people's views, and encouragement of people's responsibilities."[16]

The paternalist management style is particularly evident in the workplace. In the Maoist period, the *danwei* (单位), or "work unit," system structured urban life. In addition to stable employment, the *danwei* provided welfare and other benefits to workers, including housing, medical care, pensions, childcare, jobs for family members, and even assistance with personal matters such as finding a spouse or navigating marital discord. Although providing welfare through the company is not unique to China, the *danwei* in the Maoist period also served to cultivate loyalty to the state, thereby differing from its counterparts in Japan and elsewhere. The Maoist *danwei* was limited by state policy and the planned

13 Solinger, "Uncertain Paternalism."

14 Gregory P. Fairbrother and Zhenzhou Zhao, "Paternalism, National Citizenship, and Religiosity in Chinese State Legitimation Discourse," *Journal of Chinese Political Science* 21, no. 4 (December 2016): 428–430, https://doi.org/10.1007/s11366-016-9435-x. Patriotic education also experienced a revival after the 1989 Tiananmen Square protests and was renewed again with Xi Jinping's attention to "red army" schools in 2017. See Havier C. Hernandez, "To Inspire Young Communists, China Turns to 'Red Army' Schools," *New York Times*, October 15, 2017, www.nytimes.com/2017/10/15/world/asia/china-schools-propaganda-education.html).

15 Fairbrother and Zhao, "Paternalism, National Citizenship, and Religiosity in Chinese State Legitimation Discourse," 429–430.

16 Ibid., 431.

economy in terms of setting wages and offering benefits, but it was also responsible for political control – especially during campaigns to root out counterrevolutionaries.[17]

Although the reform period allowed enterprises greater autonomy and often led to privatization, the paternalist legacies of the *danwei* persisted. Many companies continued to offer generous gifts and perquisites, such as cash at holidays (even for retirees), medical coverage, heating subsidies, housing, childcare, and social clubs for retired workers.[18] Moreover, the enterprise would continue to assist with personal matters such as arranging funerals, visiting workers in the hospital, helping with hardships, and providing mediation for marital disputes, and in some cases "the top managers took the lead in performing a formal mourning role as heads of the enterprise family."[19] Many of these policies continued after privatization.[20] Corinna-Barbara Francis argues that, in addition to competition for labor, the "legacy of the work unit welfare system" had "shaped employees' dependence on their firms," thereby creating the expectation that firms would continue to provide similar benefits even in the reform period.[21]

In China's academic journals, scholars debate the applicability of paternalism to governance, often arguing in favor of paternalism. Xiaoxia Sun and Chunzhen Guo, for example, characterize paternalism as "coercive love from the government to citizens."[22] They argue that paternalism is an appropriate style of governance for China due to its resonance with traditional Chinese legal culture, current societal challenges, and the CCP's so-called "people as the basis" approach to governing. Therefore, they believe, it should be "widely applied in China," although they do suggest that there should be some limitations.[23] Similarly, Xiaotian Fang and Deqing Wang discuss that paternalism follows the principles of (1) care and protection, and (2) interest. They claim that individuals in modern society are "often hurt or at a disadvantage, and

[17] Anita Chan and Jonathan Unger, "A Chinese State Enterprise under the Reforms: What Model of Capitalism?" *China Journal* 62 (July 2009): 8.

[18] Chan and Unger, "A Chinese State Enterprise under the Reforms"; Corinna-Barbara Francis, "Reproduction of Danwei Institutional Features in the Context of China's Market Economy: The Case of Haidian District's High-Tech Sector," *China Quarterly* 147 (September 1996): 839.

[19] Chan and Unger, "A Chinese State Enterprise under the Reforms," 12.

[20] Ibid., 23.

[21] Francis, "Reproduction of Danwei Institutional Features in the Context of China's Market Economy," 849–850.

[22] Xiaoxia Sun and Chunzhen Guo, "法律父爱主义在中国的适用 [Application of Legal Paternalism in China]," 中国社会科学 [*Social Sciences in China*] (January 2006): 206.

[23] Sun and Guo, "法律父爱主义在中国的适用 [Application of Legal Paternalism in China]," 206.

therefore need 'parent' type of care and protection."[24] In addition, they argue that "the 'head of household' [or paternal figure] in paternalism (*jiazhangzhuyi* 家长注意) can be extended to the government and other social forces" to foster values that will support "building a modern society and the formation of order."[25] Based on their assessment, Fang and Wang suggest that the government take a paternalistic approach in order to limit the autonomy of private education.

Other Chinese scholars advocate for the role of paternalism in the legal system. Wenyi Huang, for example, advances a definition of paternalism similar to that of Fang and Wang's to argue for the appropriateness of paternalism in the legal system. Huang states that, despite negative connotations, "paternalistic legal interference" can support "economic efficiency, distributive justice, [and] basic human rights" as well as reduce social deviance such as "drug abuse, prostitution, [and] gambling," where such behavior is difficult to discover or enforce.[26] Not all Chinese scholars agree, however. Te Ma argues that residual paternalism in China's property rights regime is impinging on farmers' rights. For Ma, paternalism "comprises two characteristics: 'goodwill' and 'coercion.'" Despite possible "goodwill," Ma is concerned that paternalism in the property rights regime is excessively coercive.[27]

The paternalist provinces are the most diverse collection of provinces among those representing the three types of policy styles. Some paternalist provinces, such as Liaoning and Henan, rely much more on natural resources and agriculture than others. Geopolitically speaking, these provinces often have strategic importance for the central government, because either they have crucial natural resources in the ground, they are located on an international border, or both. For example, Inner Mongolia, which borders Mongolia and Russia, offers large deposits of rare earth metals that are crucial in the production of electric cars, cellular phones, personal computers, and other technologies. Some paternalist provinces relied on SOEs that were restructured during economic

24 Xiaotian 晓天 Fang 方 and Deqing 德清 Wang 王, "家长主义:一种政府干预民办教育的有效模式 [Paternalism: A Model of Government Intervening Non-Government Education]," 教育科学 [*Education Science*] 30, no. 2 (April 2014): 2.

25 Fang 方 and Wang 王, "家长主义:一种政府干预民办教育的有效模式 [Paternalism: A Model of Government Intervening Non-Government Education]," 2.

26 Wenyi Huang, "作为一种法律干预模式的家长注意 [Legal Paternalism as a Pattern of Legal Interference]," 法学研究 [*Chinese Journal of Law*], May 2010, 17. For a similar argument, see Xuming 旭明 Song 宋, "论家长式法律强制的人性基础与合理界限 [On the Humanistic Basis for and Reasonable Limits to Paternalistic Legal Constraints]," 重庆邮电学院学报 [*Journal of Chongqing University of Posts and Telecommunications*] 15 (June 2003): 84–86.

27 Te 特 Ma 马, "父爱主义与"还地于民 [On Paternalism and 'Returning Land to Farmers']," 北方法学 [*Northern Legal Science*] 4, no. 24 (June 2010): 41–47.

reforms, also known as the "rust belt," where many former SOE workers pressured the government to replace the "iron rice bowl" of the Maoist era. Several paternalist provinces also have large concentrations of restive ethnic minorities, including Yunnan and Tibet. These geographic and demographic conditions contribute to a relatively conservative political environment.

The border regions have been a source of concern for the government since the founding of the People's Republic, as they provide links to other restive regions beyond Chinese borders, such as central Asia. Challenges to political stability, which are prevalent in the border regions, are explicitly recognized by the government in policymaking. These provinces are often noted as a group that requires special attention from the central government. Several of them share borders with regions where a transnational criminal presence is well-established, such as the drug trade near Xinjiang. These provinces also tend to be poorer and have higher concentrations of discontented ethnic minorities who may share affinities with groups on the other side of the international border. As a result, border provinces are even more concerned with potential political instability than their counterparts elsewhere.

Several paternalist provinces have complicated histories. Take, for example, Xinjiang or Tibet. CCP rule in these places is often contested, but the nature of this contestation takes a different form from place to place. Only an in-depth analysis of each province could do justice to the complexities of their diverse cultures and histories. Other researchers have taken on this task with great success.[28] By grouping these provinces together, however, I identify some common trends facing regions with complex political challenges that are often heavily reliant on primary resources. These economic and demographic realities then impact the way local officials approach the policy process, the types of social policy that they emphasize, and how they go about implementing social policy.

## Economics, Politics, and Social Policy

Many inland provinces are less integrated with the global economy, more dependent on revenue from natural resources, and more reliant on fiscal transfers from the central government. They are also more politically conservative, partly due to rebellious populations. Because of these conditions,

[28] Barry Sautman and June Teufel Dreyer, *Contemporary Tibet: Politics, Development, and Society in a Disputed Region* (Armonk, NY: M. E. Sharpe, 2006); Parshotam Mehra, *Tibet: Writings on History and Politics* (New Delhi: Oxford University Press, 2012); K. Warikoo, *Xinjiang: China's Northwest Frontier*, Central Asia Research Forum (New York: Routledge, Taylor & Francis Group, 2016).

these provinces have maintained a paternalist style of policymaking despite changes to governing in other regions of China. With a paternalist policy style, these provinces employ more of the top-down, heavy-handed approaches to governing that we might associate with the Maoist era.

Paternalist provinces are the poorest provinces, and they are somewhat more unequal than the national average. On average, almost 35 percent of counties in paternalist provinces qualified for poverty county status during the Hu Jintao government. That number is over 50 percent in Yunnan. Yunnan is generally poorer than other paternalist provinces, with a lower GRP and income per capita. On average, income per capita in a paternalist province is about 75 percent of the national average. In Yunnan, income per capita is less than half the national average.

Paternalist provinces also have smaller average populations, although this is not the case for Yunnan, which is somewhat more populous than the national average. The most notable demographic difference between paternalist and other provinces is the large proportion of ethnic minorities. Paternalist provinces, including Yunnan, have almost twice the national average in the proportion of non-Han ethnic minorities. These provinces are also the most rural of the three policy-style groups. While about half the national population is rural, over 56 percent of the population is rural within paternalist provinces. In Yunnan, over 60 percent of the population is rural. Paternalist provinces also have a more agrarian economy and rely on natural resources more than other provinces. They rely on exports much less than the national average, but there is some variation within the group on this issue. They also receive less foreign investment – about 70 percent of the national average as a proportion of GRP, although there is substantial variation in this area. They do, however, rely on primary industry much more heavily than other provinces. Paternalist provinces report primary industry as a proportion of GRP four percentage points higher than the national average, and Yunnan is just below the paternalist group average in this regard.

Paternalist provinces are more politically conservative than their wealthier counterparts. They have fewer NGOs registered, less government innovation, and somewhat more corruption. Yunnan became increasingly restrictive of NGOs in the early 2000s, in contrast with some of the pragmatist provinces. After 2010, Yunnan instituted more stringent registration procedures and limited funding for NGOs mainly to government grants.[29] In addition, local government directly supervises

[29] Jessica C. Teets, "The Evolution of Civil Society in Yunnan Province: Contending Models of Civil Society Management in China," *Journal of Contemporary China* 24, no. 91 (January 2015): 158–175.

NGOs much more intensely than elsewhere.[30] As a group, however, paternalist provinces do have somewhat more independent newspapers than the national average, although this is likely due to newspapers catering to large ethnic minority populations such as Tibetans and Mongolians. Yunnan, however, has fewer independent newspapers than the paternalist group on average.

We might expect paternalist provinces to underperform in fiscal transparency, but, in fact, this group exhibits somewhat more fiscal transparency than the national average. Notably, Yunnan's fiscal transparency score is very low. As a group, however, paternalist provinces may report their revenue and expenditures more completely – although the accuracy of their statistics has not been verified – because they rely heavily on fiscal transfers from the central government. Provincial leaders seek to show, first, that they are using funds appropriately; second, that their revenue is still low; and, third, that they therefore continue to need transfers from the center. Despite providing somewhat more information about their revenue and expenditures than other provinces, however, paternalist provinces still experience greater challenges with corruption with respect to government funds. The paternalist group has somewhat more corruption than the national average, while Yunnan is about average (see Figure 5.1).

Yunnan's social policy spending is similar to other paternalist provinces, although Yunnan is somewhat more generous than the group average in every category (see Figure 5.2). This disparity is perhaps due to their approach to resource extraction, which entails advanced technologies.[31] On average, paternalist provinces allocate somewhat less to education than the national average and about the average for healthcare. Paternalist provinces also allocate more to social insurance, pensions, and housing than the national average.

Compared to other provinces, Yunnan and paternalist provinces face more severe social policy challenges. In 2010, for example, life expectancy was 69.5 and 73.4 years in Yunnan and other paternalist provinces, respectively, while the national average was 74.9. Illiteracy, maternal mortality rates, and infant mortality rates are all higher in paternalist provinces than the national average, and they are higher still in Yunnan (see Figure 5.3). Despite these challenges, paternalist provinces tend to allocate relatively small proportions of their small budgets to education and health. It is likely that inattention to social policy has contributed to these poor outcomes, but it is also likely that persistent poverty has

[30] Ibid.
[31] Donaldson, *Small Works*.

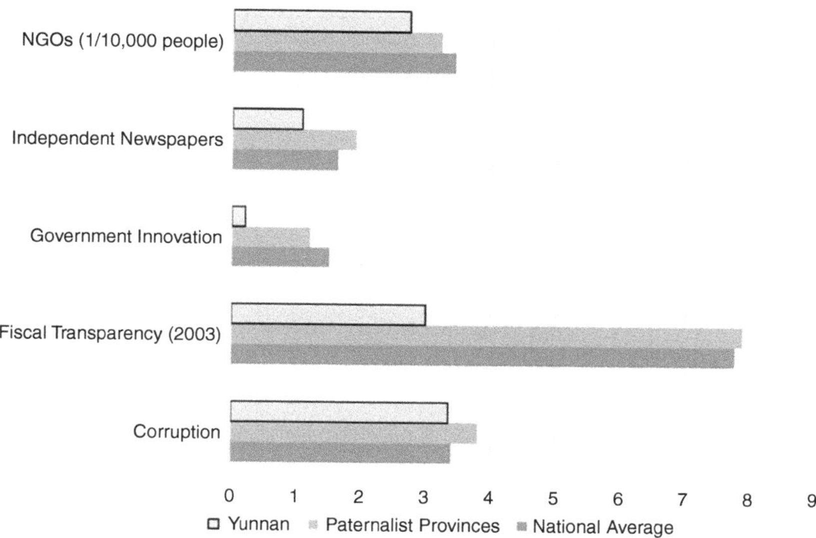


Figure 5.1 Political characteristics: Yunnan and paternalist provinces (2010, unless otherwise noted).
Note on measurement: Corruption is the number of people involved in corruption cases in the province in 2010 per 100,000 persons. Government innovation is the number of awards or finalists in national competition for government innovation from 2003 to 2012, per 10 million persons. Newspapers is measured per 10 million persons. Fiscal transparency is an original index of transparency in publishing data on provincial revenue and expenditures. Data for the fiscal transparency index is from 2003 (see Appendix A for details on calculation).

prevented these provinces from improving their population's well-being as much as wealthier coastal provinces.

## Policy Adoption and Implementation in Paternalist Provinces

Both economic and political factors constrain the policy process in paternalist provinces. These provinces are fiscally limited by their small budgets and dependence on fiscal transfers from higher levels of government, particularly the central government. They also face political challenges from restive populations, leading to a more conservative approach to

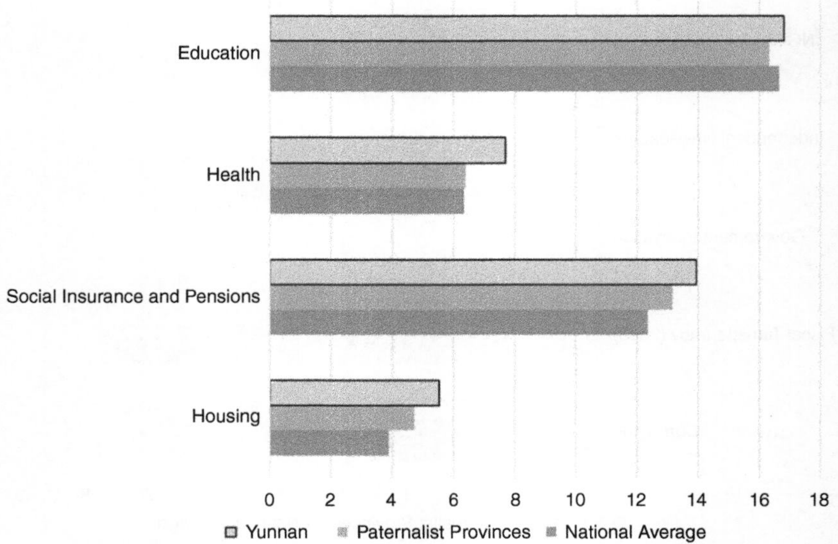


Figure 5.2 Proportion of provincial spending on social policy in Yunnan and paternalist provinces.
Sources: Data compiled by the author from *China Statistical Yearbooks*, 2009–13. Note: Data averaged over the years 2008–12, except for housing. Housing is averaged from 2010 to 2012, because data on housing prior to 2010 was not available.

policy. In this paternalist environment, the provincial government takes a top-down approach to implementation, often standardizing the details of new policies across the province. In some cases, such as poverty alleviation, paternalist provinces engage in micromanaging behavior, which is less prevalent in pragmatist provinces.

At first glance, one might assume that greater standardization and provincial intervention in local affairs might tackle inequality more effectively than a decentralized approach. However, the paternalist provinces' political conservativism reduces opportunities for local officials and non-state actors to be actively involved in the policy process, thereby reducing the likelihood of innovative solutions to policy problems. Moreover, while targeted funding to poor localities could be effective at poverty reduction, the prevalence of fiscal transfers creates the temptation for misuse of government funds in an environment of entrenched corruption. Thus, despite targeted funding and expanded programs, inequality persists, and social policy falls short of addressing underlying needs.

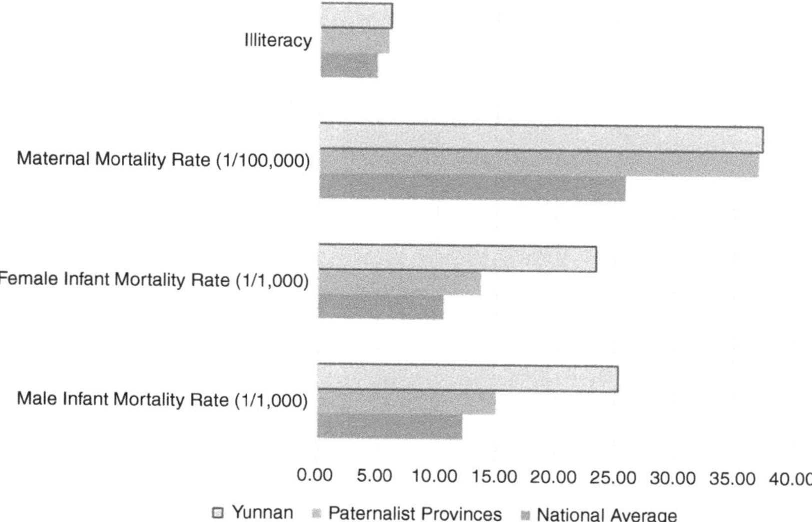


Figure 5.3 Social policy outcomes in Yunnan and other paternalist provinces.
Sources: Compiled from *China Statistical Yearbook*, 2010. Infant mortality from National Census (2010). Infant mortality rates are estimates after adjustments for underreporting.

## Health

With their smaller provincial coffers, paternalist provinces rely on central government transfers for social policy provision, including health policy. As a result, they take more direct control over policy implementation. They are more likely to standardize new policies across the province and allow less space for local officials or nonstate actors to shape policy. Thus, some policies are implemented more consistently across the province, reducing inequality in intraprovincial provision. Nonetheless, citizens in paternalist provinces expressed serious concerns about social policy in the Hu Jintao years, including mismanagement and corruption in new health policies.

The paternalist provinces' approach to the rural health insurance program known as the New Cooperative Medical System (NCMS) demonstrates their tendency to standardize the implementation of new policies with a top-down approach. Hunan and Gansu – both paternalist provinces – mainly fund the NCMS with transfers from the central

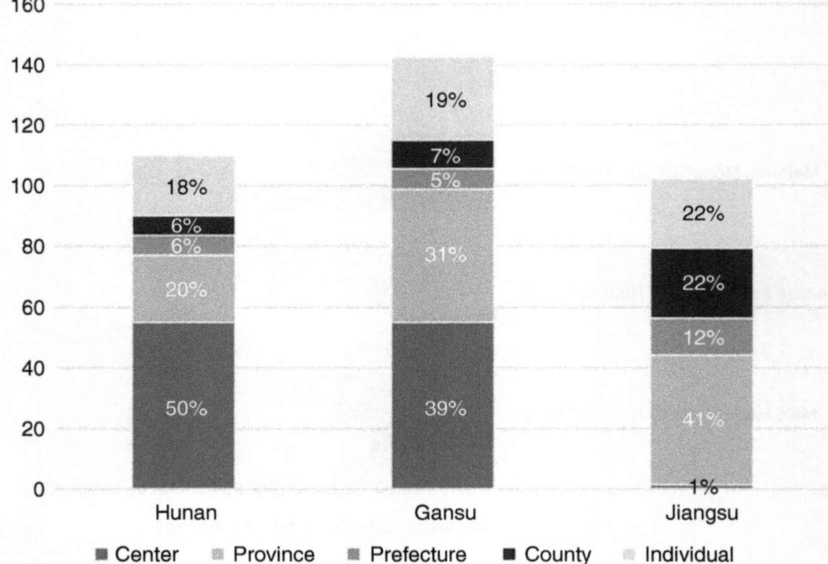


Figure 5.4 Distribution of state financing for New Cooperative Medical System (2009 RMB per enrollee).
Note: Percentages indicate the proportion of funding for the NCMS from each level of government.
Source: Author's interviews with county officials in 2009 and 2010. Author visited four counties in Hunan, four counties in Gansu, and seven counties in Jiangsu. Officials confirmed that the funding structures in the sampled counties resembled other counties in the province. For more detail on sampling and semi-structured interviews, see Appendix B.

government, supplemented by small contributions from the province, lower levels of government, and individual premiums (see Figure 5.4). Gansu's NCMS funding structure resembles that of Hunan but with greater contributions from the central government, the province, and individual premiums.[32] By contrast, pragmatist provinces such as Jiangsu mainly fund the NCMS from the provincial government, with

[32] The relatively conservative political environment in paternalist provinces inhibits researchers, too. As a result, I draw on fieldwork evidence from my survey in Yunnan as well as semi-structured interviews in Hunan and Gansu (see Appendix B for more details). Although a fuller picture of one paternalist province might offer some advantages, using examples from several paternalist provinces helps identify broader trends, since the paternalist group is also the most diverse of the three policy styles.

substantial contributions from the county and individual. Pragmatists also delegate the responsibility of implementation to the county, as discussed in the previous chapter.

While Jiangsu and pragmatist provinces allowed counties and municipalities to tailor NCMS program design to their local conditions in the Hu Jintao years, Hunan sought to standardize many features of the program across the province. These features included the proportion of funding contributed by each level of government as well as reimbursement percentages for treatment.[33] In Hunan, the requisite financial contribution from each level of government is determined by the provincial government following guidelines set by the central government pertaining to the central and western provinces.[34] In 2009, the erstwhile Ministry of Health stipulated that the NCMS contribution from lower levels of government in the central and western provinces should be at least RMB 40 per enrollee, while the individual contribution should be at least RMB 20. Regarding coastal provinces, the Ministry of Health merely stated that "the average per capita contribution level in localities in the eastern region should not be lower than the central and western regions."[35] Early in the implementation process, Hunan's Public Health Department issued provincial-level regulations that also standardized benefits, such as establishing target reimbursement levels of no less than 55 percent and 85 percent at different levels of medical facilities (see Table 4.2 for comparison with Jiangsu).[36] Thus, Hunan's NCMS program design was significantly more uniform than that of Jiangsu, even in the early stages of implementation.

Nevertheless, the degree of decentralization in the province is a contested issue among local authorities. For example, one director of a People's Hospital in Hunan (County D) thought that the village NCMS offices should assume a greater role in NCMS implementation and supervision. Yet he also remarked that the central government's

[33] "湖南新农合补偿标准进一步提高 [Hunan NCMS subsidy standards take a step further, raised]," Hunan Province People's Government Website, November 13, 2009, www.xinshao.gov.cn/info/bmlf/9290.shtml, accessed March 15, 2010.

[34] Interview HNDX14.

[35] Ministry of Health, "卫生部办公厅关于做好2009年下半年新型农村合作医疗工作的通知 [Ministry of Health General Office Notice on Proper Implementation of the New Cooperative Medical System in the Second Half of 2009]," 卫办农卫发*[2009]108*号 CLI.4.118483, June 29, 2009.

[36] Hunan Province People's Government Website, "湖南新农合补偿标准进一步提高" [Hunan NCMS Subsidy Standards Take a Step Further, Raised]," November 13, 2009, www.xinshao.gov.cn/info/bmlf/9290.shtml; Xinshao County Government Website, "湖南新农合补偿标准进一步提高, 湖南省人民政府网站 [Hunan NCMS Reimbursement Standards Raised, Hunan Provincial People's Government Website," November 13, 2009, www.xinshao.gov.cn/info/bmlf/9290.shtml.

investment in hospitals should increase substantially.[37] This director was frustrated by what he saw as insufficient funding to state-run hospitals while also seeing advantages to local actors participating more fully in policy implementation.

In paternalist provinces, the central and provincial governments intervene in health and other social policies because of concerns related to potential social instability. Prior to the NCMS, health expenditures – especially from catastrophic illnesses – were a significant cause of poverty. Because most healthcare costs were paid out of pocket, villagers often could not afford treatment and had to resort to borrowing money from friends or family. In Hunan, some villagers would seek help from the Letters and Visits Office by filing petitions for government assistance.[38] Others would beseech the public for charitable donations via the media.[39] My interview with an employee of the Letters and Visits Office in Hunan confirmed that health-related petitions were a significant problem prior to the NCMS.[40] Although the Letters and Visits Offices are an institutionalized channel for grievances, significant numbers of petitions on one issue can be perceived as an indication of social instability by higher levels of government.[41] By contrast, the link between social stability and healthcare is far more tenuous in Jiangsu. Because the general standard of living in Jiangsu Province is higher, the financial effects of catastrophic illness are less severe. Indeed, my interviews in Jiangsu did not suggest that local officials had concerns about social instability due to healthcare costs prior to the NCMS.

Paternalist provinces' top-down approach to governing does not necessarily produce more effective social policy, however. In semi-structured interviews and focus groups, villagers in Hunan revealed several difficulties with the healthcare system. For example, Hunanese villagers were more likely than their counterparts in Jiangsu to complain that their village health clinic or township hospital was unable to resolve health problems for themselves or their friends or family. As a result, they were forced to travel to the city to receive treatment – typically to the provincial capital of Changsha – where reimbursement percentages for rural insurance are much lower and a greater financial burden is thereby placed on the individual. In a similar vein, villagers in Hunan complained that they were not informed by their doctor that certain medications would not be

37 Interview HNDH18.

38 Interviews HNFV28, HNFV27. For a discussion of the Letters & Visits system, see Carl F. Minzner, "Xinfang: An Alternative to Formal Chinese Legal Institutions," *Stanford Journal of International Law* 42, no. 1 (2006): 103–180.

39 Interview HNFX23.

40 Interview HNGL29.

41 Huang, "Research Note: Administrative Monitoring in China."

covered by the NCMS, causing further financial stress. Others complained that certain procedures were not covered by the NCMS, resulting in a very small benefit to enrolling in the program. Approximately half of the villagers I interviewed in Hunan cited these issues as a weakness of the NCMS, whereas none of the villagers in Jiangsu raised these problems even when prompted. Thus, standardized policies and higher reimbursement rates at village and township medical centers have not sufficiently addressed the underlying deficiencies in healthcare in Hunan, including inadequate treatment facilities and lack of trained personnel in rural areas.

Villagers I spoke to in paternalist provinces were also more likely to express concerns about rising costs and corruption. Most complained of rising prices outstripping reimbursement rates, thereby undermining the benefit of the NCMS. According to one villager in Hunan Province:

> They [the government] have to monitor the medical market because after the NCMS some places started to increase prices. In this situation, the NCMS is of no use: [it] does not provide a benefit to villagers and the policy has no significance. So they have to control the costs of production and ensure that hospitals don't charge any inappropriate fees.[42]

In addition, rural health insurance does not always cover migrant workers when they are away from home. Finally, reimbursement percentages have a large range depending on the treatment. Some procedures are excluded, and outpatient reimbursement levels are very low.[43]

Despite myriad concerns about healthcare, villagers in paternalist provinces have very low expectations for state healthcare provision. Chinese villagers have low expectations for state healthcare provision in general,[44] but villagers in Yunnan have even lower expectations for state healthcare provision than those in Hubei (mixed province) or Jiangsu (pragmatist province). Paradoxically, even though Yunnanese villagers were the poorest in the sample, they had the most individualistic view of healthcare provision from among the three provinces in our survey. They expected the least from the state in terms of healthcare provision, despite having the most need. Villagers in Yunnan were far more likely to express the view that individuals should be responsible for the bulk of healthcare costs, with only 22 percent saying that the government should be responsible. By contrast, most villagers in Jiangsu and Hubei stated that the

[42] Interview HNDV17, December 14, 2009.
[43] Interviews with villagers in Hunan and Gansu.
[44] Ratigan, "Riding the Tiger of Performance Legitimacy?"; Martin King Whyte, *Myth of the Social Volcano: Perceptions of Inequality and Distributive Injustice in Contemporary China* (Stanford, CA: Stanford University Press, 2010).

government should be responsible for healthcare costs, at 57 and 54 percent, respectively. Village leaders living in poorer provinces were also more likely to believe that healthcare is the responsibility of the individual rather than of the state. In Yunnan, 59 percent of village leaders thought that healthcare should be the individual's responsibility, as compared to 14 percent and 27 percent in Jiangsu and Hubei, respectively.

These low expectations could be explained, at least in part, by the inadequate provision of healthcare in the past. Despite widely publicized recent reforms, for example, some Yunnanese villagers expressed the view that they did not think the government would provide healthcare because the state had not done so in the past. A few villagers (but no village leaders) stated that the government could not be relied on to pay for healthcare and that individuals therefore had no choice but to take responsibility. For example, one villager in Yunnan said, "You get sick, you pay for it. Depending on the government is not realistic."[45] Another villager in Yunnan expressed the opinion that the individual is responsible "because [healthcare] has always been out-of-pocket."[46] Since healthcare reform is incomplete and the implementation of new policies has been uneven historically, it is not surprising that some villagers do not expect the state to provide healthcare.

This group of provinces relies more heavily on earmarked transfers from the central government to implement health policy, resulting in less autonomy to tailor new policies to local conditions, as per central mandates. Officials in paternalist provinces are also more concerned about the possibility of social instability resulting from extreme poverty or inadequate social policy provision. Their response, however, is to standardize new policies at the provincial level, relegating local officials to the role of bureaucrats who carry out directives rather than shape them. The paternalist approach does not address the underlying deficiencies of social policy provision in their regions, thereby allowing inequality to persist. Nonetheless, widespread cynicism and low expectations for state healthcare may explain a relative lack of unrest in response to inadequate healthcare.

## Other Social Policies

The way paternalist provinces administered education policy during the Hu Jintao years reveals an emphasis on social control. Although investing

[45] Survey questionnaire #3288, *ziji shengbing ziji chu, kao zhengfu bu xianshi* 自己生病自己出, 靠政府不现实.

[46] Survey questionnaire #3187, *yinwei yizhi dou shi ziji fu de*因为一直都是自己付的.

in education could foster much-needed economic growth, paternalist provinces allocated relatively little funding to their schools. When these provinces turned their attention to education, city and provincial officials focused on frequent school inspections to ensure compliance with provincial regulations. However, the state did not demonstrate an interest in increasing their investment in schools or improving the quality of education.

Due to the principle of regression to the mean, one might expect that provinces already spending relatively high amounts of funds per student will not increase their funding over time as much as poorer localities. However, in general, not only were wealthier provinces spending more on education, but their growth rate for education spending was also higher even when controlling for wealth and other factors. This suggests that provincial politics were impacting financing decisions.[47] Gang Guo found that because of fiscal decentralization, and despite possible progressive fiscal transfers from the center, the gap in education spending was widening across wealthy and poor localities.[48] Guo did find a couple of exceptions, however, notably in Tibet and Xinjiang – both paternalist provinces in which education is expensive per capita due to the terrain, sparse population, and high proportion of ethnic minorities. In these cases, the center provided unusually high levels of fiscal transfers due to concerns about extreme unrest. Education is also crucial in these regions as part of the attempt to aggressively "assimilate" ethnic minorities into the CCP's national project. Yet Guo found that central subsidies associated with poverty county status did not make up for the difference between wealthy and poor counties.[49]

Paternalist provinces tend to enforce compulsory education, particularly in ethnic minority communities. Tibetan families in Yunnan and Qinghai, for example, sometimes opted out of schooling so that their children may learn farming techniques or attend a monastery. Prior to the Hu Jintao years, compulsory education regulations mandated that a designated number of children attend school from each village, but, initially, there was little oversight of the requirement. Thus, some Tibetan families would pay children from other villages to attend school in place of their own, leading to the phenomenon of "false attendance." In the 2000s, however, higher-level officials from the city or province began inspecting attendance and school infrastructure more frequently to

[47] Guo, "Decentralized Education Spending and Regional Disparities," 54–57.
[48] Ibid., 45–60.
[49] Ibid., 57–58.

ensure the implementation of guidelines.[50] While enforcing compulsory schooling certifies that the intended children are physically present in the classroom, however, it does not guarantee high-quality education. Moreover, forcing families to enroll children in school further exacerbates the rift between Tibetan communities and the state. Thus, with meagre funding and heavy-handed implementation, education policy in paternalist policies fails to reduce inequality.

Poverty alleviation also reveals how paternalist provinces tend to micromanage policy implementation through a top-down approach. In these provinces, fiscal transfers from the central government and greater involvement from the provincial level have the potential to support low-capacity localities in implementing programs to reduce poverty. However, fiscal transfers can also create a dynamic of dependency and corruption. If local leaders perceive few prospects for raising revenue, they may seek to maximize central transfers rather than work to develop a long-term economic development strategy. Indeed, paternalist provinces often micromanage policy implementation rather than encouraging local leaders to innovate. Finally, transfers are frequently misused, even when earmarked.

Yunnan's approach to poverty alleviation illustrates the paternalistic policy style that predominates in the province. China has incorporated a "point-to-point" (*dingdian fupin* 定点扶贫) strategy for poverty alleviation since 1986.[51] This approach entails linking state organizations – such as state-owned enterprises or units from the armed forces – with localities that have been identified for targeted poverty alleviation. The "linked" organization is intended to provide support for the impoverished locality by assisting local government with infrastructure creation and human capital development or offering other areas of technical expertise to foster economic growth. In a notice issued in 2010, the State Council reiterated its support for employing a "point-to-point" strategy to reduce poverty.[52]

Many localities demonstrate compliance with the central government's recommendation for a point-to-point strategy, but Yunnan implements this policy in a uniquely zealous way. In the province, each locality (county,

[50] Zhong Wei, "Research on Compulsory Education in the Tibetan Regions of Qinghai and Yunnan Provinces," in *Breaking Out of the Poverty Trap: Case Studies from the Tibetan Plateau in Yunnan, Qinghai, and Gansu*, edited by Luolin Wang and Ling Zhu (Hackensack, NJ: World Century Publishing Corporation, 2013), 149.

[51] I thank Xiaohui Gui for the apt translation of "point-to-point." This policy has occasionally been translated as "one-to-one" in Chinese sources.

[52] State Council, "中共中央办公厅、国务院办公厅关于进一步做好定点扶贫工作的通知 [Notice of the General Office of the Central Committee of the Communist Party of China and the General Office of the State Council on Further Doing a Good Job in Targeted Poverty Alleviation]," Pub. L. No. CLI.5.213783 (2010).

township, or village) that is designated for targeted poverty alleviation is assigned an official from the provincial government to monitor progress. The official visits the site regularly and administers questionnaires to assess the needs of the population and make recommendations for how local government might support poverty alleviation.[53] In a similar vein, poorer provinces tend to use the MLG more effectively to reduce poverty.[54] This could be for two reasons: greater oversight; and larger subsidies from the center. For the MLG, like health insurance, the central government provides subsidies to interior provinces but not to the coast.[55]

Despite micromanaging some policies, instances of corruption related to poverty alleviation and fiscal transfers abound in paternalist provinces. The "poverty county" policy provides a good example of how local officials sometimes abuse these programs. The State Council's Poverty Alleviation and Development Leading Group Office (*guowuyuan fupin kaifa lingdao xiaozu bangongshi* 国务院扶贫开发领导小组办公室) designates certain counties and villages for targeted development by bestowing the official designation of "Poor Counties and Villages" (*pinkun xian/cun* 贫困县/村). Ostensibly, counties are selected for targeted development based on both community and household criteria collected by local statistics offices and household surveys. Although the formula for poverty county designation is not public, counties with the designation are, on average, poorer than others based on gross regional product.[56]

Local officials are well aware that receiving this designation will entitle them to additional transfers from higher levels of government. As a result, in some cases, the process of identifying poor localities has been marred by local politics. For example, county officials in Xinshao County (新邵县) in Hunan revealed their overzealous embrace of the program when they posted an LED sign celebrating their poverty designation in late 2011. Subsequently, a photo of the sign spread widely on the internet, attracting attention and criticism. By 2012, Xinshao County was no longer included on the poverty designation list. Observers speculate that their ostentatious display led central officials to remove them

53 "云南组织40万干部定点扶贫 8月底到位 [Yunnan Organizes 400,000 Cadres for Targeted Poverty Alleviation To Be in Place by End of August]," Chinanews.com [中国新闻网], August 24, 2015, www.chinanews.com/df/2015/08-24/7485246.shtml.

54 Alfred M. Wu and M. Ramesh, "Poverty Reduction in Urban China: The Impact of Cash Transfers," *Social Policy and Society* 13, no. 2 (2014): 285–299, https://doi.org/10.1017/S1474746413000626.

55 Dorothy J. Solinger, "The Dibao Recipients," *China Perspectives*, no. 4 (April 2008): 39.

56 Kerry Ratigan, "Authoritarian Governance, Decentralization, and State Legitimacy: Healthcare Reform in Rural China" (PhD diss., University of Wisconsin–Madison, 2013), 99.

from the list. In a case from early 2013, Datong County in Shanxi Province (山西大同县) was finally reinstated as an officially poor county after having been miscategorized as "well off" since 1996.[57]

Indeed, attaining poverty status depends at least in part on actions taken by local officials. In some cases, local officials may feel that their locality was misclassified but lack the knowledge or connections to complete the application process, as local leaders in Datong eventually succeeded in doing to have their county reinstated as poor. One news report on poverty alleviation policy references a "widespread joke" that a "head of a county said his area isn't regarded as a poverty county because they are too poor," implying that they lack the resources to complete the application process.[58] Similarly, Wanlong Lin and Christine Wong found that "farm households in more advantageous positions and with more social resources have a stronger capacity to 'capture' government subsidies."[59] They find that, all else being equal, farm households are more likely to receive subsidies if the household identifies as Han, includes a CCP member, or has a head of household with a higher level of education.[60] My findings extend Lin and Wong's observations at the household level to suggest that some counties may also be more adept at attaining fiscal transfers than others, regardless of need.

Just as some local officials seek official poverty status to increase their revenue and may use funds inappropriately, there have been scattered reports of rural health insurance attracting corruption and cases of fraudulent illnesses to extract subsidies from the government (*jia bingli* 假病历).[61] This phenomenon was widely acknowledged in Hunan, but respondents in Jiangsu – a pragmatist province – were unaware of such a problem, even when prompted. Lin and Wong found that fiscal transfers for other social policies were also often diverted from their intended purpose due to corruption.[62]

[57] "小康县 '弃富逐贫'戴穷帽 '贫困'为何成香饽饽?" [Well-off county goes from rich to poor, wears 'poor hat,' how did wearing a 'poor' hat become trendy?]," 中青在线 [China Youth Online], February 25, 2013, http://article.cyol.com/yuqing/content/2013-02/25/content_7927672.htm, accessed May 15, 2013.

[58] "Counties may be incorrectly labeled as poverty stricken," *China Daily*, February 27, 2013, http://europe.chinadaily.com.cn/opinion/2013-02/27/content_16262137.htm, accessed May 15, 2013.

[59] Lin and Wong, "Are Beijing's Equalization Policies Reaching the Poor?" 44.

[60] Ibid., 43–44.

[61] "Genuine poverty alleviation," *China Daily*, February 26, 2013, www.chinadaily.com.cn/cndy/2013-02/26/content_16255617.htm, accessed May 15, 2013; interviews with hospital personnel and media reports in Hunan, 2009–10.

[62] Lin and Wong, "Are Beijing's Equalization Policies Reaching the Poor?"

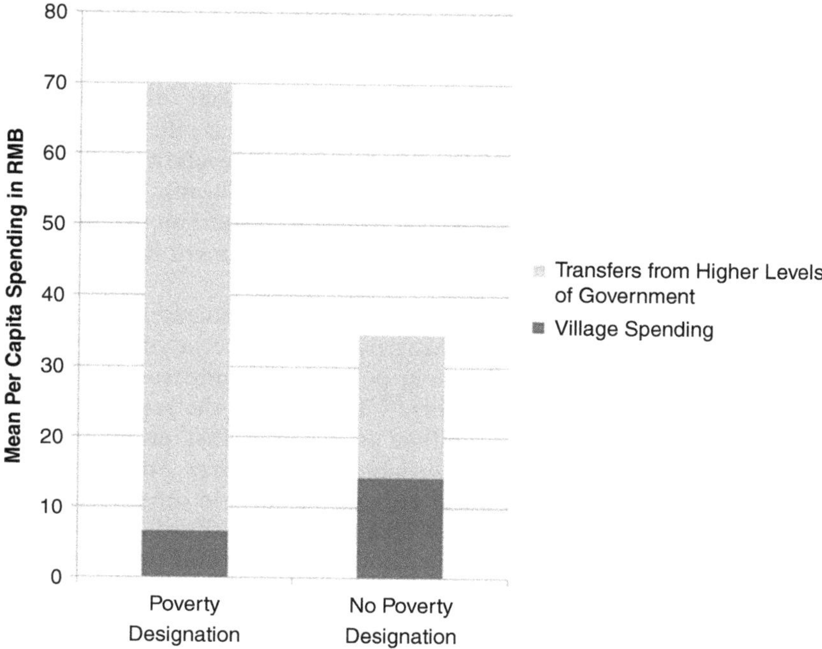


Figure 5.5 Sources of village-level health spending in Hubei and Yunnan: sampled counties with and without official designation of "poor."

Note: one village in the Yunnan sample is excluded because of enumerator error.

Source: Author's survey of village leaders. Number of observations: villages with poverty designation=35; without poverty designation=51.

Despite corruption, policies such as point-to-point and poverty counties represent targeted efforts at poverty alleviation that result in real benefits for participating areas. Localities are eligible for many more programs and subsidies once they have obtained official poverty status. In addition, villages in counties that are officially designated as "poor" receive more funding for health than villages that are not located in officially poor counties. Based on my survey of village leaders, villages that receive the official poverty designation report a substantially higher proportion of funding from higher levels of government for healthcare (which could include the county, municipal, provincial, or central government) than villages without the poverty designation. Figure 5.5 shows mean per capita spending on health at the village level grouped by villages with and without the official poverty designation.[63]

Average contributions from the village level are also lower in officially poor localities; this could either be because the village simply cannot afford to invest in health (or is not so inclined) or because they are already receiving such significant health funding from higher levels of government that they do not have an incentive to invest further in health. On average, villages in our sample with the poverty designation report more than three times as much funding from higher levels of government as do villages without the poverty designation.[64]

Similar to poverty alleviation policies, state-subsidized housing can be means-tested and targeted. Moreover, as the cost of housing is a major concern in China, housing policy might address discontent more effectively than cash transfers.[65] Thus, when the state is mainly concerned with reducing instability, as in paternalist provinces, the province tends to emphasize affordable housing over other areas of social policy even though housing prices are higher in other regions of the country. Paternalist provinces spent more on affordable housing than their pragmatist counterparts, both relatively and per capita, in the Hu Jintao years. On average, this group spent more than twice as much as pragmatist provinces on housing (see Figure 3.4). Indeed, local laws suggest that leaders in paternalist provinces had a concern for popular unrest due to lack of housing. Moreover, these concerns predated the central government's push for affordable housing, which intensified in 2010.

Local laws in Yunnan reveal a clear concern for how demolition and relocation can cause social unrest. In 2003, one "Emergency Notice from the General Office of the People's Government of Lijiang Municipality Regarding Conscientiously Implementing the State Council's Document, Relayed by the Provincial Government Office, on Safeguarding Social Stability in Urban Demolitions" concluded: "By standardizing the demolition market and strengthening the supervision and management of the demolition unit, and establishing a stable and standardized demolition and assessment team, [we must] establish a good

63 I include only villages from Hubei and Yunnan in Figure 5.5 because Jiangsu does not have any localities eligible for poverty designation and, thus, the funding structure is not comparable.

64 A student's *t*-test provides strong evidence that mean spending from higher levels of government is higher among poverty villages as compared to villages without this designation ($\alpha = 0.05$).

65 Chinese Academy of Social Sciences, "2011 General Survey of Chinese Society [2011 年度中国社会状况综合调查]."

image for the demolition industry."[66] The notice's title and content underscores the importance of social stability, and its categorization as an "emergency notice" further emphasizes the urgency of the matter. Other similar notices on demolition compensation and related issues were published in Yunnan in 2003, prior to the central government's more active interest in housing problems.

## Conclusions

Paternalist provinces have maintained a top-down, heavy-handed approach to governing that is reminiscent of the Maoist era, despite the changes of the reform era. These inland provinces comprise a diverse group, but they are generally less exposed to the global economy due to central policies that privileged the coast in the 1980s. Since inland provinces were not early beneficiaries of economic reforms, this group is less developed than their coastal counterparts. Moreover, several of these provinces face political challenges from ethnic minorities, due to the party-state's repression of these groups. The confluence of greater poverty and social unrest in these provinces has fostered a paternalist policy style that has shaped social policy provision.

Paternalist provinces tend to emphasize targeted poverty alleviation relative to other types of social policy through policies such as "point-to-point" and designated poverty counties. They allocate more funding to affordable housing, both in absolute and relative terms, than do other provinces. In healthcare, they offer somewhat more generous state-subsidized insurance programs. When they implement these policies, provincial leaders tend to micromanage the process, leaving little room for contributions from local officials or nonstate actors. Nonetheless, underlying conditions such as inadequate health infrastructure, lack of trained professionals, and corruption tend to undermine these efforts. As a result, social policy outcomes in these provinces lag behind their peers, and inequality persists.

China's differentiated approach to decentralization widens the gap in local government capacity and the quality of local governance between provinces. In Hunan, a paternalist province, counties generally followed provincial guidelines in the Hu Jintao years with little opportunity for

66 "通过规范拆迁市场和加强拆迁单位的监督管理，建立稳定规范的拆迁和评估队伍，树立拆迁行业的良好形象." Emergency Notice from the General Office of the People's Government of Lijiang Municipality Regarding Conscientiously Implementing the State Council's Document, Relayed by the Provincial Government Office, on Safeguarding Social Stability in Urban Demolitions [丽江市人民政府办公室关于认真落实省政府办公厅转发国务院办公厅关于认真做好城镇房屋拆迁工作维护社会稳定文件的紧急通知].

local officials to shape policy implementation. Whereas local officials in Jiangsu had opportunities for leadership and capacity building, their counterparts in Hunan were beholden to provincial (and central) authority, both financially and in terms of decision-making. While new policies provide an opportunity for wealthier provinces to continue building local state capacity, officials in paternalist provinces are left waiting for government transfers and do not have the autonomy or resources to tailor policies to local conditions. Paradoxically, the top-down approach to policymaking in paternalist provinces often exacerbates inequality by reducing opportunities for innovation and professional development for local officials, despite targeted policies from the center.

# 6 The Mixed Policy Style

Mixed provinces exhibit elements of pragmatism in addition to elements of paternalism. They tend to be more politically open than paternalist provinces but more restrictive than their pragmatist counterparts. This combination produces a policy style in which provincial leaders take a top-down approach to policymaking and standardize new policies across the province yet tend to be relatively frugal in their social policy allocations both in relative and per capita spending. In some cases, mixed provinces are caught in the middle – they do not generate as much revenue as coastal provinces, but they are not poor enough to be eligible for certain fiscal transfers from the central government. As a result, the budget for social policy in these provinces is often among the smallest in the country.

While coastal China was taking off economically, provinces that were not selected for early SEZs faced difficulties. Many of these provinces were home to the "losers" of economic reform – state-owned industries that were restructured or sold. As the government restructured state industry, many of the workers in mixed provinces lost their "iron rice bowl," comprising the set of social welfare benefits that SOE workers accrued during the Maoist period. Unlike in coastal provinces, these workers and the next generation of workers no longer had as many new opportunities to pursue. Many sought to stay in industry or manufacturing. Others looked to agriculture, which offered a meagre living but provided the safety net of "owning" a piece of land. From the perspective of farmers, the land could serve as a sort of pension. However, many inland residents migrated to the coast for new opportunities. Because of this different economic history, the economic profile of these middle-income, mostly central provinces diverged from pragmatist provinces in the early twenty-first century.

In these regions, the central government provides some subsidies for social policy, and the provinces tend to institute regulations to standardize social policy at the provincial level. As in paternalistic provinces, the result is less within-province variation. For example, the funding

Table 6.1 *Characteristics of the mixed policy style*

| | |
|---|---|
| Local State Resources | Medium provincial budget<br>Some central transfers for social policy<br>Medium-capacity local state |
| Institutional Approaches | Provincial standards<br>Less attentive to corruption<br>Lower transparency |
| Patterns of Policymaking | Top-down approach<br>Intermittent innovation<br>Exclusive of nonstate actors |
| Social Policy Strategy | Social control<br>Broad eligibility<br>Minimalist benefits |
| Social Policy Priorities | Social security<br>Subsidized housing |

structure from rural health insurance, including per capita contributions from the province, county, and individual, was standardized at the provincial level early in the implementation process in Hubei.[1] Of course, some variation remains, and local governments do not immediately comply with provincial-level regulations, but this effort from the provincial government does tend to reduce within-province variability. Due to the greater involvement of the provincial government, these provinces are generally later adopters of new policy and tend to exhibit less innovation at the local level than do pragmatist provinces. However, these provinces do not fully fit the model of the paternalist policy style, either. Provinces with a mixed policy style tend to take a top-down approach to policymaking, but they may not micromanage like a paternalist province. The result is pro forma implementation by local government. Table 6.1 summarizes the characteristics of the mixed policy style.

On the one hand, top-down implementation and province-wide standardization reduce within-province variation and inequality. These characteristics mitigate the effects of a postcode lottery, in which one's benefits vary based on residence. However, reduced autonomy for local government below the province level also limits opportunity to develop the capacity and capabilities of local officials in the interest of good governance. The rural health insurance program provides an illustrative

[1] Hubei Provincial Government Bulletin, "湖北省人民政府关于全面推进新型农村合作医疗制度建设的指导意见 [Hubei Province People's Government Instructive Opinion on the Full Promotion of the Construction of the New Cooperative Medical System]."

example of the implications of top-down implementation. In a pragmatist province, counties had the autonomy to set up new offices and committees to determine reimbursement percentages, thereby requiring local officials to determine the specifics of the policy (such as reimbursement percentages) at the county level. Thus, in theory, local officials were required to learn about the policy and consider the most appropriate course of action for their locality, further developing human capital within local government. By contrast, in a mixed province, counties generally followed provincial-level guidelines with little opportunity for local officials to shape policy implementation, thereby widening the gap in local government capacity and the quality of local governance between the provinces. In other words, officials in pragmatist provinces have had additional opportunities for leadership and capacity building during the Hu Jintao era, while local officials in other provinces were beholden to provincial (and central) authority, both financially and in terms of decision-making. While policies such as the rural health insurance created opportunities for pragmatist provinces to continue building local state capacity, others were left waiting for government transfers and did not have the autonomy or resources to shape policy implementation.

## Economics, Politics, and Social Policy

Mixed provinces are less integrated with the global economy than pragmatist provinces, but they have more resources than paternalist provinces. Politically, mixed provinces are not as conservative as paternalist provinces but not as open as pragmatist provinces. Mixed provinces are generally frugal in social policy, with the exception of housing.

Hubei, like other mixed provinces, is more populous than the national average. But, like pragmatist provinces, Hubei and other mixed provinces are ethnically homogenous. In fact, they are home to even fewer people identifying as non-Han ethnic minorities than are the pragmatist provinces.[2] Hubei itself has more ethnic minorities than the group average, at over 4 percent of its population. This group of provinces is also slightly more rural than the national average, although it was almost half urbanized by the early twenty-first century. Hubei and other mixed provinces are more urban than paternalist provinces but more rural than pragmatist provinces.

Mixed provinces are somewhat poorer than the national average, with income per capita at about 80 percent of the national average. Yet they are

[2] Sichuan deviates from the group average in this regard, with over 6 percent a non-Han ethnic minority.

wealthier than paternalist provinces. More than one-fifth of the counties in mixed provinces qualify for poverty county status, suggesting that there are, indeed, significant pockets of poverty that receive assistance and attention from higher levels of government. While mixed provinces are, as a group, slightly less unequal than the national average, Hubei is somewhat more unequal than the national and mixed group averages.

Mixed provinces exhibit more indications of export-oriented industrialization than their paternalist counterparts but significantly less than pragmatist provinces. Exports constitute a small proportion of gross regional product, although they account for somewhat more than in paternalist provinces. As a group, the contribution of exports to the economy of a mixed province, on average, is a little more than half of the national average. Hubei exports slightly less than the average for the mixed group. Mixed provinces attract close to the national average for foreign investment, although Hubei attracts somewhat less. Mixed provinces' reliance on primary industry is also comparable to the national average, although Hubei relies on primary industry somewhat more than the mixed group and the national average.

Net migration reveals a crucial social challenge in mixed provinces, as these provinces are exporters of labor. In the early 2000s, mixed provinces had a net migration of over 3.2 percent, and Hubei experienced almost double that loss. These migration patterns, which are closely tied to economics, impact local demands for social policy. The labor-exporting regions are often left with hollowed-out villages and towns where most of the population is not of working age – either elderly or children. Migrant workers often only return to their hometowns once per year to celebrate Lunar New Year. In many cases, elderly grandparents are taking care of left-behind children while parents are working in the city.[3] This sets up provinces like Hubei to potentially have even weaker economic performance without a strong labor force, as well as to have different social policy needs and demands.[4]

Although they are neither exceptionally politically open nor conservative (see Figure 6.1), the group of mixed provinces has about the same numbers of NGOs per population as the national average; Hubei has

[3] "China Has 61 Million Left-Behind Children … That's Almost Britain's Total Population," *South China Morning Post*, October 21, 2016, www.scmp.com/news/china/economy/article/2038731/its-official-china-has-61-million-left-behind-children-thats; John Sudworth, "Counting the Cost of China's Left-Behind Children," BBC News Beijing, www.bbc.com/news/world-asia-china-35994481, accessed July 17, 2017.

[4] Recent research suggest that migrant-sending localities might perform better at public goods provision. See Elise Pizzi, "Does Labor Migration Improve Access to Public Goods in Source Communities? Evidence from Rural China," *Journal of Chinese Political Science* 23, no. 4 (December 2018): 563–583, https://doi.org/10.1007/s11366-017-9525-4.

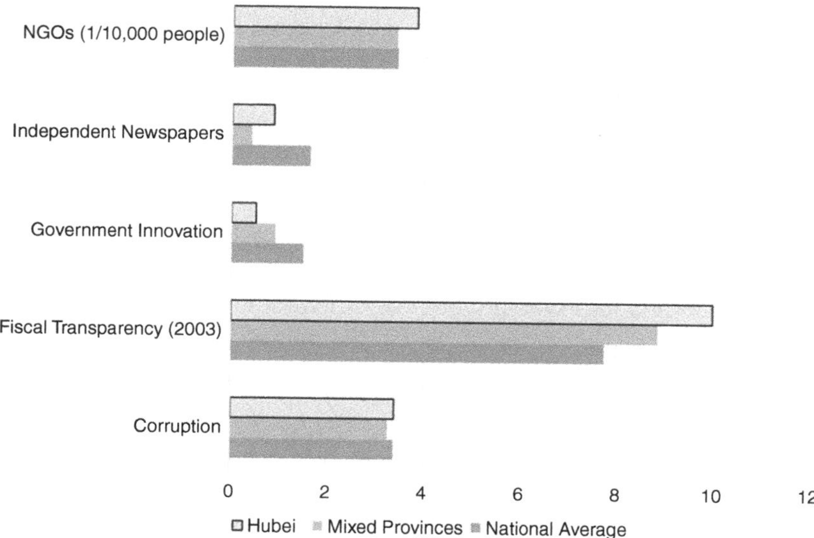


Figure 6.1 Political characteristics: Hubei and mixed provinces (2010, unless otherwise noted).
Note on measurement: Corruption is number of people involved in corruption cases in the province in 2010 per 100,000 persons. Government innovation is number of awards or finalists in national competition for government innovation from 2003 to 2012, per 10 million persons. Independent newspapers is measured per 10 million persons. Fiscal transparency is an original index of transparency in publishing data on provincial revenue and expenditures. Data for the fiscal transparency index is from 2003 (see Appendix A for details on calculation).

somewhat more. In general, the group has few independent newspapers per population, although Hubei has more than the group in this category, as well. Mixed provinces are less likely to be recognized for government innovation than the national average. Hubei fares worse than the mixed group on this measure. Mixed provinces surpass the national average for fiscal transparency, however, with Hubei exceeding its group. Hubei and the group in general exhibit about the same amount of corruption as the national average. Thus, in political openness, mixed provinces are solidly in between pragmatist and paternalist provinces.

The economic and political landscape of mixed provinces leads local officials to prioritize different types of social policy than pragmatist provinces. They also tend to be relatively frugal in their social policy allocations, both in terms of relative and per capita spending.

For the mixed group, spending on education as a proportion of the budget is slightly higher than the national average, although Hubei allocates relatively less to this area than the national average. Per capita, however, mixed provinces spend the least on education. Mixed provinces' spending on health is similar. As a proportion of the budget, this group spends slightly more than the national average, but their per capita spending is the lowest of the three groups. Similarly, mixed provinces allocate a larger proportion of their budgets to the social safety net than the national average, but they spend less per capita on these benefits than the other two groups. Indeed, mixed provinces spend less per capita on education, health, and the social safety net than paternalist provinces, even though the paternalist group comprises the poorest regions in China.

Housing spending in mixed provinces deviates somewhat from this pattern. As a proportion of social policy spending, the mixed group allocates relatively more on housing than the national average, although Hubei allocates less (see Figure 6.2). Mixed provinces spend more on housing per capita than pragmatist provinces but less than paternalist provinces (see Figure 3.4).

The complexity of social policy spending in these provinces reflects both the diversity of provinces within the group and the competing tendencies within each province. Spending suggests different priorities among mixed provinces like Hubei. However, spending fails to tell the whole story. We can observe even greater divergence within the mixed group when we look at the policy process (see Figure 6.3).

Overall, Hubei and other mixed provinces exhibit somewhat better social policy outcomes than the national average. They have slightly lower rates of illiteracy, for example, and much lower rates of maternal mortality, female infant mortality, and male infant mortality. In maternal and infant mortality, Hubei fares better than the mixed group in general. Mixed provinces have an average life expectancy of 75.2, just above life expectancy in Hubei and the national average, which are both 74.9. Thus, mixed provinces have achieved relatively positive outcomes in social policy despite being among the most frugal in terms of social policy spending.

Shenmu County in Shaanxi Province (陕西神木县) is an interesting exception to social policy provision in China and demonstrates some of the mixed qualities of governing in this group. On the one hand, Shaanxi has long been known for ideological conservativism and foot-dragging in the

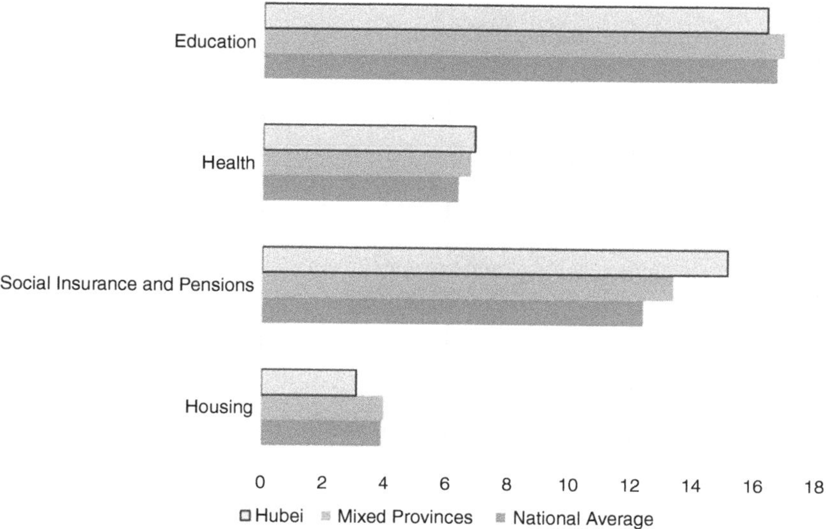


Figure 6.2 Proportion of provincial spending on social policy in Hubei and mixed provinces.
Note: Data are averaged over the years 2008–12, except for housing. Housing is averaged from 2010 to 2012 because data on housing prior to 2010 was not available.
Sources: Data compiled by the author from *China Statistical Yearbook*, 2009–13.

reform period.[5] And yet, Shenmu County has managed a different approach to innovation, as compared to that seen on the coast. It has gained notoriety for using the revenue generated by coal mining to establish an extensive social welfare system for county residents, including universal healthcare, free education through secondary school, housing subsidies, and poverty relief programs.[6] This case could certainly be considered a form of innovation of the sort we might expect of a pragmatist province. However, many of the benefits offered focus on poverty alleviation rather than cultivating a productive workforce. Moreover, these policies have been implemented

[5] Lane, "One Step Behind: Shaanxi in Reform."
[6] Typically, nine years of compulsory education are virtually free in public schools beginning at age six. Public secondary schools, however, increasingly charge various operating fees that can be a significant burden on lower-income families. In terms of the reforms made, the county has received some coverage from the state media for its efforts (see "Public welfare programs in Shenmu County, Shaanxi Province," China.org.cn, December 17, 2009, www.china.org.cn/photos/2009-12/27/content_19138418.htm).

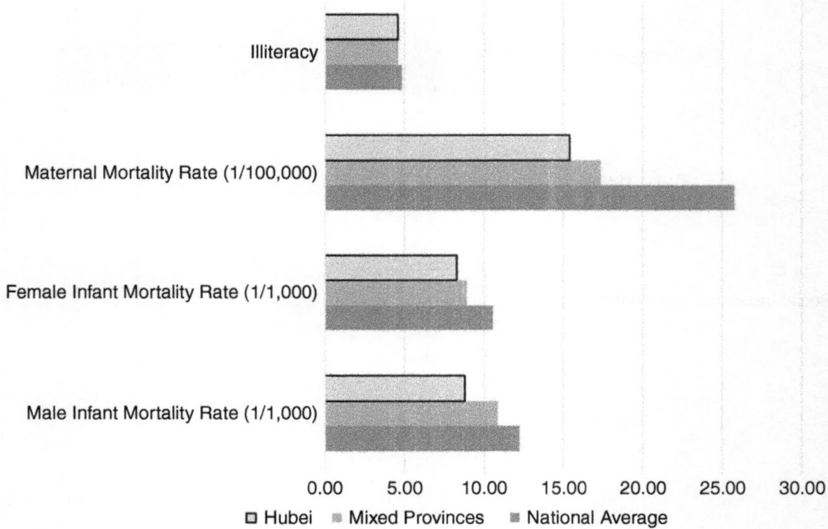


Figure 6.3 Social policy outcomes in Hubei and mixed provinces. Sources: Compiled from statistical yearbooks. Infant mortality from National Census (2010). Infant mortality rates are estimates after adjustments for underreporting.

in a top-down fashion through the county without significant involvement from nonstate actors. Meanwhile, Anhui, another province in the mixed group, served as a model for the national policy on essential drugs, although implementation was problematic.[7] Still, while there are certainly anomalies such as these, provinces in the mixed group are less likely to be policy innovators than pragmatist provinces. Nonetheless, the combination of some innovation with a concern for poverty alleviation reflects the mixed character of policymaking. Examples such as Shenmu exhibit elements associated with pragmatism as well as elements associated with paternalism.

Mixed provinces are a diverse group, comprising provinces that bear many similarities to pragmatist provinces as well as provinces that more closely resemble paternalist provinces. For example, Shandong is a coastal province. While it is not quite as wealthy or export-oriented as its coastal neighbors, it has achieved some successes in social policy that are comparable to the pragmatist group. Lin and Wong characterize Shandong as anomalous among coastal provinces. It is the poorest

[7] Huang, *Governing Health in Contemporary China*, 75.

province in the eastern region (according to the Chinese state) and was among the lowest in fiscal expenditures of all provinces in 2009.[8] Like several of the central provinces, it is too poor to adequately fund social policy, but, because of its coastal location, it is not eligible for many of the central government's fiscal transfers for social programs. For example, Shandong's per capita subsidies for the rural MLG and the NCMS were about half of those in other coastal provinces.[9] However, life expectancy and maternal and infant mortality rates in Shandong are close to the average for the pragmatist group. By contrast, Sichuan, an inland province with significant poverty, exhibits social policy outcomes close to the average for a paternalist province in terms of illiteracy and infant mortality rates, but it has slightly higher life expectancy and a lower maternal mortality rate.

## Policy Adoption and Implementation in Mixed Provinces

Like paternalist provinces, mixed provinces often take a top-down approach to implementing new policies. This group also receives more fiscal transfers from the central government for social policy than their pragmatist counterparts. Popular perceptions of the state role in social policy reveal both pragmatist and paternalist views, reflecting the mixed quality of state–society relations.

### Health

Hubei and other mixed provinces are more likely to take a top-down approach to new policies, and healthcare is no exception. For example, unlike in Jiangsu and the pragmatist provinces, the provincial government in Hubei standardized many features of the new rural health insurance program relatively early in its implementation. Starting in 2008, according to the "Hubei Province People's Government Instructive Opinion on the Full Promotion of the Construction of the New Cooperative Medical System," the program was to provide average funding of RMB 80 per person, comprised of RMB 40 from the central government and RMB 40 from local government (provincial and county levels). In designated poverty counties, the province was to provide RMB 32, while the county was to provide RMB 8 per person. In all other counties, the province was to provide RMB 30, while the county would provide RMB 10 per person. Individual premiums were to be at

[8] Lin and Wong, "Are Beijing's Equalization Policies Reaching the Poor?," 37.
[9] Ibid.

least RMB 20 per year.[10] The same opinion provided clear guidelines for reimbursement levels for in- and outpatient procedures. Of course, variation remained during the Hu Jintao years, as local governments did not immediately comply with provincial-level regulations, but this effort from the provincial government did tend to reduce within-province variability in policy implementation.

Popular perceptions of state social-policy provision illustrate how the mixed policy style is manifested in state–society relations. Survey responses from Hubei, for example, reveal different views on the role of the state in providing healthcare and the relationship of healthcare provision to other concerns. One village leader in Hubei emphatically stated that "health comes first."[11] And yet, other respondents linked the importance of good health to generating income – an orientation toward economic interests that we might expect in a pragmatist province. One villager in Hubei commented: "Only once you are healthy will you be able to earn a salary."[12] Still other comments reflect a fatalistic view of state healthcare provision and persistent paternalism. A villager in Hubei stated, for example, that "[we] don't have the money in the country; the only option is to die a slow death."[13] This type of fatalistic view might be more commonly expected in a poorer province, such as Yunnan or one of the other paternalist provinces. Hubei villagers also shared that the government should provide for healthcare in keeping with current policies or widely disseminated rhetoric. In the words of one villager, the government should be responsible for the bulk of healthcare costs because "the state really emphasizes health."[14] Like villagers in paternalistic provinces, villagers in mixed provinces tend to reflect the stated goals of the party-state and current policies when discussing their views on state responsibility for social policy provision.

Overall, the disparate comments about healthcare in Hubei suggest more conflicting ideas about state social-policy provision in mixed provinces. By contrast, comments from Yunnan (paternalist province) and Jiangsu (pragmatist province) were more consistent within each province, suggesting a more cohesive set of perceptions and expectations than exists in mixed provinces.

[10] Hubei Provincial Government Bulletin, "湖北省人民政府关于全面推进新型农村合作医疗制度建设的指导意见 [Hubei Province People's Government Instructive Opinion on the Full Promotion of the Construction of the New Cooperative Medical System]."

[11] Survey questionnaire #2303, *shouxian shi jiankang* 首先是健康.

[12] Survey questionnaire #2095, *you jiankang cai you shouru* 有健康才有收入.

[13] Survey questionnaire #2261, *nongcun genben chubuliao qian, zhi neng tuosi* 农村根本出不了钱, 只能拖死.

[14] Survey questionnaire #2244, *guojia dui yiliao feichang zhongshi* 国家对医疗非常重视.

## Other Social Policies

Although provincial leaders in mixed provinces have an interest in supporting economic growth, they invest minimally in education. Moreover, the educational goals for this group reflect the mixed character of this policy style. Government statements articulate a need to invest in education to support economic growth (like pragmatist provinces), but they also acknowledge the challenges facing schools in rural areas – an issue that is more closely associated with paternalist provinces.

Mixed provinces, on average, do not spend as much on education, relatively or per capita, as their pragmatist counterparts. Per capita, they spend even less on education than paternalist provinces, although they do allocate somewhat more of their budget to education than paternalist provinces. Nonetheless, their illiteracy rates are not as high as paternalist provinces. Thus, their lack of funding for education could be partly attributed to less costly needs in this area compared to regions with a dispersed population of ethnic minorities.

While mixed provinces seek to use education to support economic growth, they face problems of inadequate schooling in their rural areas. In 2011, for example, the Hubei provincial government articulated the goal of becoming "qualitatively and quantitatively educationally strong" (对教育强省作了定量、定性的描述) by 2015,[15] implying that there was room for improvement. On the one hand, the Hubei educational system seeks to support economic growth through cultivating human capital, as we might expect in a pragmatist province.[16] The plan emphasizes Hubei's strengths in science, technology, and industry. It also states that Hubei's educational system is its comparative advantage, and it links education with modernization and a vibrant economy. On the other hand, the provincial government is concerned about the rural–urban gap in education and aims to improve the quality of teachers in rural areas through the "rural teacher support action plan" (*nongcun jiaoshi zizhu xingdong jihua* 农村教师资助行动计划).[17] This plan includes improving the quality of rural teachers through mentorship by urban teachers and improving housing and facilities to reduce attrition with better work environments and quality of life.

The degree of decentralization in mixed provinces varies across and even within social policy areas. Although localities below the province

[15] "湖北省教育厅长陈安丽:10年进入教育强省行列_国内教育_中国教育新闻网-www.Jyb.cn 记录教育每一天 [Chen Anli, Director of the Hubei Province Education Department: 10 Years into the Ranks of Strong Education Province]," http://china.jyb.cn/gnxw/201101/t20110119_411219_1.html, accessed July 19, 2017.

[16] Ibid.

[17] Ibid.

level are often responsible for implementing much of education policy, the Hubei provincial government revoked the authority of the township to manage education in 2002, suggesting a shift toward the recentralization of education.[18]

Although mixed provinces are neither the poorest nor the most unequal in China, their citizens can be highly sensitive to inequality. As a result, the threat of unrest due to poverty incentivizes provincial and local leaders to pay close attention to poverty alleviation strategies despite objective realities. Mixed provinces receive transfers from the central government for poverty alleviation and take a top-down approach to these policies due to their population's sensitivity to inequality.

Indeed, central government policies toward inland provinces tend to be progressive. That is, inland provinces tend to receive more subsidies for social policy than the coast (with the exception of education, where key universities in the coastal provinces receive significant amounts of funding). For health and poverty alleviation, the central government tends to redistribute funds toward the inland provinces, seeking to mitigate the regional inequality that arose from coastal provinces' head start in economic development due to early access to foreign markets and capital. To compensate for these differences, the central government redistributes some subsidies to inland regions and to localities specifically designated as impoverished. The latter happens through the official "poverty counties" and, subsequently, "poverty villages" policy. Through the poverty county and "point-to-point" policies, significant benefits accrue to localities that have been officially designated as eligible.

The application process to be a poverty county is not transparent, however. Some Chinese academics have sought to reverse engineer the formula used to determine poverty counties, but the government has not released this algorithm to the public. We can speculate that the central government does not publicize the algorithm for poverty county eligibility because of reasonable suspicions that local officials might try to game the system through faulty statistical reporting if they knew how.[19] In localities with few prospects for economic growth, as in paternalist provinces and some areas of mixed provinces, officials may perceive poverty county status as a boon, despite some possible stigmatization. "Wearing a poor

18 Huarong 华蓉 Liu 刘, "乡镇教育组撤销后不留管理"真空' [Township Education Group Does Not Stay in Management 'Vacuum' after Revocation]," 中国教育报 [*China Education Daily*], July 3, 2002.

19 Jeremy L. Wallace, "Juking the Stats? Authoritarian Information Problems in China," *British Journal of Political Science* 46, no. 1 (January 2016): 11–29, https://doi.org/10.1017/S0007123414000106.

hat" has emerged as an idiom for local officials who play up poverty in their jurisdiction to gain access to preferential funding and policies such as the poverty county program. The phrase is reminiscent of "wearing a red hat" from the Maoist period, which signified feigning ideological enthusiasm for the Communist Party to get along and ahead in a system without other channels for advancement. Some local officials in mixed provinces "wear a poor hat," despite these provinces exhibiting middle levels of economic development. I provide examples of corruption related to the poverty county policy in the previous chapter on paternalist provinces.

As in health funding, the Hubei Civil Affairs and Finance Departments published relatively detailed guidelines about the implementation of poverty alleviation policies. As of 2006, the province enacted new standards for poverty relief payments of "63 yuan per person per month in cities, 59 yuan per person per month in towns [*chengzhen* 城镇], 55 yuan per person per month in rural areas."[20] These guidelines reflect some of the disparities in the cost of living between the city and the countryside, but they may not capture the contours of intraprovincial inequality.

Despite objective local economic realities, villagers in Hubei tend to be more sensitive to inequality than their counterparts in Jiangsu or Yunnan, although the latter two provinces have higher rates of inequality (see Figure 6.4). Moreover, although villagers in Yunnan are objectively much poorer, they are less concerned about inequality than their counterparts in Hubei (see Figure 6.5). Nonetheless, the perception that these provinces suffer from poverty and inequality puts additional pressure on local officials to seek support from the central government.

Local leaders in Hubei need to be more attentive to issues of poverty and inequality than their counterparts in Jiangsu. Conventional wisdom might suggest that these officials are merely responding to local needs and that, in fact, higher rates of poverty persist in Hubei than in Jiangsu. However, findings from my survey suggest that Hubei residents tend to be more sensitive to inequality than their counterparts in Jiangsu and Yunnan. Hubei does indeed have more poverty than Jiangsu but not as much as Yunnan. In terms of inequality, Hubei was actually faring the best of the three provinces as of 2012 (see Figure 6.4).

Despite a lower rate of inequality as compared to other provinces, villagers surveyed in Hubei were the most likely to identify inequality as a very serious problem, with almost half of surveyed villagers saying so. Villagers were asked to identify the severity of several problems both locally and

[20] 湖北省民政厅、湖北省财政厅关于提高社会救济对象生活补助标准的通知 [Notice of the Hubei Provincial Department of Civil Affairs and the Hubei Provincial Department of Finance on Raising the Standard of Living Subsidy for Beneficiaries of Social Assistance], CLI.12.456417,

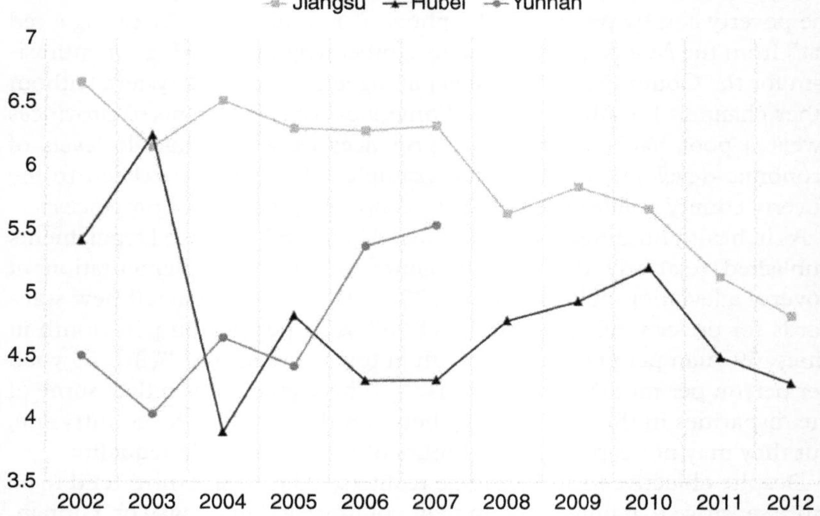


Figure 6.4 Inequality in Jiangsu, Hubei, and Yunnan.
Source: The 20:20 ratio has been calculated from provincial statistical yearbooks. See Appendix A for details.

nationally. Respondents used a "feelings thermometer" to rate the problem on a scale of 0 to 10, with 0 signifying "not a problem at all" and 10 indicating "a very serious problem." For ease of interpretation, Figure 6.5 groups a response of 7 or above as "very serious," 4–6 as "somewhat serious," and 0–3 as "not serious." Regarding local inequality, the average rating for a respondent in Hubei was 6.4, which was similar to responses in Yunnan (6.3) and higher than in Jiangsu (5.4).[21] Yet when villagers in Hubei were asked about whether inequality was a problem nationally, they were the most likely to say that it was a severe problem. The average rating of the severity of national inequality was 7.3 among villagers in Hubei, whereas it was 6.1 in Jiangsu and 6.2 in Yunnan.[22] The responses to national inequality suggest that villagers in Hubei have a heightened sensitivity to inequality compared to their counterparts elsewhere.

[21] The difference in means between Hubei and Jiangsu or Yunnan and Jiangsu is statistically significant at the 0.001 level. But the difference in means between the Hubei and Yunnan samples is not statistically significant.

[22] The difference in means between Hubei and Jiangsu or Hubei and Yunnan is statistically significant at the 0.001 level. But the difference in means between the Jiangsu and Yunnan samples is not statistically significant.

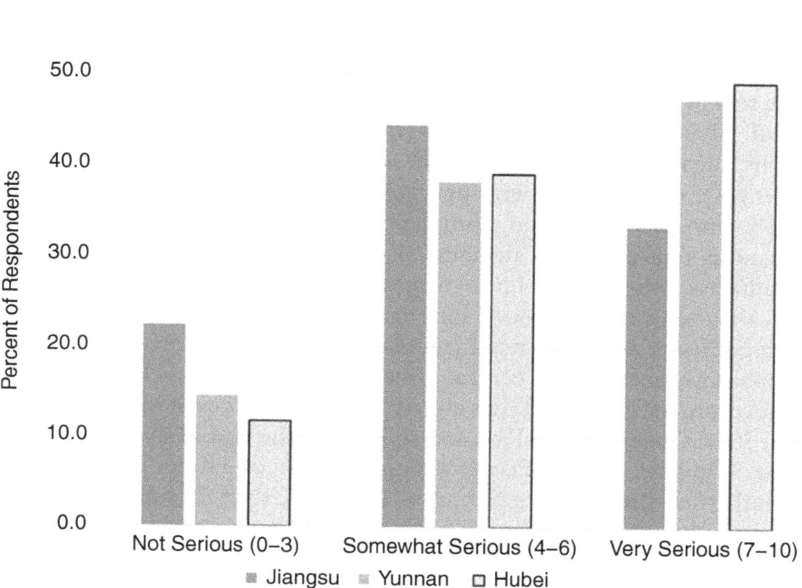


Figure 6.5 Perceptions of local inequality.
Source: Author's survey of villagers.

Because local officials are concerned with maintaining social and political stability, societal perceptions of local problems – regardless of objective reality – impact local leaders' priorities. As a result, Hubei and other mixed provinces may take stronger interventions with anti-poverty policies than we might expect given their levels of poverty and inequality.

Housing is the one area where mixed provinces tend to be somewhat more generous than their pragmatist and paternalist counterparts. In general, this group allocates relatively little funding to social policy. However, in the context of affordable housing, mixed provinces spend somewhat more per capita than pragmatist provinces, despite having smaller budgets. That said, they do not allocate as much to housing, proportionally or in total, as paternalist provinces. Notably, however, central and western provinces are targeted by the central government for housing subsidies, while coastal provinces are not.[23] Still, despite

[23] MOHURD (Ministry of Housing and Urban-Rural Development of the PRC), "中央预算内投资支持中西部新建廉租房建设 [Investment from the Central Government Budget to Support the Construction of New, Low-Rent Housing in the Central and Western

some efforts in affordable housing, mixed provinces face similar challenges in housing policy as their counterparts elsewhere.

Hubei illustrates the myriad approaches to housing represented within the group of mixed provinces. On the one hand, the province has taken an active role in promoting housing policies that are closely aligned with the central government, sometimes even issuing their regulations a few months ahead of the center. On the other hand, municipalities within Hubei have diverged in their approaches to housing, some claiming to comply with provincial and central policy while others issue their own regulations that are more stringent or specific than higher-level policy. Nonetheless, when lower levels of government issue their own regulations, they tend to focus on a state-led approach to housing provision, which contrasts with provincial guidelines in pragmatist provinces.

Apparently anticipating central policy, for example, the Hubei provincial government mandated that all city, district, and county governments create local Cheap Rental Housing (CRH) by the end of 2007, as stated in the "Opinion of the People's Government of Hubei Province on Strengthening the Housing Security Work of Urban Residents."[24] Not only does this opinion strongly reflect central government preferences, its language makes several references to "social equality" (*shehui gongping* 社会公平), "social stability" (*shehui wending* 社会稳定), and "guiding ideology" (*zhidao sixiang* 指导思想). The opinion also provides some province-wide guidelines for implementing housing policy and emphasizes the importance of housing as part of the "social security" system. In principle, these features might be more indicative of a paternalist province, as the opinion suggests a strong adherence to central policy and a top-down approach to implementing new policies. On the other hand, the opinion exhibits elements of a pragmatist approach to policymaking, as there are several references to economic development and supporting the real estate market. Moreover, after the provincial policy, several localities published their own guidelines for affordable housing, suggesting some role for lower levels of government to take initiative.

Indeed, local officials in mixed provinces sometimes take the initiative to go beyond provincial guidelines. For example, some municipalities in Hubei issued more detailed housing regulations and, occasionally, claimed to offer more generous housing benefits than mandated by the province. For example, the city government of Huanggang (黄冈市)

Regions]," January 3, 2008, www.mohurd.gov.cn/zxydt/200811/t20081125_181395.html.

24 Hubei Provincial People's Government, "湖北省人民政府关于加强城镇居民住房保障工作的意见 [Opinions of the People's Government of Hubei Province on Strengthening Housing Security for Urban Residents]," Pub. L., no. 42 (Hubei: 2007).

established a lower eligibility threshold for CRH than the previously published Hubei and State Council regulations.[25] In the Hubei "opinion," households living in dwellings smaller than 8 square meters per person were eligible for CRH, and that threshold was set to increase to 10 square meters per person by 2010. Meanwhile, a Huanggang "notice" enabled households living in dwellings smaller than 12 square meters per person to apply for CRH in 2008. Similarly, Jingmen (荆门市) began with an 8-square-meter eligibility requirement in 2008 but set a goal for 12 square meters by the end of 2012.[26] Yichang (宜昌市) also set more generous targets than the province, with CRH provided to those living in fewer than 10 square meters per person by the end of 2008 and 12 square meters by the end of 2010.[27]

However, when municipalities in Hubei issued their own guidelines, they typically still advocated a state-led approach rather than encouraging the involvement of nonstate actors in the way that Jiangsu did. An "opinion" issued by the city of Huangshi, for example, emphasized the role of the state in strengthening its monitoring of affordable housing. It did not encourage nonstate actors.[28] Although Huangshi's approach to affordable housing may have expanded the program, the city also reinforced structural inequities in housing policy in two ways. First, the Huangshi opinion restricted some affordable housing to those with a local urban *hukou*, thereby excluding migrant workers from this benefit. Second, the city encouraged the local government to rent apartments to civil servants at cost, even though civil servants are not among the lowest income residents.[29]

Despite some efforts from the province and local government, mixed provinces face similar problems with implementing housing policy as do other regions. In Hubei and elsewhere, many housing

[25] Hubei Provincial People's Government, State Council of the PRC, "国务院关于解决城市低收入家庭住房困难的若干意见 [Several Opinions of the State Council on Solving the Housing Difficulties of Urban Low-Income Families]," Pub. L., no. SC 24 (2007), www.gov.cn/zwgk/2007-08/13/content_714481.htm.

[26] Jingmen Municipal People's Government, "荆门市人民政府办公室关于印发《解决中心城区低收入家庭住房困难发展规划和年度计划》的通知 [Notice of the Jingmen Municipal People's Government Office on Disseminating the "Development Plan and Annual Plan to Solve Housing Difficulties of Low-income Families in the City Center"]," Pub. L., no. 28 (Jingmen: 2008).

[27] Yichang Muncipal Government, "宜昌市人民政府关于加强城镇居民住房保障工作的实施意见 [Implementation Opinions of the People's Government of Yichang City on Strengthening Housing Security for Urban Residents]," Pub. L., no. 017 (Yichang: 2008).

[28] "黄石市人民政府关于加强城镇居民住房保障工作的意见 [Opinions of the People's Government of Huangshi City on Strengthening Housing Security for Urban Residents]," Pub. L., no. 38 (Huangshi: 2007).

[29] Ibid.

units have been left vacant for myriad reasons, with vacancy rates ranging from 20 to 50 percent.[30] For example, the vacancy rate in Wuhan for affordable housing is about 20 percent higher than it is for commercial housing.[31] In some cases, units fail to pass safety inspections due to shoddy construction.[32] In others, affordable housing is left vacant because of its undesirable location, often far from where residents would work in the city center.[33] For example, in Chengyang District (城阳区) in Qingdao, Shandong, city residents complained in 2013 that living in the new affordable housing area, Baishawan (白沙湾片区), would entail a two-hour one-way commute to the city. In addition, the new area lacked "major hospitals, key schools, and large supermarkets."[34] Moreover, the process for selling or renting these units has been marred with corruption. Often, through bribery or connections, the affluent manage to purchase or rent units that are intended for the poor, sometimes using them as investment properties and leaving them vacant.[35] Thus, despite somewhat more provincial and local attention to housing than one sees in pragmatist provinces, Hubei has not necessarily achieved effective provision of affordable housing.

While Chinese provinces take very different approaches to implementing affordable housing policy, they clearly tend to face similar challenges. Whether the provincial government has sought to involve nonstate actors – such as private enterprise in pragmatist Jiangsu – or taken a more top-down approach as in Hubei and Yunnan, affordable housing continues to be a major social policy challenge. Across the country, affordable housing units are often sold to the affluent despite being intended for the poor. Moreover, shoddy construction and isolated locations often mean that housing projects are undesirable for their target market. Thus, current approaches to housing, despite policy style differences across provinces, have not achieved the goal of alleviating the burden of urban housing.

30 "重构住房保障_经济全局_□财经□杂志_杂志频道首页_财经网 [Rebuilding Housing Security]," caijing.com.cn, August 25, 2013, http://magazine.caijing.com.cn/20130825/2677099.shtml.

31 Ibid.

32 Ibid.

33 Ibid.; Rui Tan, "中国保障性住房体系的演进、特点与方向 [The Evolution, Characteristics and Orientation of China's Affordable Housing System]," *Journal of Shenzhen University (Humanities & Social Sciences)* 34, no. 2 (2017): 101–108.

34 "重构住房保障_经济全局_□财经□杂志_杂志频道首页_财经网 [Rebuilding Housing Security]."

35 Ibid.

## Conclusions

Mixed provinces exhibit both pragmatist and paternalist tendencies. Mixed provinces often take a top-down approach to policymaking, like paternalist provinces. Their focus on standardization appears in health policy, in particular, but is also apparent in education and poverty alleviation. Mixed provinces are particularly concerned with inequality and allocate more resources to housing than their counterparts elsewhere, even though these provinces are not among the poorest or most unequal in China. In housing, the province often takes the lead determining individuals' eligibility for subsidized housing and what these subsidies entail, but local government may offer benefits that exceed provincial mandates in their generosity. In this way, local officials may occasionally innovate like they do in pragmatist provinces, but there is still relatively little room for nonstate actors to participate in social policy provision. Yet, despite their frugality in social policy, mixed provinces have achieved relatively strong outcomes in social policy provision. With higher levels of population health and literacy, mixed provinces are well-situated to grow their economies and provide a social safety net for their citizens – if they can avoid the perils of paternalism.

# 7 Center–Local Relations, Pandemic Politics, and Local Policy Styles in Comparative Perspective

This book shows that Chinese provinces govern differently, taking divergent approaches to policy implementation. Through quantitative and qualitative research, I have identified two tendencies in provincial approaches to governance: pragmatism and paternalism. As shown in my provincial case studies in the preceding chapters, a province's dominant policy style can have implications for which social policies are prioritized and how they are implemented, even when taking into account the wealth and needs of the local population.

The gradualist, piecemeal economic reform process in China of the 1980s and 1990s created the conditions for local policy styles to have emerged in full force by the Hu Jintao years (2002–12). When the center selected coastal localities as special economic zones, those provinces prospered and established greater autonomy vis-à-vis the central government. Meanwhile, the central government tasked all provinces with funding and implementing social policy amid hard budget constraints. As a result, distinct forms of governing emerged among provinces with different economies, demographics, and relationships to the central government. Seeking to reduce the inequality that this process engendered, the central government increased targeted, earmarked fiscal transfers to poor provinces, but this approach tied the hands of local leaders and reinforced a top-down style of governing that I refer to as *paternalist*. By contrast, coastal provinces had to rely on locally generated revenue to fund social policy. Luckily for the coast, their coffers were relatively full and their exposure to foreign investors had encouraged the development of relatively functional institutions. Thus, coastal provinces developed a *pragmatic* policy style that fostered innovation and professionalism in policymaking. As they were mainly self-funding social policy, pragmatic provinces were more likely to shape central policies according to their local interests, sometimes even subverting the center's goals.

Divergent provincial policy styles have had a direct impact on the shape of social policy implementation in China, particularly during the Hu Jintao government. First, disparate provinces have prioritized different aspects of social policy through budget allocations. In Chapter 3, I examine provincial variation in social policy spending. Even when controlling for provincial wealth and social policy needs, provinces with a more pragmatic policy style are more likely to emphasize education and health spending, which are universal policies that support economic growth. Provinces with a relatively paternalist policy style are more likely to emphasize poverty alleviation and housing, which are targeted policies that are often used to mitigate social instability in China. While these trends are revealing, spending data nevertheless lacks granularity and falls short of elucidating differences in policy implementation.

In addition to differences in budget allocations, provinces diverge in how they implement what are ostensibly the same policies. Pragmatist provinces are more likely to involve local officials, private enterprise, and NGOs in designing the specifics of social policy at the implementation stage. As a result, these provinces often exhibit substantial intraprovincial inequality in terms of social policy provision, particularly in the early stages of a new policy, as they generally act with relatively greater autonomy from the central government and sometimes forgo central directives in favor of their local interests. For example, coastal provinces dragged their feet on affordable housing policy, despite a great need for these programs in their regions, and rural health insurance benefits varied significantly across provinces like Jiangsu in the early years of the policy. By contrast, paternalist provinces such as Hunan standardized these programs from their inception. Indeed, because paternalist provinces often rely on earmarked fiscal transfers from the central government, they are more constrained in their policy choices. Provincial authorities in Yunnan, for example, may micromanage programs such as point-to-point poverty alleviation. Paternalist provinces are more likely to take a top-down approach to implementation and closely follow central guidelines, with little innovation or participation from nonstate actors.

By unpacking the different approaches to social policy among China's provinces, this analysis resolves apparent contradictions in previous research. Scholars have characterized Chinese authoritarianism in a variety of ways, including fragmented, experimentalist, consultative, and populist.[1] These seemingly distinct interpretations are reconcilable by taking regional variation into account. By considering China as an authoritarian regime with multiple governing styles that manifest themselves at the local level, this book offers a new lens through which to view

[1] Heilmann and Perry, *Mao's Invisible Hand*; Lieberthal, "Introduction"; Wenfang Tang, *Populist Authoritarianism: Chinese Political Culture and Regime Sustainability* (New York: Oxford University Press, 2016); Teets, *Civil Society under Authoritarianism*; Mertha, "Fragmented Authoritarianism 2.0."

Chinese politics. China is indeed fragmented, as Kenneth Lieberthal and others contend.[2] The institutional fragmentation that they have identified has fostered divergence in how local actors approach the policy process. Provinces have developed distinct policy styles, and this divergence is not random. In this book, I have identified regional variations and how these distinct approaches impact policy implementation.

Examining how subnational policy styles function furthers our understanding of Chinese state legitimacy by unpacking the regional differences in center–local relations. Scholars have examined center–local relations in China, but they have not sought to explain and describe the nature of regional differences. Yumin Sheng, for example, has shown how the central government strategically places regime loyalists in coastal provinces. Perhaps because of their long time horizons and ambitions to move to central-level posts, these loyalists comply with central policy to send local revenue from wealthy coastal regions to the central government.[3] Meanwhile, the central government redistributes some of this revenue in the form of subsidies to central and western provinces to reduce poverty and quell unrest. Sheng focuses on compliance with tax policy, but his argument implies that coastal provinces may be more predisposed to comply with central policy in general due to the loyalist disposition of their leaders.

Building on Sheng's insightful observations, I find that coastal provinces are more likely to *deviate* from central directives in social policy or to find innovative ways to implement – or shirk – policies mandated by Beijing despite compliance with tax policy. We might speculate that coastal loyalists feel empowered to exercise their autonomy because they are aware that the center needs the revenue that they provide. In addition, it is likely that provincial officials with personal connections in the central government feel that they have greater familiarity with the center's "true" priorities, and therefore they are more willing to take risks with policy areas that they perceive as less politically sensitive.[4] This dynamic suggests yet another way that the center maintains loyalty on the coast. In policy areas that are not deemed politically sensitive, the center tolerates greater local autonomy in policy implementation in pragmatist provinces. By contrast, constrained by earmarked fiscal transfers and monitoring from Beijing, officials in central and western provinces tend to stick more closely to the letter of the law. The result is less policy

[2] Lieberthal, "Introduction."

[3] Sheng, *Economic Openness and Territorial Politics in China.*

[4] Bulman and Jaros's analysis of concurrent appointments at the provincial level also suggests that regime loyalists may have greater autonomy to selectively implement policy. Bulman and Jaros, "Leninism and Local Interests."

innovation, greater pro forma compliance, and less intraprovincial variation. Since central and western provinces benefit from fiscal transfers for social policy, their officials must follow central policy more closely. Selectively tolerating regional autonomy provides another way that the central government can manage a large, complex, decentralized Leninist party-state.

Provincial autonomy vis-à-vis the central government has ebbed and flowed since the founding of the PRC. Linda Chelan Li's account of recentralization in the early economic reform period (1978–93) proves instructive for understanding current center–province relations in China. In her study of Guangdong in the early economic reform period, Li found that "implementation discretion required more calculation and strategic analysis on the part of provincial officials." She noted that provincial officials "first had to assess the suitability of central policies for local application, and subsequently undertake the course of action which would bring the most benefit and incur the least cost, in terms of 'penalties.'"[5] When the central government sought to recentralize in the early 1990s, Li observed that "provincial governments, once having tasted the benefits of enhanced power, were thus naturally all the more resentful of such threats to their authority."[6]

Reflecting this ebb and flow, the Hu Jintao government in the early 2000s was then characterized by an unusually – some may say excessively – high degree of decentralization. Some CCP elites felt that Hu's commitment to collective decision-making and tendency to tolerate local officials asserting their autonomy was weakening party discipline and creating opportunities for corruption. In the wake of this shift toward decentralization, observers may surmise that some degree of recentralization – reducing the amount of discretion afforded to local officials – was practically inevitable. Indeed, by the 2010s, scholars noted a trend toward recentralization in China that intensified under Xi Jinping and had myriad implications for policy implementation.

As the aphorism goes, "history doesn't repeat itself, but it often rhymes." Since taking office in 2013, Xi Jinping has initiated increased recentralization, initially with the consent of elites who were seeking a course correction after Hu. "Recentralization" encompasses various changes in how the party-state governs, including fiscal recentralization (some of which occurred even prior to Xi's ascendance to power), less discretion for policy implementation, increased use of coercion and repression, consolidation of power by the party, increased emphasis on

[5] Li, *Centre and Provinces*, 177. [6] Ibid., 291.

ideological correctness, and further developments in digital monitoring.[7] For example, at the 19th Party Congress in 2017, the central government directed that village governance would be adjusted so that the two positions of village head and village party secretary would be filled by the same individual. The impacts of recentralization for local official behavior have been palpable. Researchers have found that Xi's recentralization directives have affected local officials' behavior and reduced overall policy innovation, even in pragmatist localities such as Shenzhen and Zhejiang.[8]

This book offers insights into the range of possible reactions to recentralization, as initiatives to recentralize the policy process are likely to be received very differently depending on provincial policy style. Indeed, Lewis, Teets, and Hasmath find that some local officials have continued innovating, despite strong signals to follow central directives.[9] Extrapolating from my findings, efforts at recentralization are likely to be more smoothly implemented in paternalist provinces, as compared to a province such as Jiangsu where local officials have become accustomed to significant autonomy when it comes to tailoring policy to local conditions. Moreover, following Yumin Sheng's logic regarding the relative leverage of wealthy provinces vis-à-vis the center, pragmatist officials may resent tightened controls and perhaps find ways to resist recentralization.

On December 8, 2019, on the cusp of the high-traffic travel season to celebrate Lunar New Year, doctors reported a case of "unknown

[7] See, for example, Jean C. Oi et al., "Shifting Fiscal Control to Limit Cadre Power in China's Townships and Villages," *China Quarterly* 211 (September 2012): 649–675; Xueguang Zhou, "Organizational Response to COVID-19 Crisis: Reflections on the Chinese Bureaucracy and Its Resilience," *Management and Organization Review* 16, no. 3 (July 2020): 473–484, https://doi.org/10.1017/mor.2020.29; Xiang Gao, "State–Society Relations in China's State-Led Digitalization: Progress and Prospects," *China Review* 20, no. 3 (August 2020): 1–12; Diana Fu and Greg Distelhorst, "Grassroots Participation and Repression under Hu Jintao and Xi Jinping." *China Journal* 79 (January 1, 2018): 100–122, https://doi.org/10.1086/694299; Sheena Chestnut Greitens, "Surveillance, Security, and Liberal Democracy in the Post-COVID World." *International Organization* 74, no. S1 (December 2020): E169–190, https://doi.org/10.1017/S0020818320000417.

[8] Orion A. Lewis, Jessica C. Teets, and Reza Hasmath, "Exploring Political Personalities: The Micro-Foundation of Local Policy Innovation in China," *Governance* (January 2021), https://doi.org/10.1111/gove.12573; Jessica C. Teets, Reza Hasmath, and Orion A. Lewis, "The Incentive to Innovate? The Behavior of Local Policymakers in China," *Journal of Chinese Political Science* 22, no. 4 (December 2017): 505–517, https://doi.org/10.1007/s11366-017-9512-9.

[9] Lewis, Teets, and Hasmath, "Exploring Political Personalities"; Teets, Hasmath, and Lewis, "The Incentive to Innovate?" Lewis, Teets, and Hasmath find that some local officials continue to innovate despite pressures from the central government, and they identify several factors that help explain why some officials persist in innovating despite overall recentralization. They also explore the interaction between individual-level propensity to innovate and changing structural conditions.

pneumonia" in the city of Wuhan in Hubei Province.[10] Several doctors, including Dr. Li Wenliang who later died of the virus, sounded the alarm through social media channels about the possibility of a new SARS-like virus. However, not only were the warnings not heeded, but eight individuals – including some doctors – were chastised by local officials on national television. The first death from the novel coronavirus (SARS-CoV-2) was recorded on January 9, 2020. Local authorities resisted taking action until after human-to-human transmission was confirmed on January 20, 2020. The city of Wuhan was placed under lockdown three days later.

By the time the lockdown was ordered, more than six weeks had passed since doctors' initial warnings of the new virus, and the window of opportunity for containment had closed. However, once the severity of the new virus was abundantly apparent, China's central government initiated an aggressive campaign to mitigate the effects of the epidemic. This campaign was largely successful in maintaining low numbers of cases and deaths in China throughout 2020 and 2021.[11] Nonetheless, as of the time of this writing, the subsequent pandemic has led to almost 400 million cases of COVID-19 and over 5.6 million deaths worldwide.

Local officials in Wuhan have been judged harshly for their handling of the initial warnings of the novel coronavirus, but, unfortunately, their behavior and the tragic outcome in Wuhan should not have been surprising. First, as other scholars have established, local officials continued to follow the incentives established by the cadre evaluation system and upward accountability, which would include suppressing undesirable outcomes. Had local officials incorrectly sounded the alarm in the weeks leading up to Lunar New Year, disrupting holiday plans and economic activity, the consequences would have been severe. Thus, the decision to declare the virus to be dangerous and transmissible among humans was high-stakes. Second, Hubei and Wuhan were not likely to have a highly professionalized corps of local officials. Even during the heyday of decentralization in the early 2000s, local officials in Hubei expected to take orders from higher levels of government in many policy areas rather than developing their own professional expertise. Third, under Xi Jinping, there are indications that loyalty to the party has been

[10] In 2020, Lunar New Year occurred on January 25.

[11] Alex Jingwei He, Yuda Shi, and Hongdou Liu, "Crisis Governance, Chinese Style: Distinctive Features of China's Response to the Covid-19 Pandemic," *Policy Design and Practice* 3, no. 3 (July 30, 2020): 242–258, https://doi.org/10.1080/25741292.2020.1799911.

prized over expertise, thereby exacerbating a challenge that Hubei was likely already facing during the Hu Jintao years.[12] Fourth, Hubei had even tighter budgets for social policy and healthcare than its coastal counterparts and faced myriad challenges in its healthcare system. Hubei had already experienced excessive flu in 2019 immediately prior to COVID-19, and their healthcare system was strained. Despite the resources marshalled by the central government to respond to the epidemic in late January, the loss of life was likely larger due to the lack of preparation in the province's healthcare system overall and the tendency of local officials to focus on politics over expertise.

What if SARS-CoV-2 had first been discovered in a city with a more developed, well-resourced healthcare system? What if the virus had been discovered in a city where local officials were accustomed to a certain degree of autonomy? Or where they frequently used their professional judgment to make difficult decisions on the ground? Of course, we can never know whether these counterfactuals would have changed the outcome, either locally or globally. But perhaps if doctors had been reporting the new virus to local officials who were more professional and valued expertise, the party-state may have reacted more quickly and saved lives.

The response to the novel coronavirus highlighted structural features of the Chinese political system that are problematic for good governance. The hierarchical Leninist party-state disincentivizes local officials from reporting problems to higher levels of government, and ideological fealty is increasingly valued over expertise. Both features have been exacerbated under Xi Jinping's leadership due to the recentralization of political power and a renewed emphasis on ideological correctness, reminiscent of the Maoist era. Furthermore, these features are likely to be more pronounced among local officials in provinces that had taken a paternalist approach to governing even prior to Xi's tenure as paramount leader.

These subnational differences in governing point to new ways to examine social policy that could be applied beyond the context of China. In studies of social welfare in electoral democracies, political party is often used as a proxy for local preferences. That approach is not feasible in a single-party state. Instead, I use independent variables that capture economic strategy, political unrest, needs, and wealth. In this way, my analysis drills down past political party to look at the roots of local preferences and approaches to governing. Using a similar approach in an electoral democracy, scholars could examine the role of local

[12] Zhou, "Organizational Response to COVID-19 Crisis."

preferences without relying on the proxy of political parties. Rather, researchers might use data on civil society organizations, the ideological leanings of local media, religiosity, or the degree of decentralization within a province or state to examine regional differences. By demonstrating the extent of subnational variation in social welfare in China, my research suggests possibilities for exploring these questions elsewhere.

Cases in the United States suggest instances where a similar approach could be applied to better understand local variation in social policy provision. For example, Sarah Bruch and her coauthors find that the decentralization of social policy under the Personal Responsibility and Work Opportunity Reconciliation Act (PRWORA) led to greater variation in implementation across US states: "The weaker the federal role, the further apart are the states with respect to both the share of the needy they help and the level of assistance they provide."[13] Going further, Margaret Weir and Jessica Schirmer argue that the United States has developed "two worlds of welfare," which can be traced to regional differences in demographics and urban growth.[14] Similar to my argument regarding provincial policy styles in China, they demonstrate how different regions can develop divergent approaches to social policy, leading to less effective institutions for poverty alleviation in the American South and Mountain West. Beyond the study of social policy, path-breaking research by Princess Williams examines the implications of regional identities for American politics.[15]

The impact on policy implementation of centralized versus decentralized approaches to social policy are also illustrated by the US case. Byungkyu Kim and Richard Fording, for example, found that US states that devolved the implementation of Temporary Assistance for Needy Families (TANF) to local government had better results for TANF recipients finding employment and increasing their earnings. However, these states were also more likely to end an enrollee's TANF benefits as a punitive measure.[16] By contrast, Dallas Elgin and David Carter find that, within US states, decentralized and centralized approaches to child

[13] Sarah K. Bruch, Marcia K. Meyers, and Janet C. Gornick, "The Consequences of Decentralization: Inequality in Safety Net Provision in the Post-Welfare Reform Era," *Social Service Review* 92, no. 1 (March 2018): 23, https://doi.org/10.1086/696132.

[14] Margaret Weir and Jessica Schirmer, "America's Two Worlds of Welfare: Subnational Institutions and Social Assistance in Metropolitan America," *Perspectives on Politics* 16, no. 2 (June 2018): 380–399, https://doi.org/10.1017/S1537592717004248.

[15] Princess Williams, *The Politics of Place: How Southern Identity Shapes American Political Behavior* (Doctoral dissertation, University of Michigan: 2021).

[16] Byungkyu Kim and Richard C. Fording, "Second-Order Devolution and the Implementation of TANF in the US States," *State Politics & Policy Quarterly* 10, no. 4 (Winter 2010): 341–367.

welfare services are similarly effective.[17] And, of course, leaders in Beijing are not alone in the challenge of eliciting compliance from lower levels of government. In 2019, California Governor Gavin Newsom took legal action against California cities that resisted implementing affordable housing laws, costing one city millions of dollars in state grants. In response, the California cities began to comply with affordable housing.[18] By contrast, when the central government noticed foot-dragging on affordable housing during the Hu Jintao years, Beijing implemented stronger directives (in contrast to vague targets), signaling the importance of the policy, and provinces responded with improved compliance.

My research suggests that practitioners in public policy, economics, and development should take regional differences more seriously. An economist's predictions that the wealth of coastal China will inevitably spread to the poorer western regions could be stymied by local politics. NGOs and development agencies will encounter distinct ideas about local needs and priorities, social welfare, and even the role of government in different localities, thereby impacting the feasibility of new projects. For example, if an NGO were seeking to expand their work into affordable housing, a pragmatist province like Jiangsu might be more welcoming, as stated policy has explicitly provided a larger role for nonstate actors. Yet the organization would need to be mindful of the interests of local government, as local officials may depend on real estate for revenue. In other words, understanding regional variation is the key to effectively assessing useful strategies and likely outcomes for policy-related decision-making and philanthropic action.

If Chinese politics are as cyclical as some suggest, the role of local states in shaping social policy in China is likely to persist and eventually reemerge, despite recent trends toward recentralization.[19] This book furthers our understanding of how local politics can impact social welfare,

[17] Dallas J. Elgin and David P. Carter, "Administrative (de)Centralization, Performance Equity, and Outcome Achievement in Rural Contexts: An Empirical Study of US Child Welfare Systems," *Governance* 32, no. 1 (January 2019): 23–43, https://doi.org/10.1111/gove.12343.

[18] Liam Dillon, "After Huntington Beach Lawsuit, Newsom Warns Cities He'll Continue Housing Law Crackdown," *Los Angeles Times*, www.latimes.com/politics/la-pol-ca-gavin-newsom-housing-cities-summit-20190219-story.html, accessed March 10, 2020; Jeff Collins, "Southern California cities can soon object to giant increases in housing goals," *Orange County Register*, September 3, 2020, www.ocregister.com/2020/09/03/southern-california-cities-can-soon-object-to-giant-increases-in-housing-goals, accessed January 31, 2020.

[19] On Chinese politics' cyclical nature, see Susan L. Shirk, "China in Xi's 'New Era': The Return to Personalistic Rule," *Journal of Democracy* 29, no. 2 (April 2018): 22–36, https://doi.org/10.1353/jod.2018.0022.

even in an authoritarian regime. This research yields insights for both scholars and practitioners, particularly those working in developing countries. Not only do these findings suggest new avenues of research for scholars of social policy in developing countries by focusing on local welfare regimes, but they also offer a theoretical framework that can help us understand regional variation in greater depth across different political contexts.

# Appendix A: Construction of Policy Styles Index

## Export-Oriented Industrialization Index

I designed the index for economic development strategy to capture the degree to which provinces are engaging in export-oriented industrialization (EOI). To standardize across a wide variety of scales, I used the provinces' z-scores for each measure. All measures for this index were from 2010. The index includes each province's z-score for the following measures: the value of exports per gross regional product; the value of foreign direct investment per gross regional product; the number of patents filed per 10,000 people;[1] and the value of primary industry in the provincial economy per gross regional product. For all measures, a higher z-score represents a greater degree of EOI as the provincial economic development strategy. For all measures except primary industry, a higher value suggests greater emphasis on EOI. However, a greater reliance on primary industry suggests a lesser degree of EOI. Thus, for this measure, I reversed the z-score so that its direction would be consistent with the other measures: a higher z-score suggests greater emphasis on EOI. I then averaged the z-scores of these four measures to produce an index that captures the extent to which each province relies on EOI as an economic development strategy.

[1] Patents are included as an indication of innovation, which is likely to be associated with an outward-looking economic strategy. Previous research has examined the importance of patents and innovation for economic growth in China and beyond. See Raeyoon Kang, Taehyun Jung, and Keun Lee, "Intellectual Property Rights and Korean Economic Development: The Roles of Patents, Utility Models and Trademarks," *Area Development and Policy* 5, no. 2 (April 2020): 189–211, https://doi.org/10.1080/23792949.2019.1585889; Julie T. Miao, "Definition and Typologies of Local Innovation Systems: A Case Study of Optics Valley in Central China," *Area Development and Policy* 5, no. 2 (April 2020): 212–232, https://doi.org/10.1080/23792949.2019.1672572.

## Political Openness Index

I included seven different measures that capture different factors signaling political openness or, conversely, suggesting the potential for internal political or social unrest in the province that would tend to lead to a less open political climate. To standardize across a wide variety of scales, I used provinces' z-scores for each measure. All measures were from the 2010 *China Statistical Yearbook* unless otherwise noted. The index includes each province's z-score for the following measures: public security spending per capita; the number of newspapers per 10 million people; the number of nongovernmental organizations registered in the province per 10,000 people; the percentage of the population that identifies as an ethnic minority; anti-corruption; government innovation; and fiscal transparency.

The number of newspapers per 10 million people was calculated by compiling a list of newspapers in each province according to the 2010 *China Journalism Yearbook*. A research assistant and I examined each newspaper's website and counted those that were not explicitly mouthpieces of the party-state (excluding publications such as *China Daily* and *People's Daily*, which focus on reporting official policy).[2] This number is somewhat inflated in provinces with large numbers of ethnic minorities, as there are many newspapers in ethnic minority languages. Although newspapers in ethnic minority languages may seem independent of the party-state, it is safe to assume that information is tightly controlled in regions such as Tibet and Xinjiang, where high concentrations of ethnic minorities reside. Thus, I do not expect these newspapers to publish the same degree of investigative journalism, plurality of opinion, and debate as newspapers in majority-Han provinces.

Anti-corruption was measured as the total number of people involved in corruption cases per 100,000 people. This measure was reversed so that a higher z-score means fewer corruption cases in the province.

Government innovation is measured by using a national competition for innovative policies. Because of the small number of prizes, I used the number of prizes awarded each year from 2003 to 2012. I gave each province one point if it was a finalist in the competition and two points if it won an award for government innovation. I then divided this number per 10 million people in the province based on the 2010 population to obtain a score for provincial government innovation standardized by population. For example, during the time period under study, Beijing had six finalists and three winners for a total of nine points. Beijing had a population of over 19.6 million people in 2010. Dividing 9 points by 1.96 gave a score of 4.59

[2] Many thanks to Alice Yang for her assistance.

for government innovation. As with the other measures, I then calculated a z-score for each province. A higher government-innovation score and associated z-score suggests a more open political climate.

I also created an original measure of fiscal transparency. Fiscal transparency is broadly defined as how forthcoming a government is in reporting revenue and expenditures. China's provincial governments vary in the types of revenues and expenditures they report in their statistical yearbooks. Because these yearbooks have become increasingly standardized over time, I examined variation in reporting from the 2003 set of yearbooks. In the 2003 set, all provinces reported their total revenue and expenditure, so I did not take this into consideration. Almost all provinces reported revenue in three to five broad categories, such as major industries and personal income tax, but only some reported detailed sources. I gave each province one point per each detailed source of revenue reported. The detailed sources of revenue include: revenue collected for the central government versus the province; revenue by level of government; and sources of revenue (e.g., specific taxes such as VAT, real estate tax, stamp tax, slaughter tax).

For expenditures, all provinces reported the same broad categories of spending, but they varied in reporting on detailed categories. Each province received one point for reporting expenditures in each of the detailed categories, which include: expenditures by level of government; detailed breakdown of the Culture, Education, Science, and Health (文教科卫) category; detailed breakdown of the Agriculture, Rural Production, Forestry, and Water (农业, 农村生产, 农林水) category; detailed breakdown of the Industry and Trade (工交商) category; detailed breakdown of the Pension, Social Welfare, and Social Security (抚恤, 社会福利, 社会保障) category; policy price subsidies (政策性价格补助); policy price subsidies by broad categories (usually grain, cotton, oil, meat [粮棉油肉] and "other"); and breakdown of at least some of the broad categories of policy price subsidies. Some detail was provided for both revenue and expenditures for the following categories: general budgetary versus fund budgetary revenue and expenditures; extrabudgetary totals for revenue and expenditures; total revenue and expenditures for each city, county, or district; and breakdown of each city's revenue and expenditures into categories. I then added up the points for each province to calculate its fiscal transparency score and z-score. I propose that more transparent provinces will also be more politically open.

## Descriptive Statistics

Table A.1 provides descriptive statistics for the variables used in the analysis of provincial data in Chapter 3.

Table A.1 *Descriptive statistics*

| Variable | Observations | Mean | Standard Deviation | Minimum | Maximum |
|---|---|---|---|---|---|
| **Dependent Variables** | | | | | |
| Education spending* | 150 | 428.20 | 278.09 | 47.08 | |
| Education as a proportion of total spending | 150 | 16.60 | 2.65 | 10.26 | 1,501.22 |
| Health spending* | 150 | 167.29 | 103.97 | 16.35 | 22.22 |
| Health as a proportion of total spending | 150 | 6.61 | 1.72 | 3.90 | 505.14 |
| Social safety net spending* | 150 | 298.11 | 153.96 | 27.90 | 16.61 |
| Social safety net as a proportion of total spending | 150 | 12.44 | 3.36 | 5.77 | 727.71 |
| Minimum Livelihood Guarantee (MLG) spending* | 150 | 28.70 | 17.40 | 1.40 | 25.49 |
| MLG as a proportion of total spending | 150 | 1.25 | 0.69 | 0.24 | 82.00 |
| Housing spending* | 90 | 101.02 | 55.51 | 6.32 | 3.30 |
| Housing as a proportion of total spending | 90 | 3.79 | 1.92 | 0.45 | 248.58 |
| **Independent Variables** | | | | | 10.97 |
| Policy style | 150 | 0.52 | 1.03 | −0.68 | |
| Earmarked education transfers† | 141 | 1,549,066.00 | 2,350,200.00 | 39.00 | 2.70 |
| Key universities | 150 | 3.83 | 4.92 | 1.00 | 12,000,000.00 |
| Earmarked health transfers† | 150 | 33,316.53 | 26,075.59 | 842.00 | 26.00 |
| Earmarked social safety net transfers† | 144 | 312,752.40 | 230,156.60 | 12,926.00 | 123,067.00 |
| Earmarked MLG transfers† | 144 | 233,952.80 | 183,416.50 | 3,014.00 | 1,042,890.00 |

Table A.1 *(cont.)*

| Variable | Observations | Mean | Standard Deviation | Minimum | Maximum |
|---|---|---|---|---|---|
| Fiscal transfers[†] | 120 | 1,013.91 | 535.26 | 215.72 | 789,270.00 |
| Population[‡] | 150 | 4,308.51 | 2,711.43 | 287.00 | 2,664.51 |
| Log of Gross Regional Product* | 150 | 9.20 | 1.03 | 5.98 | 9,893.48 |
| Dependency ratio | 150 | 35.86 | 6.11 | 25.01 | 10.95 |
| Inequality ratio | 131 | 4.88 | 0.94 | 2.88 | 49.41 |
| Percent urban | 150 | 49.41 | 14.58 | 23.80 | 9.08 |
| | | | | | 88.60 |

Units: * RMB 100,000,000; † RMB 10,000; ‡ 10,000 people

*Sources:* Social policy spending data from *China Statistical Yearbook* (2013). Education transfer data from *China Educational Finance Statistical Yearbook* (2013). Other fiscal transfer data from *China Civil Affairs Statistical Yearbook* (2013). Data on key universities from China Education Online. Inequality measure calculated based on data from provincial yearbooks (2008–12). All others from *China Statistical Yearbook* (2008–12).

# Appendix B: Research Methods

***with Leah Rabin***

This book relies on both qualitative and quantitative evidence, including semi-structured interviews conducted with county-level officials, hospital personnel, and villagers, as well as an original survey of over 1,000 villagers and village officials. I also gathered information from statistical yearbooks, national and local laws and regulations, newspapers, provincial websites, and other government websites. By triangulating information collected from various sources, I examine the politics of healthcare despite the limitations on data collection in China.

I conducted semi-structured interviews in three provinces from 2009 to 2010 with the support of a Foreign Language and Area Studies Fellowship from the US Department of Education. Respondents for these interviews included local government officials (particularly county-level health officials), hospital personnel, and villagers in three provinces: Jiangsu, Hunan, and Gansu. I visited seven counties in Jiangsu and four counties each in Hunan and Gansu. Given the importance of economic conditions in social policy implementation, I purposefully chose three provinces that vary in their levels of economic development. I also selected counties within each province to reflect salient intra-provincial cleavages, including wealth and degree of urbanization. The provinces selected for fieldwork are depicted in Figure A.1. In addition, archival research was conducted between 2009 and 2012. I gathered information on healthcare reform and health policy implementation from local provincial libraries and the Universities Service Centre at the Chinese University of Hong Kong, as well as through national and regional statistical yearbooks, laws and regulations, provincial websites, and the media.

Finally, I conducted a survey of villagers and village officials in collaboration with Leah Rabin in 2012 in three provinces: Jiangsu, Hubei, and Yunnan (Figure A.1). The survey was funded by the National Science Foundation's Doctoral Dissertation Research Improvement Grant

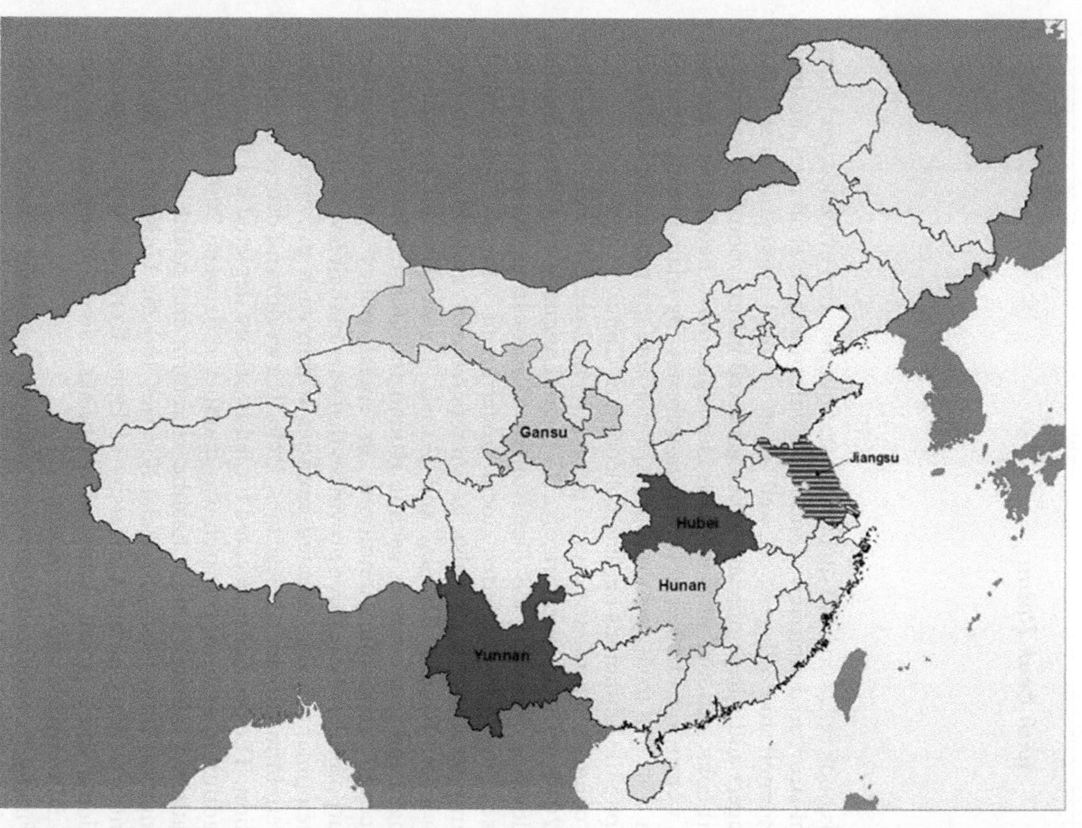


Figure A.1 Map of fieldwork provinces.

(awarded to the author) and by the Southwest China IGERT program at the University of Wisconsin–Madison (awarded to Rabin), as well as through additional support from the Summer Initiative Fund of the University of Wisconsin–Madison's Department of Political Science and the Vilas Research Travel Grant from the Graduate School at the University of Wisconsin–Madison.

This appendix is organized as follows: first, I discuss the impact of the political and social context on conducting research on healthcare reform in China; second, I detail the process of conducting semi-structured interviews; third, I describe the survey, including sampling, development of the survey instrument, enumerator training, and the resulting data.

## Mixed Methods in a Challenging Research Environment

Social science research in China remains challenging despite an increased openness to policy evaluation research and a wider dissemination of social scientific research methods in Chinese universities. Because China's political system is authoritarian and economic development is uneven, access to information is highly contingent on local politics, and the reliability of official statistics is dubious.[1] The logistical challenges of

[1] Official estimates placed the Gini coefficient at around 0.47 in 2012. See Kevin Yao and Aileen Wang, "China Lets Gini out of the Bottle; Wide Wealth Gap," Reuters, January 17, 2013, www.reuters.com/article/us-china-economy-income-gap-idINBRE90H06L20130118?edition-redirect=in. One of the difficulties in analyzing official statistics in China is that there are competing incentives for local leaders. On the one hand, some officials seek to demonstrate their success in promoting economic growth by inflating gross regional product figures. On the other hand, officials in impoverished areas may deflate economic indicators in order to elicit the coveted official "poverty designation" from the central government (see discussion in Chapter 5), which makes the locality eligible for additional subsidies from the central government. In terms of social indicators, local officials face severe repercussions if they are unsuccessful at implementing family planning policies or if there are significant incidents of social unrest in their locality. These incentives can lead to misreporting of crucial data by local officials. For a few examples, see Thomas Orlik, *Understanding China's Economic Indicators* (Upper Saddle River, NJ: FT Press, 2012); or Thomas Orlik, "China's Puzzling Numbers," *Wall Street Journal*, September 15, 2011, http://online.wsj.com/article/SB10001424053111904353504576565893924294066.html. See also William Wan, "China's economic data drew sharp scrutiny from experts analyzing global trends," *Washington Post*, February 4, 2013, www.washingtonpost.com/world/asia_pacific/chinas-economic-data-draw-sharp-scrutiny-from-experts-analyzing-global-trends/2013/02/04/f4de4b84-6ae0-11e2-af53-7b2b2a7510a8_story.html. Regarding discrepancies in official environmental statistics, see Brad Plumer, "China could be hiding an entire Japan's worth of carbon emissions," *Washington Post*, June 12, 2012, www.washingtonpost.com/blogs/wonkblog/post/china-could-be-hiding-an-entire-japans-worth-of-carbon-emissions/2012/06/12/gJQA3zuTXV_blog.html. Regarding village statistics, see Lily L. Tsai, "Understanding the Falsification of Village Income Statistics," *China Quarterly* 196 (December 2008): 805–826. On which data are more likely to be manipulated and

conducting research in a developing country can be significant, but they can be resolved with proper planning. The lack of political freedom, however, generates two major obstacles to research. First, interviewees are less likely to give honest and complete answers because of the potential for pressure and retribution from local officials. Among poorer populations, individuals are even more vulnerable, as they are dependent on the benevolence of local officials. Second, while all scholars – Chinese and foreign – are limited in what is permissible research, foreign scholars are subject to greater suspicion and even more limits, both de facto and de jure. Between 1999 and 2004, the Measures for the Administration of Foreign-Affiliated Surveys generated increasingly restrictive requirements to obtain survey permits.[2] Moreover, there are specific regulations that prohibit non-Chinese scholars from certain types of independent research within China. For example, survey research by foreign scholars without direct oversight by Chinese researchers is not officially authorized and may be considered "gathering sensitive information."[3] Even in those cases where research proposals have earned proper clearance, the lack of strong legal institutions results in ad hoc decision-making by local officials who may prohibit research that could be considered sensitive.

Perceptions of whether health policy is a politically sensitive topic are also germane to whether respondents will be willing to speak with researchers and what type of information they are willing to divulge. In general, health policy was not a politically sensitive topic in China at the time I was doing my research. Scholars, officials, the media, and the public at large could have relatively frank and open discussions about the need to invest more in health infrastructure or the ways in which current policy could be improved. For example, the central government posted the proposal for the 2009 health reform on an internet forum for public commentary. This method of soliciting public comment on policy proposals has been utilized in other policy arenas as well. In fact, as

when, see Jeremy L. Wallace, "Juking the Stats? Authoritarian Information Problems in China." *British Journal of Political Science* 46, no. 1 (January 2016): 11–29, https://doi.org/10.1017/S0007123414000106.

[2] National Bureau of Statistics, "涉外调查管理办法," National Bureau of Statistics of the People's Republic of China, www.stats.gov.cn/statsinfo/auto2072/201310/t20131031_450864.html, accessed July 29, 2017.

[3] Attention paid to "illegal surveys" generally pertains to geographic mapping of national resources with commercial or national security implications. See, for example, Qian Wang, "Tougher Penalties Mapped out to Fight Illegal Surveys," *China Daily*, October 23, 2012, http://europe.chinadaily.com.cn/china/2012-10/23/content_15837733.htm, accessed March 28, 2013. Nonetheless, in the context of a "rule by law" legal system, the Chinese government has been known to apply the law selectively and instrumentally. See Randall Peerenboom, *China's Long March toward Rule of Law* (Cambridge: Cambridge University Press, 2002).

evident in the sources cited throughout this book, Chinese scholars also conduct research on the effectiveness of health policy. Health policy design and implementation is generally not considered politically sensitive as long as one does not suggest that the party-state is implicated in existing problems or that regime change would be necessary for effective policy reform. Within these parameters, relatively open discussion of the healthcare system can occur and, thus, the details of policymaking can be accessible for research.

Although health policy is generally not considered a politically sensitive topic, conducting interviews with officials as a foreigner was nevertheless far more challenging than approaching villagers. When I had a direct introduction to an official, such as through that official's former university professor, we often engaged in relatively frank conversations about local affairs. However, when I arrived without an introduction or when the introduction was made through a more tenuous connection (a friend of a friend), officials would withhold ostensibly public information or would prevaricate in response to straightforward questions by saying "hard to say," "not sure," "[let's] talk about it later" (*bu hao shuo* 不好说/*hen nan shuo* 很难说, *bu qingchu* 不清楚, *yihou zai shuo* 以后再说) or giving similarly oblique responses. In a couple of cases, a county-level official assured me that he would send me requested information via email, which I correctly interpreted as yet another form of evasion. In all cases, I made notes of the conditions of the interview and the attitude of the interviewee, and I considered the implications regarding the likely veracity of the information obtained. Furthermore, local officials were more forthcoming with information in some regions than others. Local officials in less wealthy counties were more reticent in general.

Given the uneven quality of information collected from interviews and official documents, as well as the difficulty in obtaining information from less wealthy counties, I also conducted a survey of over 1,000 villagers and village leaders in three provinces to further examine the effect of local state–society relations on health policy implementation. The survey enabled me to test the generalizability of key hypotheses as well as create a controlled environment where the same questions were asked of everyone. The item nonresponse rate was very low for most questions (often less than 10 percent, even for politically sensitive questions), and I was able to gather information about health policy, villagers' expectations, and perceptions of government that would not have been possible through interviews. As the survey was conducted with help from a local university in each province, local officials were more consistently forthcoming with our enumerators than when I approached them independently as a foreign researcher. We also encouraged enumerators to provide as much supplementary, qualitative information as they could, including, for example, whether there were other individuals present (an issue that has emerged as a source of reliability problems in politically restrictive environments). Therefore, we were able to gather a more complete picture of respondents' views and any extenuating circumstances that may have affected responses.

The issue of protecting informants, respondents, and field assistants is of utmost importance for a social scientist. Being identified as foreign researcher can matter in the perceived risk calculation and can have additional bias effects, which will be discussed in the following section on semi-structured interviews. To protect those who participated in my research, I did not record our conversations; rather, my field assistant and I took copious notes on each conversation and the general demeanor of the interviewee. I present the list of interviews with officials in Table A.2, but I have withheld the names of individuals or counties to protect informants.

Table A.2 *Interviews with local officials and hospital personnel*

| Interview Code | County Code | Province | Date | Institution | Position |
|---|---|---|---|---|---|
| JSAW01 | A | Jiangsu | 11/30/09 | County Health Bureau | Bureau Head |
| JSAH02 | A | Jiangsu | 11/30/09 | County People's Hospital | Doctor |
| JSBW07 | B | Jiangsu | 12/01/09 | County Health Bureau | Bureau Head |
| JSBH08 | B | Jiangsu | 12/01/09 | County People's Hospital | Doctor |
| JSCW10 | C | Jiangsu | 12/02/09 | County Health Bureau | Bureau Head |
| JSCH11 | C | Jiangsu | 12/02/09 | Hospital | Administrator |
| HNDX14 | D | Hunan | 12/14/09 | NCMS Office | Administrator |
| HNDH15 | D | Hunan | 12/14/09 | People's Hospital 1 | Doctor |
| HNDH18 | D | Hunan | 12/14/09 | People's Hospital 2 | Doctor |
| HNEW19 | E | Hunan | 12/15/09 | County Health Bureau | Bureau Head |
| HNEV20 | E | Hunan | 12/15/09 | Village Committee | Village Leader |
| HNEV21 | E | Hunan | 12/15/09 | Village Committee | Village Head |
| HNEH22 | E | Hunan | 12/15/09 | County People's Hospital | Doctor |

Table A.2 *(cont.)*

| Interview Code | County Code | Province | Date | Institution | Position |
|---|---|---|---|---|---|
| HNFW23 | F | Hunan | 12/17/09 | County Health Bureau | Administrator |
| HNFH24 | F | Hunan | 12/17/09 | County People's Hospital | Hospital Director |
| HNGL29 | G | Hunan | 01/14/09 | Office of Letters and Visits | Administrator |
| HNGW30 | G | Hunan | 01/14/09 | County Health Bureau | Bureau Head |
| HNGH31 | G | Hunan | 01/14/09 | County People's Hospital | Doctor |
| JSHW34 | H | Jiangsu | 03/04/09 | County Health Bureau | Administrator |
| JSHH35 | H | Jiangsu | 03/04/09 | County People's Hospital | Doctor |
| JSHH37 | H | Jiangsu | 03/04/09 | Village Clinic | Administrator |
| JSIW39 | I | Jiangsu | 03/05/09 | County Health Bureau | Bureau Head |
| JSIH40 | I | Jiangsu | 03/05/09 | County People's Hospital | Doctor |
| JSIH42 | I | Jiangsu | 03/05/09 | Village Clinic | Administrator |
| JSJW44 | J | Jiangsu | 03/08/09 | County Health Bureau | Bureau Head |
| JSJW45 | J | Jiangsu | 03/08/09 | County Health Bureau | Administrator |
| JSJH46 | J | Jiangsu | 03/08/09 | County People's Hospital | Doctor |
| JSKW49a | K | Jiangsu | 03/09/09 | County Health Bureau | Deputy Head of Bureau |
| JSKW49b | K | Jiangsu | 03/09/09 | County Health Bureau | Administrator |
| JSKW49 c | K | Jiangsu | 03/09/09 | County Health Bureau | Administrator |
| JSKH50 | K | Jiangsu | 03/09/09 | County People's Hospital | Administrator |
| JSLW53 | L | Jiangsu | 03/10/09 | NCMS Office | Administrator |
| GSW54 | M | Gansu | 6/24/10 | County Health Bureau | Bureau Head |
| GSH55 | M | Gansu | 6/24/10 | Township Hospital | Managing Director |
| GSH56 | M | Gansu | 6/24/10 | Township Hospital | Hospital Director |
| GSW57 | N | Gansu | 6/24/10 | County Health Bureau | Bureau Head |
| GSW58 | O | Gansu | 6/29/10 | NCMS Office | Administrator |
| GSW59 | P | Gansu | 6/30/10 | NCMS Office | Administrator |

Because of the challenges of conducting social science research in an authoritarian, developing country, social scientists must rely on multiple sources of information and aim to triangulate to generate a more accurate and complete picture of political dynamics.[4] Incorporating semi-structured interviews and survey data in addition to official statistics and media reports has enabled me to examine the politics of health policy adoption and implementation. In the next two sections, I will detail the process of conducting field research.

## Qualitative Evidence

Having gathered archival data and official statistics, I utilized face-to-face, semi-structured interviews with local officials (policy implementers) and villagers. The main goal of these interviews was to make a qualitative assessment: how were the reforms functioning in practice, what challenges had arisen, what was the response, and what were the factors that affected implementation across different regions and different socioeconomic levels. The latter was particularly significant because previous research had shown that there is a major divergence between coastal and interior regions in China, largely resulting from variation in socioeconomic development. Because the information I was seeking was related to processes and people's experiences with health systems, the method for gathering the data necessitated a flexible and open-ended approach to interviews.[5]

In 2009 and 2010, I conducted thirty-eight semi-structured interviews with county-level officials and hospital personnel. I conducted conversations and focus groups with villagers in each county. I also had conversations with local scholars in each province and in Beijing regarding healthcare reform. These scholars have researched health policy, and some of them have served as government advisers for healthcare reform. The respondents chosen for interviews were mainly a convenience sample developed through introductions from local scholars. I conducted interviews in a total of fifteen counties in three provinces: seven counties in Jiangsu and four counties each in Gansu and Hunan. In Gansu, I gained permission from the provincial Health Bureau to approach local officials

[4] Allen Carlson et al., *Contemporary Chinese Politics: New Sources, Methods, and Field Strategies* (New York: Cambridge University Press, 2010).

[5] Herbert J. Rubin, *Qualitative Interviewing: The Art of Hearing Data* (Thousand Oaks, CA: Sage, 2012); Benjamin L. Read, "More Than an Interview, Less Than Sedaka: Studying Subtle and Hidden Politics with Site-Intensive Methods," in Contemporary Chinese Politics: New Sources, Methods, and Field Strategies, edited by Allen Carlson, Mary E. Gallagher, Kenneth G. Lieberthal, and Melanie Manion (New York: Cambridge University Press, 2010), 145–161.

in nearby counties. Official permission facilitated access in some cases, but it also may have influenced local officials' responses because they might have perceived official permission as a signal that what they shared would then be reported back to their superiors.

As my interview targets were local officials, formal introductions were crucial to gaining access to potential respondents. Therefore, I utilized contacts established through my colleagues at the University of Wisconsin–Madison and during research in China. I developed an interview protocol for county-level officials, hospital personnel, and villagers based on previous research. However, I also allowed the conversation to flow naturally, when appropriate, and gained important insights about local officials through informal interactions.

In Hunan Province, I chose localities to visit based on variation in socioeconomic conditions, and I was able to obtain informal introductions in some cases. In other cases, interviewees were essentially "cold-called"; that is, I visited local officials without a formal or informal introduction. In these cases, a research assistant and I would approach local officials, explain our purpose as academic researchers, and obtain whatever information officials were willing to proffer. However, without a formal introduction – whether I had an informal introduction or no introduction – the quantity and quality of information gathered was inconsistent. In general, local officials were more forthcoming if I had an introduction from a close friend or former professor. These interviews were, in general, the most successful and informative.

Respondents' willingness to be forthcoming varied substantially. In some localities, officials would say that information related to health policy implementation was "[politically] sensitive" (*min'gan* 敏感) or "classified" (*baomi* 保密), whereas officials in other areas would say "this is not sensitive" or "this is public" (*gongkai* 公开) information. Officials were undoubtedly more reticent with a foreign researcher because of the potential to be perceived as revealing "state secrets" (which has an ambiguous and constantly shifting definition and scope) to a foreigner. Nonetheless, officials' reactions as respondents provided interesting insight into local political climate variation and into whether local officials felt empowered to take initiative and discuss policy with a foreigner. As previously stated, health policy is not generally considered particularly sensitive relative to other political topics.

In selecting local officials to interview, I sought respondents in county-level Health Bureaus and New Cooperative Medical System (NCMS) offices; in some areas, I also sought out other local officials, such as the village representative of the All-China Women's Federation (often tasked with implementing village-level family planning policy). The county

NCMS office is responsible for implementing the NCMS health insurance program. Although the NCMS is ostensibly an insurance program, there is institutional overlap between the NCMS and local providers. Therefore, NCMS officials also tend to have knowledge of health policy implementation more broadly. Which official was interviewed often depended on officials' availability and, sometimes, the strength of my connection to the target official through an introduction. In some counties, I spoke to several officials together, which was useful because they were able to corroborate information or assist each other in recalling specific details. Most officials were also able to corroborate their accounts with official party documents or reports, of which they could provide me copies.

Interviewing villagers was easier in most cases. Villagers were generally more forthcoming – willing to tell me about their lives and tribulations – and seemed less wary of my identity as a foreigner. In the majority of cases, local officials were not present when I interviewed villagers. Thus, villagers could speak relatively freely. In a few villages, local officials insisted on accompanying me to interview villagers or organized an impromptu focus group with villagers of their selection. In these cases, villagers' comments were clearly influenced by the presence of local officials. For example, when I asked a question, villagers in these groups would look at the official for an answer, or they would respond but look to the official for confirmation that their answer was "correct." In these cases, I interpreted the information with extreme care and generally excluded responses that seemed to have been heavily influenced by the presence of local officials.

I chose which villages to visit randomly, with some consideration for local connections when available (e.g., if my research assistant had relatives in a local village) and accessibility (e.g., some locations would have been dangerous to visit due to poor infrastructure), except in the few cases in which officials insisted that I visit a specific village. In general, I did not notice anything particularly unusual about the villages that I visited; I was not taken to conspicuously "model" villages except, perhaps, in one case where I was taken to an urban district that was a special economic zone with a recently constructed hospital and medical facility. This instance was instructive, however, since the Chinese government has made a concerted effort to invest more in health infrastructure, particularly at the local level. Thus, while investment in new clinics and hospitals may not occur in a majority of villages, it does occur in the context of the recent increase in healthcare investment.

In addition to interviewing local officials, I also spoke to available hospital personnel in the counties that I visited. In most cases, I was able to speak to doctors, nurses, and low-level administrators. In some cases, I was able to speak to the hospital director. Most hospital personnel were able to corroborate or provide greater nuance to the experiences that villagers had shared.

Over the course of qualitative work, I gained a plethora of fascinating information about health policy implementation at the local level, as well as information about villagers' perceptions of government. I also achieved "saturation"[6] on many different issues, although interview experiences varied across provinces. For example, in poorer provinces, villagers consistently complained of inadequate health infrastructure. Moreover, they often stated that the new rural health insurance policy constituted an improvement over the previous out-of-pocket payment system. However, many people complained that the medicines and treatments that they had been prescribed either were not covered by the new insurance policy or were not available in local pharmacies or local medical clinics. These were the most common complaints regarding rural health insurance. However, these problems were not as salient in Jiangsu, the wealthiest province included in my fieldwork.

Villagers in most localities also indicated that recent policies, such as the new rural health insurance program, demonstrated that the central government cared about improving health policy, but that either local governments were not implementing the policies correctly or adequately or else local corruption was interfering with proper implementation. This resilient trust in the central government in combination with criticism of local government is consistent with previous research on trust in government in China.[7]

In conducting this type of research, interviewer effects are inevitable. Certainly, the information that I gathered as a white, female American differed from what a researcher of another race, gender, or nationality might have found. It is not clear, however, that the bias introduced by researcher effects in China is consistent across respondents. While some respondents were clearly reticent in the presence of a foreigner for fear that they might be divulging "classified information," other respondents seemed to be more open with me given that I do not have formal ties to the Chinese government or Communist Party. More often than not, conversations with villagers transpired fluidly without noticeable reference to or

[6] In social science research, "saturation" refers to when you hear similar accounts from various interviewees to the extent that the researcher is confident that these accounts represent a common or typical experience for many people.

[7] Lianjiang Li, "Political Trust in Rural China," *Modern China* 30, no. 2 (2004): 228–258; Tianjian Shi, "Cultural Values and Political Trust: A Comparison of the People's Republic of China and Taiwan," *Comparative Politics* 33, no. 4 (July 2001): 401–419.

interest in the fact that I am a foreigner. These observations are not made to assert that my identity and its implicit effect on responses should be discounted, but rather to suggest that my easily identifiable status as a foreigner had varying effects. Some interviewees even seemed more willing to talk to me and my research assistants because we were outsiders not from the village or region.[8] In cases where villagers have had conflicts with local officials, they may be more willing to talk to people whom they do not perceive to be part of the local power structure. Had I been a known confidante of local officials, some villagers may have been more reticent to discuss their problems with health policy implementation or daily life in general. In all cases, I made note of the respondent's demeanor, and I take this into consideration in my analysis.

#### *Conversations with Villagers*

In each county, I visited at least one village in which I spoke to villagers individually and in small groups. I used a semi-structured interview format while allowing for greater flexibility depending on the situation.[9] The conversations with villagers were generally more informal, but they enabled me to better understand interactions with the healthcare system from villagers' perspectives.

#### *Conversations with Scholars*

I had numerous conversations, formal and informal, with scholars from Chinese universities whose research examines health policy. Some of these scholars have advised the government on healthcare reform. While rarely quoted directly in this book, their views have informed both my fieldwork and my analysis.

### Survey Data

In addition to semi-structured interviews and other qualitative research, I conducted a survey of over 1,000 villagers and village leaders in Jiangsu, Hubei, and Yunnan provinces in collaboration with Leah Rabin (PhD, University of Wisconsin–Madison). By utilizing archival and qualitative research from our separate dissertation projects, we were able to design and implement the survey to maximize internal and external validity

[8] I often enlisted a local graduate student to accompany me to conduct interviews. She (almost all of my field assistants were women) would take notes and translate local dialect into standard Mandarin when necessary.

[9] Rubin, *Qualitative Interviewing*.

under challenging research conditions. By subsequently employing survey data to complement my archival and qualitative research, I was able to assess the relationship between state–society dynamics and health policy implementation. I analyzed survey data to test the generalizability of hypotheses generated in earlier stages of my research and was also able to gather information from village officials that had been elusive during my semi-structured interviews. Rabin and I were also able to collect useful demographic and village-level information that is not publicly available: when enumerators interviewed village leaders, they inquired about village-level characteristics such as population and village health facilities.

### *Sample of Localities*

For the results of a sample survey to be generalizable to a broader population, the sample must be representative of the target population. In this project, I sought to understand expectations and perceptions of healthcare provision in rural China. While limited resources precluded a nationally representative sample, Rabin and I were able to sample villagers and village leaders from rural localities in three provinces that vary significantly across socioeconomic conditions. In a large, developing country such as China, social policy implementation in general – and healthcare policy in particular – relies heavily on local government's capacity to implement policy effectively. Additionally, local government often bears a significant responsibility in funding healthcare in China. Therefore, sampling localities with variation in wealth was fundamental to this study.

In addition, the three provinces chosen vary in their approaches to health policy implementation as a whole. Jiangsu has taken a more decentralized approach to health policy implementation compared to Hubei and Yunnan. As discussed in Chapter 4, both funding and policy decisions for healthcare occur at lower levels of government in Jiangsu – generally at the county or municipal level – whereas the provincial governments of Hubei and Yunnan have taken a more active role in standardizing how health policy is implemented. Hubei and Yunnan also rely on central government funds for healthcare to a greater degree than Jiangsu.

With key independent variables such as wealth and the degree of decentralization of health policy in mind, we purposefully chose a convenience sample of three provinces: Jiangsu, Hubei, and Yunnan. We chose these provinces for three primary reasons. First, these provinces represent some of the salient socioeconomic, demographic, and geographic diversity of the country. Jiangsu is the wealthiest, Hubei is middle income, and Yunnan is the poorest and most agrarian. Jiangsu is located in the littoral region, while Hubei is in central China and Yunnan is in southwestern China. Jiangsu and Hubei do not have significant populations of ethnic minorities, whereas Yunnan has a large (but varied) ethnic minority population. Having ethnic minorities often changes the dynamics of local politics in Chinese provinces. Therefore, we sought to include Yunnan to examine the extent to which the politics of ethnic minorities might impact social policy and local state–society relations, although a nuanced analysis of the politics of ethnic minorities in China is beyond the scope of this book. The second motivation for choosing these three provinces was that Rabin and I had previously conducted extensive qualitative research in two of the three provinces. We thus had an understanding of the local context regarding healthcare and environmental issues, as well as which topics would be politically sensitive. Third, we secured a partnership in each province with professors at a local university who agreed to facilitate any necessary local permissions to conduct a survey as well as to assist us in recruiting students as survey enumerators.[10]

We then utilized a multistage, nested sampling design. Within each province, we chose three municipalities to represent the province's socioeconomic diversity.[11] Each province has between thirteen and sixteen municipalities. Initial conditions for effective healthcare infrastructure are highly associated with the wealth of the local government, so I therefore sought to ensure variation in this characteristic. Furthermore, since local government is often responsible for funding a substantial proportion of healthcare initiatives – and in some cases funding the majority of them, as in wealthier provinces – capturing this variation was crucial to understanding how implementation varies when controlling for wealth. We measured wealth by using the most recent statistics available for each municipality's gross regional product per capita – these are published by the provincial government in statistical yearbooks. Below the municipality, localities were chosen in a nested, randomized fashion. Specifically, three counties were selected randomly within each municipality, and then three townships and two back-up townships were selected within each county. Finally, three villages and two back-up villages were selected within each township. We instructed

[10] For example, Yunnan has unusually stringent regulations related to survey research that required the official support of a local university.

[11] Municipalities, also sometimes translated as prefectures or prefecture-level cities (地级市), constitute an administrative unit one level below the province that comprises counties, towns and townships, and villages (or cities and districts in urban areas).

teams to visit three townships per county and two villages per township, where possible. Some teams were able to visit the additional villages and townships that had been selected as back-up localities. We included data from those localities in the dataset since those villages were also selected according to the same nested, randomized sampling method.

Publicly available lists of counties and townships were reliable, but additional information that would have been required for a probability sample or a stratified sample was not reliably and consistently available for all provinces. Therefore, we elected to select counties, townships, and villages within each municipality randomly. At the village level, sampling presented additional complications. Through publicly available sources, we compiled lists of village names within the townships selected, and we then sought to identify and confirm village names and locations through satellite mapping.[12] However, a fair amount of flux has occurred with village boundaries, and villages sometimes change names or get amalgamated when local authorities see fit. Therefore, occasionally, the names of villages in our sampling frame were inaccurate. Further information at the village level, even basic demographic information such as population, is not consistently publicly available without permission from local government (usually the township government). Obtaining this type of information from over eighty townships would not have been feasible given the resources available. Therefore, we selected villages randomly rather than probabilistically. However, because lists of village names were not always updated and because some villages were so remote that they were inaccessible or dangerous to travel to, we sampled back-up villages. Teams of enumerators were instructed to attempt to visit the villages that were sampled first and then visit back-up villages in the event that sampled villages were not accessible or village officials refused to participate. In fact, no team encountered a village where all officials refused to participate, nor did any officials express concern about official permission; thus, the latter possibility was not a problem. The final sample visited by enumerators comprised three provinces, nine municipalities, twenty-seven counties, eighty-three townships, and 170 villages, with 299 village leaders and 801 villagers.

### *Sample of Individuals*

We were not able to gain access to local registries of villages or households and, therefore, had to rely on limited – and sometimes outdated – public records to create the sampling frame of localities. For individual-level

[12] We used Google Earth, which we found to be highly reliable and as current as possible.

sampling, certain teams were designated as enumerators for officials while others were responsible for villagers. For officials, enumerator teams went to the village committee's office and spoke to at least one village leader. In most cases, enumerators were able to interview two or more village officials. In most villages, there are between five and fifteen people on the village committee who are chosen through a combination of nomination and popular election by villagers. Previous research has examined the quality and consequences of village elections for local government accountability and democracy.[13] Enumerators were instructed to speak to whichever officials were available and could provide the basic village-level information that appears in the questionnaire. Thus, the sample of officials is not a probability sample. The other enumerator teams were instructed to find the main village road intersections and fan out in different directions, seeking willing respondents at every fifth door until they had completed two interviews each or time was up. Our goal per village was two interviews with officials and four interviews with villagers. Sometimes the enumerator teams were unable to meet this target because of lack of access to willing respondents or time constraints. At other times, they exceeded the target.

Enumerators reported few difficulties with nonresponse. In fact, although we had been advised by local scholars to avoid some topics because they might be politically sensitive, villagers and officials were, by and large, more forthcoming than we and the enumerators expected. There were only a few regions where enumerators encountered significant problems with response. In Suzhou (Jiangsu), the wealthiest municipality in the sample, enumerators reported that residents were standoffish, unfriendly, and often unwilling to participate in the survey. According to enumerators, residents were not enticed by the small gifts offered for participation because they were relatively wealthy. In Zhaotong (昭通) in Yunnan, one of the poorest municipalities in China, enumerators were not always able to travel to the counties and villages in the sample due to lack of infrastructure, bad weather, and precarious travel conditions such as landslides. They had to go to back-up localities instead. In Yuxi (玉溪) municipality (Yunnan), some interviews were cut short because farmers were in the midst of a harvest and had to return to their crops after about twenty to thirty minutes. In general, however, the completion rate was very high, even for questions that may have been deemed politically sensitive or personal.

[13] Melanie Manion, "Democracy, Community, Trust: The Impact of Elections in Rural China," *Comparative Political Studies* 39, no. 3 (April 2006): 301–324; Renfu Luo et al., "Village Elections, Public Goods Investments and Pork Barrel Politics, Chinese-Style," *Journal of Development Studies* 46, no. 4 (April 2010): 662–684.

*Implementation*

We collaborated with local universities in each of the three provinces to implement the survey. In each province, at least one local professor assisted us in recruiting appropriate students to apply as enumerators. In Jiangsu, all students were graduate students, and students from one university had previous experience conducting health-related surveys in local hospitals. In Hubei, students were advanced undergraduates from a variety of majors with no previous survey experience. In Yunnan, students were a mix of advanced undergraduates and graduates, and approximately one-third had experience conducting surveys on health policy in rural areas. The majority of students were from the provinces in which the survey was being conducted. Many students were also local to the prefectures and counties that contained the target villages, which improved communication and comprehension in villages where villagers only spoke a local dialect. In addition, there were almost always two students – one male and one female – conducting each questionnaire together.[14] This allowed the enumerators greater flexibility and improved accuracy in communication and note-taking. It also helped to neutralize potential bias introduced in those communities where gender roles affected villagers' willingness to participate and/or share honestly about more sensitive issues. The questionnaire took an average of about fifty minutes to complete. In cases where the interview occurred during daily chores, such as washing clothes, preparing dinner, or returning from work in the fields, it may have taken longer.

In each province, we conducted a three-day training for enumerators, which included an exam to test students' knowledge and a pretest in a local village. In addition, we reserved the right to dismiss students who did not meet our criteria. The three-day training included an introduction to survey methods, sensitivity training for conducting research in rural China, and practice administering the survey instrument to each other. The culminating pretest in a local village enabled us both to refine the survey instrument to local conditions and to evaluate the enumerators' performance. For students without previous experience conducting a survey, the pretest was essential to dispel some of the trepidation they felt in asking questions of strangers and reassured many who were concerned about whether respondents might perceive the questions as personally or politically sensitive.

When beginning the questionnaire, enumerators would record the village name and sex of the interviewee, take descriptive notes about the

[14] In a few cases, a team member fell ill, which led to some questionnaires being administered by only one enumerator.

appearance of the household, record the date of the interview and the time it started, and note concerns about the interviewee's attitude (in the case of any question about the perceived enthusiasm of the interviewee to participate), apparent language barriers, and whether there were any other people (including children) present. Respondents were compensated with a small gift as a gesture of appreciation for their participation. Gifts were chosen to be appropriate to the income level of the locality, such as a bar of soap, high-quality winter socks, or a thermos for tea. In the wealthiest municipality sampled, villagers declined gifts.

Surveys in China often suffer from low-quality responses, and there have been incidents reported of fraudulent data where enumerators fill in the questionnaires themselves. In addition, since enumerators were travelling to areas with which they were not familiar, we felt that it was important for enumerators to conduct each interview as a pair and to travel in small groups of three to five pairs (six to ten students). The safety of our enumerators was of utmost importance, and we wanted to ensure that they would not be put in difficult or dangerous situations by being alone, particularly in the case of young women. Having enumerators conduct interviews in pairs, generally a man and a woman, thus ensured safety and improved reliability of the data collected. In rare cases, gender parity was not possible. In addition, most pairs included one person who could speak the local dialect to facilitate communication. We then grouped three or four pairs into a small team, and each small team was responsible for the villages sampled in a particular municipality. The team traveled together and visited each village together.

The target of the survey included both village leaders (officials) and villagers.[15] However, we were concerned that, if village officials learned of the survey, they would either accompany enumerators to conduct the interviews or would suggest which villagers to interview, as had occurred at times during my qualitative research. To avoid this problem, we instructed each small group of enumerators to travel to villages together and interview village officials and villagers simultaneously. One pair interviewed village officials while the other three or four pairs interviewed villagers. By conducting the interviews simultaneously, we were able to prevent officials from influencing villagers' responses.

In consultation with local collaborators, we determined that the most appropriate time to conduct the survey would be toward the end of the universities' winter vacations during Lunar New Year – or Spring Festival, as it is generally known in China. This timing had two principal

[15] I use the term "village leader" to denote an individual who is serving on the village committee or a village "cadre" (*ganbu* 干部).

advantages. First, since enumerators were university students, they could participate in the project without disrupting their studies. Second, rural areas are generally in a festive state during this period. Therefore, villagers and officials have fewer work- or farming-related demands. In addition, some migrant workers return home at this time, allowing us to gain a fuller understanding of the village dynamics. While migrant workers were not the target of this project, those who were in the village at the time of the survey could have been chosen as respondents. In accordance with the university schedules of our local collaborators, the survey was administered during Spring Festival of 2012.

### *Measurement and the Process of Drafting the Survey Instrument*

The questionnaire, sampling, and preparation for the survey were likewise informed by data accumulated through archival research and the semi-structured interviews from my own research, as well as Rabin's independent research on environmental, political, and social dynamics in rural China. The majority of questions in the instrument were closed-ended questions. However, the instrument did include some open-ended questions, and we encouraged enumerators to provide supplemental information. Enumerators also had a full page to write additional notes and/or anecdotes that interviewees shared with them, as well as any concerns, such as interruptions by the interviewee's superior or other people who may have joined the interview or influenced the interviewee's responses.

The survey instrument was divided into eight sections: personal characteristics and demographic information; local environmental conditions; healthcare usage and perceptions; the legal system; trust and relationships with others; sources of news and information; attitudes about social issues and the government; salary; political participation; and other sensitive questions. We chose this order to ensure that data of particular relevance to our two projects would be more likely to be completed along with demographic information. It also ensured that if the respondent's attitude was affected by the more politically sensitive questions, any resulting discomfort would not increase item nonresponse on the other sections or cause the respondent to end the interview prematurely.

The pretest in each of the three provinces enabled us to adapt the survey instrument in both form and content. First, the questionnaire needed to be revised to reflect local conditions and to ensure that questions were worded as clearly as possible in plain language that villagers could readily understand. In addition to our own experiences conducting qualitative fieldwork, discussions with our local collaborators and local enumerators provided additional perspectives regarding which questions might be considered politically sensitive. Generally, we excluded questions that were deemed highly politically sensitive by our local collaborators. Moreover, multiple pretests allowed us to revise the questionnaire and reduce its length so that the average time for completion was under an hour.[16] The questionnaire needed to be a reasonable length so that the time for participation would not be unduly onerous for villagers and officials; this improved the survey response rate and facilitated the work of the enumerators.

Most of the survey instrument was administered to both villagers and village officials. However, a few questions related to the village – such as village population – were asked only of village officials. Opinion questions related to perceptions of government and local leaders were modified to reflect the position of a villager or village leader. Thus, we have been able to conduct analysis related to the differences in perspectives between villagers and village officials.

By conducting extensive training of enumerators, communicating with enumerators while they administered the survey, and utilizing three pretests to revise the instrument, we sought to ensure that the data collected were as reliable as possible.

### *Limitations and Potential Sources of Bias*

To the extent that there was nonresponse, whether item nonresponse or selected individuals refusing to participate in the survey, one may argue that villagers who are more satisfied with the regime would be more likely to participate. On the one hand, this is possible. But on the other hand, enumerators consistently found that villagers who had problems with government (local or national) would try to complain to them and try to get enumerators to intervene or inform the media on their behalf. On several occasions, enumerators had to explain that they were there only in a research capacity and not to advocate on behalf of villagers. It is possible, however, that people in communities that have suffered extreme political repression may be reticent to respond openly to a survey. Despite having taken precautionary measures to reduce bias introduced by, for example, the presence of local officials during interviews with villagers, we could not completely eliminate this possibility. The survey was conducted in an authoritarian country. Therefore, I interpret the

[16] The mean time for completion was 55 minutes with a standard deviation of 15 minutes, a minimum of 15 minutes (an incomplete questionnaire), and a maximum of 128 minutes.

Table A.3 *Demographic characteristics of respondents*

| | Jiangsu | | Hubei | | Yunnan | | Total | |
|---|---|---|---|---|---|---|---|---|
| Villagers | Count | Percent | Count | Percent | Count | Percent | Count | Percent |
| Women | 118 | 46% | 134 | 46% | 129 | 51% | 381 | 48% |
| CCP | 22 | 9% | 32 | 11% | 17 | 7% | 71 | 9% |
| Ethnic Minorities | 0 | 0% | 28 | 10% | 47 | 19% | 75 | 9% |
| Total | 258 | 100% | 292 | 100% | 251 | 100% | 801 | 100% |
| | Jiangsu | | Hubei | | Yunnan | | Total | |
| Village Leaders | Count | Percent | Count | Percent | Count | Percent | Count | Percent |
| Women | 20 | 19% | 27 | 28% | 10 | 11% | 57 | 20% |
| CCP | 85 | 80% | 80 | 82% | 68 | 78% | 233 | 80% |
| Ethnic Minorities | 0 | 0% | 8 | 8% | 16 | 18% | 24 | 8% |
| Total | 106 | 100% | 97 | 100% | 87 | 100% | 290 | 100% |

*Source*: Author's original survey.

Table A.4 *Age of respondents*

| | Obs. | Mean | Std. Dev. | Min. | Max. |
|---|---|---|---|---|---|
| Jiangsu | | | | | |
| Villagers | 257 | 48.03 | 14.19 | 19 | 93 |
| Village Leaders | 105 | 44.69 | 11.75 | 21 | 81 |
| Hubei | | | | | |
| Villagers | 290 | 48.26 | 13.81 | 18 | 87 |
| Village Leaders | 97 | 46.46 | 11.79 | 24 | 86 |
| Yunnan | | | | | |
| Villagers | 243 | 43.57 | 16.63 | 18 | 81 |
| Village Leaders | 87 | 45.02 | 8.43 | 25 | 67 |

*Source*: Author's original survey.

results with caution and assume that there may be some bias in favor of the government. Another way in which we sought to reduce this was to ensure that the majority of questions in the survey instrument were not generally considered politically sensitive. Those questions that may be considered politically sensitive were relegated to the final section of the

Table A.5 *Education level of respondents*

| | Jiangsu | | | |
|---|---|---|---|---|
| | Villagers | | Village Leaders | |
| | Count | Percent | Count | Percent |
| 1: No Schooling | 40 | 16% | 2 | 2% |
| 2: Primary School | 64 | 25% | 5 | 5% |
| 3: Junior High School | 90 | 35% | 20 | 20% |
| 4: High School | 48 | 19% | 41 | 41% |
| 5: College and Above | 12 | 5% | 32 | 32% |
| 6: Other* | 3 | 1% | 0 | 0% |
| Total | 257 | 100% | 100 | 100% |
| | **Hubei** | | | |
| | Villagers | | Village Leaders | |
| | Count | Percent | Count | Percent |
| 1: No Schooling | 22 | 9% | 1 | 1% |
| 2: Primary School | 77 | 30% | 5 | 5% |
| 3: Junior High School | 117 | 46% | 35 | 35% |
| 4: High School | 59 | 23% | 39 | 39% |
| 5: College and Above | 12 | 5% | 16 | 16% |
| 6: Other* | 4 | 2% | 0 | 0% |
| Total | 291 | 113% | 96 | 96% |
| | **Yunnan** | | | |
| | Villagers | | Village Leaders | |
| | Count | Percent | Count | Percent |
| 1: No Schooling | 47 | 18% | 0 | 0% |
| 2: Primary School | 82 | 32% | 7 | 7% |
| 3: Junior High School | 79 | 31% | 42 | 42% |
| 4: High School | 28 | 11% | 34 | 34% |
| 5: College and Above | 15 | 6% | 4 | 4% |
| 6: Other* | 2 | 1% | 0 | 0% |
| Total | 253 | 98% | 87 | 87% |

* Responses to option 6 included three graduate or professional school responses, five descriptions that were unclear, and one "self-educated" response.

*Source*: Author's original survey.

instrument. Although bias from political pressure is not completely unavoidable (much as pressure to deceive enumerators for social, psychological, or political reasons would be present in a democratic setting), we sought to reduce this as much as possible. Significant proportions of respondents were willing to rate the government (local and national) unfavorably in different categories, suggesting that many respondents were willing and able to express their views, including negative opinions of the government.

Overall, our sample of villagers roughly reflects the demographic composition of rural China (Tables A.3, A.4, and A.5). There is one noticeable discrepancy, however, that could have implications for our analysis: our enumerators disproportionately interviewed Communist Party members. Communist Party members comprise about 6 percent of the population in China (and much less in rural areas), but 9 percent in our sample of villagers. This slight over-representation of relatively "elite" villagers certainly affects inference drawn from our survey data. However, given that my main research questions are related to state legitimacy and state–society relations, the over-representation of CCP members does not preclude useful analysis of these data. CCP members tend to be more politically active, more educated, but also more critical of state policies. In addition, as CCP members are leaders in their communities, I expect that their views have a greater effect on other villagers and the potential for anti-government action than non-CCP members. Therefore, by including a slightly higher proportion of CCP members than is representative, our survey data more closely reflect the positions of those villagers who play a leadership role in their communities. Also, party membership is always used as a control variable in my analysis; thus, I do not anticipate that this would preclude inference from our data.

# References


Battaglini, Monica, and Olivier Giraud. "Policy Styles and the Swiss Executive Federalism: Comparing Diverging Styles of Cantonal Implementation of the Federal Law on Unemployment." *Swiss Political Science Review* 9, no. 1 (April 2003): 285–308. https://doi.org/10.1002/j.1662-6370.2003.tb00408.x.

Beck, Nathaniel, and Jonathan N. Katz. "What to Do (and Not to Do) with Time-Series Cross-Section Data." *American Political Science Review* 89, no. 3 (September 1995): 634–647.

Bernstein, Thomas P., and Xiaobo Lü. *Taxation without Representation in Contemporary Rural China*. Cambridge: Cambridge University Press, 2003.

Blumenthal, David, and William Hsiao. "Privatization and Its Discontents – The Evolving Chinese Health Care System." *New England Journal of Medicine* 353, no. 11 (September 2005): 1165–1170.

Brown, Philip H., Alan de Brauw, and Du Yang. "Understanding Variation in the Design of China's New Co-operative Medical System." *China Quarterly* 198 (June 2009): 304–329.

Bruch, Sarah K., Marcia K. Meyers, and Janet C. Gornick. "The Consequences of Decentralization: Inequality in Safety Net Provision in the Post–Welfare Reform Era." *Social Service Review* 92, no. 1 (March 2018): 3–35. https://doi.org/10.1086/696132.

Bulman, David J., and Kyle A. Jaros. "Leninism and Local Interests: How Cities in China Benefit from Concurrent Leadership Appointments." *Studies in Comparative International Development* 54, no. 2 (June 2019): 233–273. https://doi.org/10.1007/s12116-019-09279-0.

Butler, Patrick. "Q&A: Postcode Lottery." *The Guardian*, November 9, 2000. www.theguardian.com/society/2000/nov/09/NHS.

Cai, Hongbin, and Daniel Treisman. "State Corroding Federalism." *Journal of Public Economics* 88, no. 3–4 (March 2004): 819–843.

caijing.com.cn. "重构住房保障_经济全局_《财经》杂志_杂志频道首页_财经网 [Rebuilding Housing Security]." August 25, 2013. http://magazine.caijing.com.cn/20130825/2677099.shtml.

*Caixin Global*. "Liaoning Government Admits False Growth Data from 2011–14." January 18, 2017. www.caixinglobal.com/2017-01-18/101046468.html (accessed April 26, 2017).

Cao, Xuebing. "The Chinese Medical Doctor Association: A New Industrial Relations Actor in China's Health Services?" *Relations Industrielles* 66, no. 1 (Winter 2011): 74–97.

Carlson, Allen, Mary E. Gallagher, Kenneth G. Lieberthal, and Melanie Manion. *Contemporary Chinese Politics: New Sources, Methods, and Field Strategies*. New York: Cambridge University Press, 2010.

Chan, Anita, and Jonathan Unger. "A Chinese State Enterprise under the Reforms: What Model of Capitalism?" *China Journal* 62 (July 2009): 1–26.

Chan, Chak Kwan, King Lun Ngok, and David Phillips. *Social Policy in China: Development and Well-Being*. Bristol, UK: Policy Press, 2008.

Chan, Kam Wing. "The Chinese Hukou System at 50." *Eurasian Geography and Economics* 50, no. 2 (2009): 197–221.

Chan, Kam Wing. "The Household Registration System and Migrant Labor in China: Notes on a Debate." *Population and Development Review* 36, no. 2 (June 2010): 357–364. https://doi.org/10.2307/25699064.

Chan, Kam Wing, and Will Buckingham. "Is China Abolishing the Hukou System?" *China Quarterly* 195 (September 2008): 582–606.

*China Daily*. "Counties May Be Incorrectly Labeled as Poverty Stricken." *China Daily*, February 27, 2013. http://europe.chinadaily.com.cn/opinion/2013-02/27/content_16262137.htm.

China Education Online (中国教育在线). "全国重点大学名单-中国教育在线 [List of National Key Universities]." June 29, 2005. www.eol.cn/article/20050629/3142081.shtml.

China Law Translate. *National Security Law* (blog), July 1, 2015. http://chinalawtranslate.com/2015nsl/?lang=en.

Chinanews.com (中国新闻网). "云南组织40万干部定点扶贫 8月底到位 [Yunnan Organizes 400,000 cadres for Targeted Poverty Alleviation To Be in Place by End of August]." August 24, 2015. www.chinanews.com/df/2015/08-24/7485246.shtml.

China.org.cn. "Public Welfare Programs in Shenmu County, Shaanxi Province." December 17, 2009. www.china.org.cn/photos/2009-12/27/content_19138418.htm.

Chinese Academy of Social Sciences. "2011 General Survey of Chinese Society [2011 年度中国社会状况综合调查]." 2012. www.sdccass.cn/pic/Upload/Files/baogao/201203/F6346722794823612054106.pdf.

Chung, Jae Ho. "Reappraising Central–Local Relations in Deng's China: Decentralization, Dilemmas of Control, and Diluted Effects of Reform." In *Remaking the Chinese State: Strategies, Society, and Security*, edited by Chien-min Chao and Bruce J. Dickson, 46–75. New York: Routledge, 2001.

Clarke, Donald. "Hong Kong's National Security Law: A First Look." *The China Collection*, June 30, 2020. https://thechinacollection.org/hong-kongs-national-security-law-first-look/.

Collins, Jeff. "Southern California Cities Can Soon Object to Giant Increases in Housing Goals." *Orange County Register*, September 3, 2020. www.ocregister.com/2020/09/03/southern-california-cities-can-soon-object-to-giant-increases-in-housing-goals (accessed January 31, 2020).

Deng, Xiaoping. *Selected Works of Deng Xiaoping, 1938–1965*. Beijing: Intercultural Publishing, 2011.

Deng, Xiaoping. *Selected Works of Deng Xiaoping, 1975–1982*. Beijing: Foreign Languages Press, 1984.

Deng, Xiaoping. The Bureau for the Compilation and Translation of Works of Marx, Engels, Lenin, and Stalin Under the Central Committee of the Communist Party of China, trans. *Selected Works of Deng Xiaoping (1938–1965)*. Beijing: Foreign Language Press, 1992.

Devlin, Kate. "Healthcare Postcode Lottery Means Patients Losing Out on Cancer Treatments." *The Telegraph*, September 8, 2008. www.telegraph.co.uk/news/health/2700686/Healthcare-postcode-lottery-means-patients-losing-out-on-cancer-treatments.html.

Dewey, John. *Lectures in China, 1919–1920*. Honolulu: University Press of Hawaii, 1973.

Dillon, Liam. "After Huntington Beach Lawsuit, Newsom Warns Cities He'll Continue Housing Law Crackdown." *Los Angeles Times*, February 19, 2020. www.latimes.com/politics/la-pol-ca-gavin-newsom-housing-cities-summit-20190219-story.html.

Dillon, Nara. *Radical Inequalities: China's Revolutionary Welfare State in Comparative Perspective*. Harvard East Asian Monographs 383. Cambridge, MA: Harvard University Asia Center, 2015.

Djukanovic, Vojin, and Edward P. Mach, eds. *Alternative Approaches to Meeting Basic Health Needs in Developing Countries: A Joint UNICEF/WHO Study*. Geneva: World Health Organization, 1975.

Donaldson, John A. *Small Works: Poverty and Economic Development in Southwestern China*. Ithaca, NY: Cornell University Press, 2011.

Donaldson, John A. "Why Do Similar Areas Adopt Different Development Strategies? A Study of Two Puzzling Chinese Provinces." *Journal of Contemporary China* 18, no. 60 (June 2009): 421–444.

Duckett, Jane. "Challenging the Economic Reform Paradigm: Policy and Politics in the Early 1980s' Collapse of the Rural Co-operative Medical System." *China Quarterly* 205 (March 2011): 80–95.

Duckett, Jane. *The Chinese State's Retreat from Health: Policy and the Politics of Retrenchment*. New York: Routledge, 2010.

Duckett, Jane. "International Influences on Policymaking in China: Network Authoritarianism from Jiang Zemin to Hu Jintao." *China Quarterly* 237 (March 2019): 15–37. https://doi.org/10.1017/S0305741018001212.Edin, Maria. "Remaking the Communist Party-State: The Cadre Responsibility System at the Local Level in China." *China: An International Journal* 1, no. 1 (March 2003): 1–15.

Eggleston, Karen, Ling Li, Qingyue Meng, and Magnus Lindelow. "Health Service Delivery in China: A Literature Review." Policy Research Working Paper 3978. *World Bank*, 2006.

Elgin, Dallas J., and David P. Carter. "Administrative (de)Centralization, Performance Equity, and Outcome Achievement in Rural Contexts: An Empirical Study of U.S. Child Welfare Systems." *Governance* 32, no. 1 (January 2019): 23–43. https://doi.org/10.1111/gove.12343.

*English. News. Cn*. "China to Allow Two Children for All Couples – Xinhua." www.xinhuanet.com/english/2015-10/29/c_134763645.htm (accessed March 26, 2018).

Esping-Andersen, Gøsta. *The Three Worlds of Welfare Capitalism*. Princeton, NJ: Princeton University Press, 1990.

Ewig, Christina. "Piecemeal but Innovative: Health Sector Reform in Peru." In *Crucial Needs, Weak Incentives: Social Sector Reform, Democratization, and Globalization in Latin America*, edited by Robert R. Kaufman and Joan M. Nelson, 217–246. Baltimore, MD: Woodrow Wilson Center with Johns Hopkins University Press, 2004.

Fairbrother, Gregory P., and Zhenzhou Zhao. "Paternalism, National Citizenship, and Religiosity in Chinese State Legitimation Discourse." *Journal of Chinese Political Science* 21, no. 4 (December 2016): 417–434. https://doi.org/10.1007/s11366-016-9435-x.

Fang 方, Xiaotian 晓天, and Deqing 德清 Wang 王. "家长主义:一种政府干预民办教育的有效模式 [Paternalism: A Model of Government Intervening in Non-Government Education]." 教育科学 [*Education Science*] 30, no. 2 (April 2014): 1–8.

Feick, Jürgen. "L'Analyse Comparative Des Politiques Publiques: Un Chemin Vers L'Intégration Des Résultats? [Comparative Analysis of Public Policy: A Path towards Integrating Findings?]" *L'Année Sociologique* 40 (1990): 179–225.

Fewsmith, Joseph. "The Elusive Search for Effective Sub-County Governance." In *Mao's Invisible Hand: The Political Foundations of Adaptive Governance in China*, edited by Sebastian Heilmann and Elizabeth J. Perry, 297–320. Cambridge, MA: Harvard University Asia Center, 2011.

Francis, Corinna-Barbara. "Reproduction of Danwei Institutional Features in the Context of China's Market Economy: The Case of Haidian District's High-Tech Sector." *China Quarterly* 147 (September 1996): 839–859.

Frazier, Mark W. *Socialist Insecurity: Pensions and the Politics of Uneven Development in China*. Ithaca, NY: Cornell University Press, 2010.

Freeman, Gary P. "National Styles and Policy Sectors: Explaining Structured Variation." *Journal of Public Policy* 5, no. 4 (October 1985): 467–496.

Friedman, Edward, Paul G. Pickowicz, and Mark Selden. *Revolution, Resistance, and Reform in Village China*. New Haven, CT: Yale University Press, 2005.

Fu, Diana, and Greg Distelhorst. "Grassroots Participation and Repression under Hu Jintao and Xi Jinping." *China Journal* 79 (January 1, 2018): 100–122, https://doi.org/10.1086/694299.

Gallagher, Mary Elizabeth. *Contagious Capitalism: Globalization and the Politics of Labor in China*. Princeton, NJ: Princeton University Press, 2007.

Gao, Xiang. "State–Society Relations in China's State-Led Digitalization: Progress and Prospects." *China Review* 20, no. 3 (August 2020): 1–12.

Gerring, John. "What Is a Case Study and What Is It Good For?" *American Political Science Review* 98, no. 2 (May 2004): 341–354.

Glaser, Bonnie S., and Phillip C. Saunders. "Chinese Civilian Foreign Policy Research Institutes: Evolving Roles and Increasing Influence." *China Quarterly* 171 (September 2002): 597–616. https://doi.org/10.1017/S0009443902000372.

Goodman, David S.G. , and Gerald Segal. *China Deconstructs: Politics, Trade, and Regionalism*. New York: Routledge, 1994.

Gough, Ian, and Geof Wood. *Insecurity and Welfare Regimes in Asia, Africa and Latin America: Social Policy in Development Contexts*. New York: Cambridge University Press, 2004.

Greitens, Sheena Chestnut. "Surveillance, Security, and Liberal Democracy in the Post-COVID World." *International Organization* 74, no. S1 (December 2020): E169–190, https://doi.org/10.1017/S0020818320000417.

Guo, Gang. "Decentralized Education Spending and Regional Disparities: Evidence from Chinese Counties 1997–2001." *Journal of Chinese Political Science* 11, no. 2 (September 2006): 45–60.

Haeder, Simon F., and David L. Weimer. "You Can't Make Me Do It: State Implementation of Insurance Exchanges under the Affordable Care Act." *Public Administration Review* 73, no. s1 (September 2013): S34–47. https://doi.org/10.1111/puar.12065.

Haggard, Stephan, and Robert R. Kaufman. *Development, Democracy, and Welfare States: Latin America, East Asia, and Eastern Europe*. Princeton, NJ: Princeton University Press, 2008.

Han, Jun. "The Emergence of Social Corporatism in China: Nonprofit Organizations, Private Foundations, and the State." *China Review* 16, no. 2 (2016): 27–53.

Hanson, Marta E. "Conceptual Blind Spots, Media Blindfolds: The Case of SARS and Traditional Chinese Medicine." In *Health and Hygiene in Chinese East Asia: Policies and Publics in the Long Twentieth Century*, edited by Angela Leung Ki Che and Charlotte Furth, 228–254. Durham, NC: Duke University Press, 2010.

Hernández, Javier C. "To Inspire Young Communists, China Turns to 'Red Army' Schools." *New York Times*, October 15, 2017. www.nytimes.com/2017/10/15/world/asia/china-schools-propaganda-education.html.

He, Alex Jingwei. "Maneuvering within a Fragmented Bureaucracy: Policy Entrepreneurship in China's Local Healthcare Reform." *China Quarterly* 236 (December 2018): 1088–1110.

He, Alex Jingwei, Yuda Shi, and Hongdou Liu. "Crisis Governance, Chinese Style: Distinctive Features of China's Response to the Covid-19 Pandemic." *Policy Design and Practice* 3, no. 3 (July 2020): 242–258, https://doi.org/10.1080/25741292.2020.1799911.

He, Henry Yuhuai. *Dictionary of the Political Thought of the People's Republic of China*. Armonk, NY: M. E. Sharpe, 2001.

Heilmann, Sebastian. "Policy Experimentation in China's Economic Rise." *Studies in Comparative International Development* 43, no. 1 (Spring 2008): 1–26. https://doi.org/10.1007/s12116-007-9014-4.

Heilmann, Sebastian. "Policy-Making through Experimentation: The Formation of a Distinctive Policy Process." In *Mao's Invisible Hand: The Political Foundations of Adaptive Governance in China*, edited by Sebastian Heilmann and Elizabeth J. Perry, 62–101. Cambridge, MA: Harvard University Asia Center, 2011.

Heilmann, Sebastian, and Elizabeth J. Perry, eds. *Mao's Invisible Hand: The Political Foundations of Adaptive Governance in China*. Cambridge, MA: Harvard University Asia Center, 2011.

Henochowicz, Anna. "Chinese Wikipedia Blocked by Great Firewall." *China Digital Times (CDT)* (blog), May 20, 2015. http://chinadigitaltimes.net/2015/05/chinese-wikipedia-blocked-by-great-firewall/.

Hornby, Lucy. "What's up, Doc? Investors Knock at China Hospitals." Reuters News, September 1, 2011. www.reuters.com/article/idINIndia-59106920110902.

Howlett, Michael, and Evert Lindquist. "Policy Analysis and Governance: Analytical and Policy Styles in Canada." *Journal of Comparative Policy Analysis* 6, no. 3 (December 2004): 225–249.

Huang, Wenyi. "作为一种法律干预模式的家长注意 [Legal Paternalism as a Pattern of Legal Interference]." 法学研究 *[Chinese Journal of Law]* (May 2010): 3–17.

Huang, Xian. "Four Worlds of Welfare: Understanding Subnational Variation in Chinese Social Health Insurance." *China Quarterly* 222 (June 2015): 449–74. https://doi.org/10.1017/S0305741015000399.

Huang, Yanzhong. *Governing Health in Contemporary China*. New York: Routledge, 2013.

Huang, Yanzhong. "The SARS Epidemic and Its Aftermath in China: A Political Perspective." In *Learning from SARS: Preparing for the Next Disease Outbreak: Workshop Summary*, edited by Stacey Knobler, Adel Mahmoud, Stanley Lemon, Alison Mack, Laura Sivitz, and Katherine Oberholtzer, 116–136. Washington, DC: National Academies Press, 2004. www.ncbi.nlm.nih.gov/books/NBK92479/.

Huang, Yasheng. "Research Note: Administrative Monitoring in China." *China Quarterly* 143 (September 1995): 829–834.

Huang, Youqin. "Low-Income Housing in Chinese Cities: Policies and Practices." *China Quarterly* 212 (December 2012): 941–964. https://doi.org/10.1017/S0305741012001270.

Hubei Provincial Government Bulletin. "湖北省人民政府关于全面推进新型农村合作医疗制度建设的指导意见 [Hubei Province People's Government Instructive Opinion on the Full Promotion of the Construction of the New Cooperative Medical System]." May 2008.

Hubei Provincial People's Government. "湖北省人民政府关于加强城镇居民住房保障工作的意见 [Opinions of the People's Government of Hubei Province on Strengthening Housing Security for Urban Resident]." Pub. L., no. 42 (Hubei: 2007).

Huber, Evelyne, and John D. Stephens. "State Economic and Social Policy in Global Capitalism." In *A Handbook of Political Sociology: States, Civil Societies, and Globalization*, edited by Thomas Janoski, Robert Alford, Alexander M. Hicks, and Mildred Schwartz, 607–629. New York: Cambridge University Press, 2005.

Hunan Province People's Government Website. "湖南新农合补偿标准进一步提高 [Hunan NCMS Subsidy Standards Take a Step Further, Raised]." November 13, 2009. www.xinshao.gov.cn/info/bmlf/9290.shtml.

Jingmen Municipal People's Government. 荆门市人民政府办公室关于印发《解决中心城区低收入家庭住房困难发展规划和年度计划》的通知. Pub. L., no. 28 (Jingmen: 2008).

Beach, Sophie. "Proposed Internet Security Law Raises Concerns." *China Digital Times (CDT)*, July 8, 2015. https://chinadigitaltimes.net/2015/07/proposed-internet-security-law-raises-concerns/ (accessed February 26, 2020).

Kang, Raeyoon, Taehyun Jung, and Keun Lee. "Intellectual Property Rights and Korean Economic Development: The Roles of Patents, Utility Models and Trademarks." *Area Development and Policy* 5, no. 2 (April 2020): 189–211. https://doi.org/10.1080/23792949.2019.1585889.

Kaufman, Robert R., and Joan M. Nelson. *Crucial Needs, Weak Incentives: Social Sector Reform, Democratization, and Globalization in Latin America*. Baltimore, MD: Woodrow Wilson Center Press with Johns Hopkins University Press, 2004.

Kay, Stephen J. "Unexpected Privatizations: Politics and Social Security Reform in the Southern Cone." *Comparative Politics* 31, no. 4 (July 1999): 403–422.

Kim, Byungkyu, and Richard C. Fording. "Second-Order Devolution and the Implementation of TANF in the US States." *State Politics & Policy Quarterly* 10, no. 4 (Winter 2010): 341–367.

Kornreich, Yoel, Ilan Vertinsky, and Pitman B. Potter. "Consultation and Deliberation in China: The Making of China's Health-Care Reform." *China Journal* 68 (July 2012): 176–203.

Kung, James, Yongshun Cai, and Xiulin Sun. "Rural Cadres and Governance in China: Incentive, Institution and Accountability." *China Journal* 62 (2009): 61–77.

Kurtz, Marcus J. "Understanding the Third World Welfare State after Neoliberalism: The Politics of Social Provision in Chile and Mexico." *Comparative Politics* 34, no. 3 (April 2002): 293–313.

Kwon, Huck-ju. "Advocacy Coalitions and Health Politics in Korea." *Social Policy and Administration* 41, no. 2 (April 2007): 148–161.

Lane, Kevin P. "One Step Behind: Shaanxi in Reform." In *Provincial Strategies of Economic Reform in Post-Mao China: Leadership, Politics, and Implementation*, edited by Peter T. Y. Cheung, Chae-ho Chŏng, and Zhimin Lin, 212–250. Studies on Contemporary China. Armonk, NY: M. E. Sharpe, 1998.

Lei, Xiaoyan, and Wanchuan Lin. "The New Cooperative Medical Scheme in Rural China: Does More Coverage Mean More Service and Better Health?" *Health Economics* 18, supplement 2 (July 2009): S25–46.

Lewis, Orion A., Jessica C. Teets, and Reza Hasmath. "Exploring Political Personalities: The Micro-Foundation of Local Policy Innovation in China." *Governance* (January 2021). https://doi.org/10.1111/gove.12573.

Li, Hongbin, and Li-An Zhou. "Political Turnover and Economic Performance: The Incentive Role of Personnel Control in China." *Journal of Public Economics* 89, no. 9–10 (2005): 1743–62.

Li, Jun and Weiping Ye. "直接登记制下的社会组织行政监管研究 [Research on the Administrative Supervision of Social Organizations under the Direct Registration System]." 天府新论 [*Tianfu Xinlun*] 5 (2014): 8–13.

Li, Lianjiang. "Political Trust in Rural China." *Modern China* 30, no. 2 (April 2004): 228–258.

Li, Linda Chelan. *Centre and Provinces – China 197–1993: Power as Non-Zero-Sum*. Studies on Contemporary China. Oxford: Clarendon Press, 1998.

Li, Yang, Yinjun Zhao, Danhui Yi, Xiaojun Wang, Yan Jiang, Yu Wang, Xinchun Liu, and Shuangge Ma. "Differences Exist across Insurance Schemes in China Post-Consolidation." *PloS ONE* 12, no. 11 (November 2017): 1–13. https://doi.org/10.1371/journal.pone.0187100.

Li, Yushang. "The Elimination of Shistosomiasis in Jiaxing and Haining Counties, 1948–58: Public Health as Political Movement." In *Health and Hygiene in Chinese East Asia*, edited by Angela Leung Ki Che and Charlotte Furth, 204–227. Durham, NC: Duke University Press, 2010.

Lieberthal, Kenneth G. "Introduction: The 'Fragmented Authoritarianism' Model and Its Limitations." In *Bureaucracy, Politics, and Decision Making in Post-Mao China*, edited by Kenneth G. Lieberthal and David M. Lampton, 1–25. Berkeley, CA: University of California Press, 1992.

Liebman, Benjamin L. "Watchdog or Demagogue? The Media in the Chinese Legal System." *Columbia Law Review* 105, no. 1 (January 2005): 1–157.

Lim, Meng-Kin, Hui Yang, Tuohong Zhang, Zijun Zhou, Wen Feng, and Yude Chen. "China's Evolving Health Care Market: How Doctors Feel and What They Think." *Health Policy* 69, no. 3 (September 2004): 329–337. https://doi.org/10.1016/j.healthpol.2004.01.001.

Lin, Tingjin. *The Politics of Financing Education in China*. Basingstoke, UK: Palgrave Macmillan, 2013.

Lin, Vivian, and David Legge. *Health Policy in and for China*. Beijing: Peking University Press, 2010.

Lin, Wanlong, and Christine Wong. "Are Beijing's Equalization Policies Reaching the Poor? An Analysis of Direct Subsidies Under the 'Three Rurals' (Sannong)." *China Journal* 67 (January 2012): 23–46.

Liu, Derek Tai-wei. "Top-Down Accountability and the Politics of Social Spending in China." APSA 2010 Annual Meeting Paper. 2014.

Liu, Mingxing, Victor Shih, and Dong Zhang. "The Fall of the Old Guards: Explaining Decentralization in China." *Studies in Comparative International Development* 53, no. 4 (December 2018): 379–403. https://doi.org/10.1007/s12116-018-9267-0.

Liu 刘, Huarong 华蓉. "乡镇教育组撤销后不留管理'真空' [Township Education Group Does Not Stay in Management 'Vacuum' after Revocation]." 中国教育报 [*China Education Daily*], July 3, 2002.

Long, Cheryl, Jin Yang, and Jing Zhang. "Institutional Impact of Foreign Direct Investment in China." *World Development* 66 (February 2015): 31–48. https://doi.org/10.1016/j.worlddev.2014.08.001.

Lu, Ming, and Yiran Xia. "Migration in the People's Republic of China." ADBI Working Paper Series. Tokyo: Asian Development Bank Institute, September 2016. www.adb.org/publications/migration-people-republic-china/.

Lucas, AnElissa. *Chinese Medical Modernization: Comparative Policy Continuities, 1930–1980s*. New York: Praeger, 1982.

Luo, Renfu, Linxiu Zhang, Jikun Huang, and Scott Rozelle. "Village Elections, Public Goods Investments and Pork Barrel Politics, Chinese-Style." *Journal of Development Studies* 46, no. 4 (April 2010): 662–684.

Lynch, Elizabeth M. "China Passes National Security Law." *China Law & Policy* (blog), July 1, 2015. http://chinalawandpolicy.com/2015/07/01/china-passes-national-security-law/.

Ma 马, Te 特. "父爱主义与"还地于民 [On Paternalism and 'Returning Land to Farmers']." 北方法学 [*Northern Legal Science*] 4, no. 24 (June 2010): 41–47.

Malesky, Edmund J. "Foreign Direct Investors as Agents of Economic Transition: An Instrumental Variables Analysis." *Quarterly Journal of Political Science* 4, no. 1 (March 2009): 59–85. https://doi.org/10.1561/100.00008068.

Manion, Melanie. "Democracy, Community, Trust: The Impact of Elections in Rural China." *Comparative Political Studies* 39, no. 3 (April 2006): 301–324.

Manion, Melanie. "The Cadre Management System, Post-Mao: The Appointment, Promotion, Transfer and Removal of Party and State Leaders." *China Quarterly* 102 (June 1985): 203–233.

Mao Zedong. *Chairman Mao Talks to the People; Talks and Letters: 1956–1971*, edited by Stuart R. Schram. The Pantheon Asia Library. New York: Pantheon Books, 1975. https://catalog.hathitrust.org/Record/001258672.

Martínez Franzoni, Juliana. "Welfare Regimes in Latin America: Capturing Constellations of Markets, Families, and Policies." *Latin American Politics and Society* 50, no. 2 (Summer 2008): 67–100.

Martinez-Vazquez, Jorge, Baoyun Qiao, and Li Zhang. "The Role of Provincial Policies in Fiscal Equalization Outcomes in China." *China Review* 8, no. 2 (Fall 2008): 135–167.

Maskin, Eric, Yingyi Qian, and Chenggang Xu. "Incentives, Information, and Organizational Form." *Review of Economic Studies* 67, no. 2 (April 2000): 359–378.

McCall, Leslie, and Christine Percheski. "Income Inequality: New Trends and Research Directions." *Annual Review of Sociology* 36 (August 2010): 329–347. https://doi.org/10.1146/annurev.soc.012809.102541.

Mehra, Parshotam. *Tibet: Writings on History and Politics*. New Delhi: Oxford University Press, 2012.

Mertha, Andrew. "'Fragmented Authoritarianism 2.0': Political Pluralization in the Chinese Policy Process." *China Quarterly* 200 (December 2009): 995–1012. https://doi.org/10.1017/S0305741009990592.

Mertha, Andrew C. "China's 'Soft' Centralization: Shifting Tiao/Kuai Authority Relations." *China Quarterly* 184 (December 2005): 791–810.

Miao, Julie T. "Definition and Typologies of Local Innovation Systems: A Case Study of Optics Valley in Central China." *Area Development and Policy* 5, no. 2 (April 2020): 212–232. https://doi.org/10.1080/23792949.2019.1672572.

Ministry of Health. "Notification of the Opinion of the State Council General Office Published by the Health Bureau and Other Departments Related to Establishing the New Cooperative Medical System" CLI.2.45115, January 16, 2003.

Ministry of Health. "卫生部办公厅关于做好2009年下半年新型农村合作医疗工作的通知 [Ministry of Health General Office Notice on Proper Implementation of the New Cooperative Medical System in the Second Half of 2009]." 卫办农卫发[2009] 108号 CLI.4.118483, June 29, 2009.

Ministry of Health and Ministry of Finance. "关于做好新型农村合作医疗试点有关工作的通知 [Notice on Proper Implementation of the New Cooperative Medical System Pilot Projects]." 319 (2005).

Ministry of Health of the People's Republic of China. *China Public Health Statistical Yearbook* [中国卫生统计年鉴]. Beijing: Peking Union Medical College Publishing House, 2010.

Minzner, Carl F. "Xinfang: An Alternative to Formal Chinese Legal Institutions." *Stanford Journal of International Law* 42, no. 1 (2006): 103–180.

MOHURD (Ministry of Housing and Urban-Rural Development of the PRC). "中央预算内投资 支持中西部新建廉租房建设 [Investment from the Central Government Budget to Support the Construction of New, Low-Rent Housing the Central and Western Regions]." January 3, 2008.

Montinola, Gabriella, Yingyi Qian, and Barry R. Weingast. "Federalism, Chinese Style: The Political Basis for Economic Success in China." *World Politics* 48, no. 1 (January 1996): 50–81.

National Bureau of Statistics. "涉外调查管理办法 [Measures for the Administration of Foreign-Affiliated Surveys]." National Bureau of Statistics of the People's Republic of China. www.stats.gov.cn/statsinfo/auto2072/201310/t20131031_450864.html, (accessed July 29, 2017).

Naughton, Barry. "China's Economic Think Tanks: Their Changing Role in the 1990s." *China Quarterly* 171 (September 2002): 625–635. https://doi.org/10.1017/S0009443902000396.

Nelson, Joan. "The Politics of Health Sector Reform: Cross-National Comparisons." In *Crucial Needs, Weak Incentives*, edited by Richard Kaufman and Joan Nelson, pp. 23–64. Washington, DC: Woodrow Wilson Center Press, 2004.

Sudworth, John. "Counting the Cost of China's Left-behind Children." BBC News, Beijing, April 12, 2016. www.bbc.com/news/world-asia-china-35994481 (accessed July 17, 2017).

Ngok, Kinglun, and Weiqing Guo. "The Quest for World Class Universities in China: Critical Reflections." *Policy Futures in Education* 6, no. 5 (October 2008): 545–557. https://doi.org/10.2304/pfie.2008.6.5.545.

O'Brien, Kevin J., and Lianjiang Li. *Rightful Resistance in Rural China*. New York: Cambridge University Press, 2006.

Oi, Jean C. "Fiscal Reform and the Economic Foundations of Local State Corporatism in China." *World Politics* 45, no. 1 (October 1992): 99–126. https://doi.org/10.2307/2010520.

Oi, Jean C., Kim Singer Babiarz, Linxiu Zhang, Renfu Luo, and Scott Rozelle. "Shifting Fiscal Control to Limit Cadre Power in China's Townships and Villages." *China Quarterly* 211 (September 2012): 649–675.

Oksenberg, Michel. "Economic Policy-Making in China: Summer 1981." *China Quarterly* 90 (June 1982): 165–194. https://doi.org/10.1017/S0305741000000308.

Orlik, Thomas. "China's Puzzling Numbers." *Wall Street Journal*, September 15, 2011. http://online.wsj.com/article/SB10001424053111904353504576565893924294066.html.

Orlik, Thomas. *Understanding China's Economic Indicators*. Upper Saddle River, NJ: FT Press, 2012.

Pan, Jay, and Gordon G. Liu. "The Determinants of Chinese Provincial Government Health Expenditures: Evidence from 2002–2006 Data." *Health Economics* 21, no. 7 (July 2012): 757–777. https://doi.org/10.1002/hec.1742.

Pappas, Gregory. "The Centrality of Dewey's Lectures in China to His Socio-Political Philosophy." *Transactions of the Charles S. Peirce Society: A Quarterly Journal in American Philosophy* 53, no. 1 (Winter 2017): 7–28.

Peerenboom, Randall. *China's Long March toward Rule of Law*. Cambridge: Cambridge University Press, 2002.

Pizzi, Elise. "Does Labor Migration Improve Access to Public Goods in Source Communities? Evidence from Rural China." *Journal of Chinese Political Science* 23, no. 4 (December 2018): 563–583. https://doi.org/10.1007/s11366-017-9525-4.

Plumer, Brad. "China Could Be Hiding an Entire Japan's Worth of Carbon Emissions." *Washington Post*, June 12, 2012. www.washingtonpost.com/blogs/wonkblog/post/china-could-be-hiding-an-entire-japans-worth-of-carbon-emissions/2012/06/12/gJQA3zuTXV_blog.html.

Pribble, Jennifer. "Women and Welfare: The Politics of Coping with New Social Risks in Chile and Uruguay." *Latin American Research Review* 41, no. 2 (2006): 84–111.

Pribble, Jennifer. "Worlds Apart: Social Policy Regimes in Latin America." *Studies in Comparative International Development* 46, no. 2 (November 2010): 191–216. https://doi.org/10.1007/s12116-010-9076-6.

"Project 211: A Brief Introduction (II)." www.edu.cn/20010101/21852.shtml (accessed June 26, 2018).

Qian, Jiwei. "Anti-Poverty in China: Minimum Livelihood Guarantee Scheme." *East Asian Policy* 5, no. 4 (2013): 53–64. https://doi.org/10.1142/S1793930513000366.

Ratigan, Kerry. "Authoritarian Governance, Decentralization, and State Legitimacy: Healthcare Reform in Rural China." PhD diss., University of Wisconsin–Madison, 2013.

Ratigan, Kerry. "Disaggregating the Developing Welfare State: Provincial Social Policy Regimes in China." *World Development* 98 (October 2017): 467–484. https://doi.org/10.1016/j.worlddev.2017.05.010.

Ratigan, Kerry. "Riding the Tiger of Performance Legitimacy? Chinese Villagers' Satisfaction with State Healthcare Provision." *International Political Science Review*, August 6, 2020. https://doi.org/10.1177/0192512120927482.

Read, Benjamin L. "More Than an Interview, Less Than Sedaka: Studying Subtle and Hidden Politics with Site-Intensive Methods." In *Contemporary Chinese Politics: New Sources, Methods, and Field Strategies*, edited by Allen Carlson, Mary E. Gallagher, Kenneth G. Lieberthal, and Melanie Manion, 145–161. New York: Cambridge University Press, 2010.

Richardson, Jeremy, Gunnel Gustafsson, and Grant Jordan. "The Concept of Policy Style." In *Policy Styles in Western Europe*, edited by Jeremy Richardson, 1–16. London: George Allen & Unwin, 1982.

Rittberger, Berthold, and Jeremy Richardson. "Old Wine in New Bottles? The Commission and the Use of Environmental Policy Instruments." *Public Administration* 81, no. 3 (September 2003): 575–606. https://doi.org/10.1111/1467-9299.00362.

Rubin, Herbert J. *Qualitative Interviewing: The Art of Hearing Data*. Thousand Oaks, CA: SAGE, 2012.

Rudra, Nita. "Globalization and the Decline of the Welfare State in Less-Developed Countries." *International Organization* 56, no. 2 (Spring 2002): 411–45.

Rudra, Nita. *Globalization and the Race to the Bottom in Developing Countries: Who Really Gets Hurt?* New York: Cambridge University Press, 2008.

Rudra, Nita. "Welfare States in Developing Countries: Unique or Universal?" *Journal of Politics* 69, no. 2 (May 2007): 378–396.

Saich, Tony. "Social Policy Development in the Era of Economic Reform." In *AIDS and Social Policy in China*, edited by Joan Kaufman, Arthur Kleinman, and Tony Saich, 15–46. Cambridge, MA: Harvard University Asia Center, 2006.

Sautman, Barry, and June Teufel Dreyer. *Contemporary Tibet: Politics, Development, and Society in a Disputed Region*. Armonk, NY: M. E. Sharpe, 2006.

Shaffer, Gregory, and Henry S. Gao. "China's Rise: How It Took on the US at the WTO." Legal Studies Research Paper Series No. 2017–15. Rochester, NY: Social Science Research Network, March 20, 2017. https://papers.ssrn.com/abstract=2937965.

Shambaugh, David. "China's International Relations Think Tanks: Evolving Structure and Process." *China Quarterly* 171 (September 2002): 575–596. https://doi.org/10.1017/S0009443902000360.

Shen, Yimin (申毅敏), and Huiqin (侯慧琴) Hou. "医生收红包'潜规则'探秘 [Probing the 'Hidden Rule' That Doctors Accept Red Envelopes]." *Procuratorial Daily*, 2004. http://review.jcrb.com/zyw/n273/ca258338.htm.

Sheng, Yumin. "Central-Provincial Relations at the CCP Central Committees: Institutions, Measurement and Empirical Trends, 1978–2002." *China Quarterly* 182 (June 2005): 338–355.

Sheng, Yumin. *Economic Openness and Territorial Politics in China*. New York: Cambridge University Press, 2010. http://assets.cambridge.org/97805211/95386/cover/9780521195386.jpg.

Shi, Tianjian. "Cultural Values and Political Trust: A Comparison of the People's Republic of China and Taiwan." *Comparative Politics* 33, no. 4 (July 2001): 401–419.

Shirk, Susan L. *The Political Logic of Economic Reform in China*. California Series on Social Choice and Political Economy 24. Berkeley, CA: University of California Press, 1993.

Shue, Vivienne. *The Reach of the State: Sketches of the Chinese Body-Politic*. Stanford, CA: Stanford University Press, 1988.

Singh, Prerna. *How Solidarity Works for Welfare: Subnationalism and Social Development in India*. Cambridge Studies in Comparative Politics. Cambridge: Cambridge University Press, 2016.

Smith, William C., and Devin K. Joshi. "Public vs. Private Schooling as a Route to Universal Basic Education: A Comparison of China and India." *International Journal of Educational Development* 46 (January 2016): 153–165. https://doi.org/10.1016/j.ijedudev.2015.11.016.

Solinger, Dorothy J. "Politics in Yunnan Province in the Decade of Disorder: Elite Factional Strategies and Central–Local Relations, 1967–1980." *China Quarterly* 92 (December 1982): 628–662.

Solinger, Dorothy J. "The Dibao Recipients: Mollified Anti-Emblem of Urban Modernization." *China Perspectives* 4 (2008): 36–46.

Solinger, Dorothy J. "Uncertain Paternalism: Tensions in Recent Regional Restructuring in China." *International Regional Science Review* 11, no. 1 (1987). https://doi.org/10.1177/016001768701100103.

Solinger, Dorothy J., and Yiyang Hu. "Welfare, Wealth, and Poverty in Urban China: The Dibao and Its Differential Disbursement." *China Quarterly* 211 (September 2012): 741–764.

Solinger, Dorothy J., and Ting Jiang. "When Chinese Central Orders and Promotion Criteria Conflict." *Modern China* 42, no. 6 (March 2016): 571–606. https://doi.org/10.1177/0097700416635507.

Song 宋, Xuming 旭明. "论家长式法律强制的人性基础与合理界限 [On the Humanistic Basis for and Reasonable Limits to Paternalistic Legal Constraints]." 重庆邮电学院学报 [*Journal of Chongqing University of Posts and Telecommunications*] 15 (June 2003): 84–86.

*South China Morning Post*. "China Has 61 Million Left-behind Children ... That's Almost Britain's Total Population." October 21, 2016. www.scmp.com/news/china/economy/article/2038731/its-official-china-has-61-million-left-behind-children-thats.

State Council. 中共中央办公厅、国务院办公厅关于进一步做好定点扶贫工作的通知 [Notice of the General Office of the Central Committee of the Communist Party of China and the General Office of the State Council on Further Doing a Good Job in Targeted Poverty Alleviation]. Pub. L., no. CLI.5.213783 (2010).

State Council Development Research Center. "李克强在国务院发展研究中心调研时强调 [Li Keqiang Emphasizes Research at the State Council Development Research Center]," November 10, 2011.

State Council of China. Opinions of the State Council on the Integration of the Basic Medical Insurance for Urban and Rural Residents [国务院关于整合城乡居民基本医疗保险制度的意见]. Pub. L., no. CLI.2.262352 (2016).

State Council of the PRC. 国务院关于解决城市低收入家庭住房困难的若干意见 [Several Opinions of the State Council on Solving the Housing Difficulties of Urban Low-income Families]. Pub. L., no. SC 24 (2007). www.gov.cn/zwgk/2007-08/13/content_714481.htm.

Su, Min, Zhongliang Zhou, Yafei Si, Xiaolin Wei, Yongjian Xu, Xiaojing Fan, and Gang Chen. "Comparing the Effects of China's Three Basic Health Insurance Schemes on the Equity of Health-Related Quality of Life: Using the Method of Coarsened Exact Matching." *Health and Quality of Life Outcomes* 16, no. 1 (March 2018). https://doi.org/10.1186/s12955-018-0868-0.

Sun, Xiaoxia, and Chunzhen Guo. "法律父爱主义在中国的适用 [Application of Legal Paternalism in China]." 中国社会科学 [*Social Sciences in China*] (January 2006): 47–58.

Tan, Rui. "中国保障性住房体系的演进、特点与方向 [The Evolution, Characteristics and Orientation of China's Affordable Housing System]."

*Journal of Shenzhen University (Humanities & Social Sciences)* 34, no. 2 (2017): 101–108.

Tang, Wenfang. *Populist Authoritarianism: Chinese Political Culture and Regime Sustainability*. New York: Oxford University Press, 2016.

Tanner, Murray Scot. "Changing Windows on a Changing China: The Evolving 'Think Tank' System and the Case of the Public Security Sector." *China Quarterly* 171 (September 2002): 559–574.

Teets, Jessica C. *Civil Society under Authoritarianism: The China Model*. New York: Cambridge University Press, 2014.

Teets, Jessica C. "The Evolution of Civil Society in Yunnan Province: Contending Models of Civil Society Management in China." *Journal of Contemporary China* 24, no. 91 (January 2015): 158–175.

Teets, Jessica C., Michael Gao, Mika Wysocki, and Weiru Ye. "The Promise of 'Payment for Ecosystem Services': An Analysis of Watershed Eco-Compensation Policy Design in China." 2018.

Teets, Jessica C., Reza Hasmath, and Orion A. Lewis. "The Incentive to Innovate? The Behavior of Local Policymakers in China." *Journal of Chinese Political Science* 22, no. 4 (December 2017): 505–517. https://doi.org/10.1007/s11366-017-9512-9.

Teichman, Judith. "Redistributive Conflict and Social Policy in Latin America." *World Development* 36, no. 3 (March 2008): 446–460.

Thireau, Isabelle, and Linshan Hua. "One Law, Two Interpretations: Mobilizing the Labor Law in Arbitration Committees and in Letters and Visits Offices." In *Engaging the Law in China: State, Society, and Possibilities for Justice*, edited by Neil J. Diamant, Stanley B. Lubman, and Kevin J. O'Brien, pp. 84–107. Stanford, CA: Stanford University Press, 2005.

Tsai, Lily L. *Accountability without Democracy: Solidary Groups and Public Goods Provision in Rural China*. Cambridge Studies in Comparative Politics. New York: Cambridge University Press, 2007.

Tsai, Lily L. "Understanding the Falsification of Village Income Statistics." *China Quarterly* 196 (December 2008): 805–826.

Tsai, Wen-Hsuan, and Nicola Dean. "Experimentation under Hierarchy in Local Conditions: Cases of Political Reform in Guangdong and Sichuan, China." *China Quarterly* 218 (June 2014): 339–358.

"Two Chinese Provinces Faked Economic Data, Inspectors Say." Bloomberg.com, June 12, 2017. www.bloomberg.com/news/articles/2017-06-12/two-chinese-provinces-falsified-economic-data-inspectors-say.

World Bank and the Development Research Center of the State Council, the People's Republic of China. *Urban China: Toward Efficient, Inclusive, and Sustainable Urbanization*. Washington, DC: World Bank Group, 2014.

van der Kamp, Denise, Peter Lorentzen, and Daniel Mattingly. "Racing to the Bottom or to the Top? Decentralization, Revenue Pressures, and Governance Reform in China." *World Development* 95 (July 2017): 164–176. https://doi.org/10.1016/j.worlddev.2017.02.021.

Wallace, Jeremy L. "Juking the Stats? Authoritarian Information Problems in China." *British Journal of Political Science* 46, no. 1 (January 2016): 11–29. https://doi.org/10.1017/S0007123414000106.

Wan, William. "China's Economic Data Drew Sharp Scrutiny from Experts Analyzing Global Trends." *Washington Post*, February 4, 2013. www.washingtonpost.com/world/asia_pacific/chinas-economic-data-draw-sharp-scrutiny-from-experts-analyzing-global-trends/2013/02/04/f4de4b84-6ae0-11e2-af53-7b2b2a7510a8_story.html.

Wang, Hongman. 大国卫生之论 [*Arguments about Our Country's Health*]. Beijing: Peking University Press, 2006.

Wang, Qian. "Tougher Penalties Mapped out to Fight Illegal Surveys." *China Daily*, October 23, 2012. http://europe.chinadaily.com.cn/china/2012-10/23/content_15837733.htm.

Wang, Sangui, Zhou Li, and Yanshun Ren. "The 8–7 National Poverty Reduction Program in China – The National Strategy and Its Impact." A case study from Reducing Poverty, Sustaining Growth – What Works, What Doesn't, and Why: A Global Exchange for Scaling Up Success. Washington, DC: International Bank for Reconstruction and Development/World Bank, 2004.

Wang, Shaoguang. "China's 1994 Fiscal Reform: An Initial Assessment." *Asian Survey* 37, no. 9 (September 1997): 801–817. https://doi.org/10.2307/2645698.

Wang, Ya Ping, Lei Shao, Alan Murie, and Jianhua Cheng. "The Maturation of the Neo-Liberal Housing Market in Urban China." *Housing Studies* 27, no. 3 (April 2012): 343–359. https://doi.org/10.1080/02673037.2012.651106.

Warikoo, K. *Xinjiang: China's Northwest Frontier*. Central Asia Research Forum. London: Routledge, 2016.

Wedeman, Andrew H. *From Mao to Market: Rent Seeking, Local Protectionism, and Marketization in China*. Cambridge: Cambridge University Press, 2003.

Wedeman, Andrew Hall. *Double Paradox: Rapid Growth and Rising Corruption in China*. Ithaca, NY: Cornell University Press, 2012.

Wei, Zhong. "Research on Compulsory Education in the Tibetan Regions of Qinghai and Yunnan Provinces." In *Breaking Out of the Poverty Trap: Case Studies from the Tibetan Plateau in Yunnan, Qinghai, and Gansu*, edited by Luolin Wang and Ling Zhu, 143–163. Hackensack, NJ: World Century Publishing Corporation, 2013.

Weingast, Barry R., Yingyi Qian, and Gabriella Montinola. "Federalism, Chinese Style: The Political Basis for Economic Success in China." *World Politics* 48, no. 1 (October 1995): 50–81.

Weir, Margaret, and Jessica Schirmer. "America's Two Worlds of Welfare: Subnational Institutions and Social Assistance in Metropolitan America." *Perspectives on Politics* 16, no. 2 (June 2018): 380–399. https://doi.org/10.1017/S1537592717004248.

Weyland, Kurt. *Democracy without Equity: Failures of Reform in Brazil*. Pittsburgh, PA: University of Pittsburgh Press, 1996.

Weyland, Kurt. "From Leviathan to Gulliver? The Decline of the Developmental State in Brazil." *Governance* 11, no. 1 (1998): 51–75.

Weyland, Kurt. "'Growth with Equity' in Chile's New Democracy?" *Latin American Research Review* 32, no. 1 (1997): 37–67.

Whyte, Martin King. *Myth of the Social Volcano: Perceptions of Inequality and Distributive Injustice in Contemporary China*. Stanford, CA: Stanford University Press, 2010.

Williams, Princess. *The Politics of Place: How Southern identity Shapes American Political Behavior*. PhD diss., University of Michigan: 2021.

Wilson, Sven E., and Daniel M. Butler. "A Lot More to Do: The Promise and Peril of Panel Data in Political Science." Unpublished manuscript, Department of Political Science, Brigham Young University, 2004. www.stanford.edu/class/polisci353/2004spring/reading/wilson_butler.pdf.

Wilson, Sven E., and Daniel M. Butler. "A Lot More to Do: The Sensitivity of Time-Series Cross-Section Analyses to Simple Alternative Specifications." *Political Analysis* 15, no. 2 (March 2007): 101–123. https://doi.org/10.1093/pan/mpl012.

Wong, Christine. "Fiscal Reform: Paying for the Harmonious Society." *China Economic Quarterly* 14, no. 2 (June 2010): 22–27.

Wong, Joseph. *Healthy Democracies: Welfare Politics in Taiwan and South Korea*. Ithaca, NY: Cornell University Press, 2004.

Poverty Reduction and Economic Management Unit – East Asia and Pacific Region. "China National Development and Sub-National Finance: A Review of Provincial Expenditures." World Bank, April 9, 2002. www1.worldbank.org/publicsector/LearningProgram/Decentralization/ChinaNatlDevSubNatFinance.pdf.

Wu, Alfred M., and M. Ramesh. "Poverty Reduction in Urban China: The Impact of Cash Transfers." *Social Policy and Society* 13, no. 02 (April 2014): 285–299. https://doi.org/10.1017/S1474746413000626.

Wu, Bin, Aijuan Chen, and Hongfei Ji. "The Isomorphism of Chinese Universities: An Analysis of Higher Education Expansion and Consequences." Discussion Paper 55. China Policy Institute, University of Nottingham, December 2009. www.nottingham.ac.uk/cpi/documents/discussion-papers/discussion-paper-55-isomorphism-universities.pdf.

Xiao, Xiangchen [潇湘晨]. "我国严禁医生收入与药品收入挂钩 [China Prohibits Linking Doctors' Salaries to Prescriptions]." *Xinhua News*, 2013. http://news.xinhuanet.com/fortune/2013-02/21/c_124371680.htm.

Xing, Hua [辛华]. "苏州允许设立私营医院 [Suzhou Allows Establishment of Private Hospitals]." 人民日报 [*People's Daily*], 华东新闻 [*Xinhua News*], 2002. www.people.com.cn/GB/paper40/5749/581937.html.

Xinshao County Government Website. "湖南新农合补偿标准进一步提高, 湖南省人民政府网站 [Hunan NCMS Reimbursement Standards Raised, Hunan Provincial People's Government Website]." November 13, 2009. www.xinshao.gov.cn/info/bmlf/9290.shtml.

Xu, Jianchu, and Jesse Ribot. "Decentralisation and Accountability in Forest Management: A Case from Yunnan, Southwest China." *European Journal of Development Research* 16, no. 1 (March 2004): 153–173. https://doi.org/10.1080/09578810410001688789.

Yao, Kevin, and Aileen Wang. "China Lets Gini out of the Bottle; Wide Wealth Gap." Reuters, January 17, 2013. www.reuters.com/article/uk-china-economy-income-gap/china-lets-gini-out-of-the-bottle-wide-wealth-gap-idUKBRE90H06R20130118.

Yichang Muncipal Government. 宜昌市人民政府关于加强城镇居民住房保障工作的实施意见 [Implementation Opinions of the People's Government of

Yichang City on Strengthening Housing Security for Urban Residents]. Pub. L., no. 017. Yichang: 2008.

Yip, Ka-che. *Health and National Reconstruction in Nationalist China: The Development of Modern Health Services, 1928–1937*. Monograph and Occasional Paper Series 50. Ann Arbor, MI: Association for Asian Studies, 1995.

Yip, Winnie. "Disparities in Healthcare and Health Status: The Rural–Urban Gap and Beyond." In *One Country, Two Societies: Rural-Urban Inequality in Contemporary China*, edited by Martin King Whyte, 147–165. Harvard Contemporary China Series 16. Cambridge, MA: Harvard University Asia Center, 2010.

Yu, Hong, and Yongnian Zheng. "The Resource Boom in China's Resource-Rich Provinces: The Role of the State-Owned Enterprises and Associated Problems." *Asian Survey* 56, no. 2 (April 2016): 270–300. https://doi.org/10.1525/as.2016.56.2.270.

Zhang, Changdong. "Reexamine Regional Models of China's Economic Growth: Toward an Integrated Analytical Framework." *Sociology Compass* 14, no. 5 (May 2020): e12781. https://doi.org/10.1111/soc4.12781.

Zhang, Le-Yin. "Chinese Central-Provincial Fiscal Relationships, Budgetary Decline and the Impact of the 1994 Fiscal Reform: An Evaluation." *China Quarterly* 157 (March 1999): 115–141.

Zhang, Mingmin [张明敏]. "江苏 从太仓试点到全省推进 [Jiangsu: From the Pilot of Taicang to the Whole Province]." *China Philanthropy Times* [公益时报], October 28, 2013. www.gongyishibao.com/html/yaowen/2411.html.

Zhang, Qian, and Roy Brouwer. "Is China Affected by the Resource Curse? A Critical Review of the Chinese Literature." *Journal of Policy Modeling* 42, no. 1 (January–February 2020): 133–152. https://doi.org/10.1016/j.jpolmod.2019.06.005.

Zhao, Litao, and Jinjing Zhu. "China's Higher Education Reform: What Has Not Been Changed?" *East Asian Policy* 2, no. 4 (December 2010): 115–125.

Zhao, Yuezhi, and Wusan Sun. "Public Opinion Supervision: Possibilities and Limits of the Media in Constraining Local Officials." In *Grassroots Political Reform in Contemporary China*, edited by Elizabeth J. Perry and Merle Goldman, 300–324. Cambridge, MA: Harvard University Press, 2007.

Zhen, Bizhao. *Population and Health Policy in the People's Republic of China*. Occasional Monograph Series 9. Washington, DC: Interdisciplinary Communications Program, Smithsonian Institution, 1976.

Zhou, Xueguang. "Organizational Response to COVID-19 Crisis: Reflections on the Chinese Bureaucracy and Its Resilience." *Management and Organization Review* 16, no. 3 (July 2020): 473–484.

Zhu, Xufeng. 政策变迁中的专家参与 [*The Participation of Experts in Policy Change*]. Beijing: China Remin University Publishing, 2012.

Zou, Yonghua. "Contradictions in China's Affordable Housing Policy: Goals vs. Stucture." *Habitat International* 41 (January 2014): 8–16. https://doi.org/10.1016/j.habitatint.2013.06.001.

Zuo, Cai (Vera). "Promoting City Leaders: The Structure of Political Incentives in China." *China Quarterly* 224 (December 2015): 955–984. https://doi.org/10.1017/S0305741015001289.

Zweig, David. *Internationalizing China: Domestic Interests and Global Linkages*. Ithaca, NY: Cornell University Press, 2002.

"中共中央关于加强和改进党的作风建设的决定(全文) [Decision of the CPC Central Committee on Strengthening and Improving the Party's Working Style (Full Text)]." www.people.com.cn/GB/shizheng/16/20011007/575835.html (accessed June 28, 2017).

"关于改进党的作风 [On Improving the Party's Style]." www.cctv.com/special/733/-1/47004.html (accessed June 28, 2017).

"南京医生自曝送红包经历 医患关系岂能为交易 [Nanjing Doctors Expose Their Experiences of Accepting Red Envelopes; How Can the Doctor-Patient Relationship Be Based on Under-the-Table Deals?]." *Xinhua Net*, 2006. http://news.xinhuanet.com/politics/2006-03/22/content_4332282.htm.

"开展群众路线教育 大力加强作风建设 [Carry Out Mass Line Education and Strengthen Construction of Work Style]." www.miit.gov.cn/n11293472/n11293877/n15329799/n15369909/index.html (accessed June 29, 2017).

"江苏教育改革发展显著特点-徐州教研网 [Remarkable Features of Educational Reform and Development in Jiangsu]." http://jys.xze.cn/Item/32.aspx (accessed June 22, 2016).

"江苏省政府办公厅关于加快保障性安居工程建设的意见 [Opinions of the General Office of the Jiangsu Provincial Government on Accelerating the Construction of Affordable Housing Projects]." www.law110.com/law/32/jiangsu/law1102006215260.html (accessed November 24, 2015).

"湖北省教育厅长陈安丽:10年进入教育强省行列_国内教育_中国教育新闻网-www.jyb.cn 记录教育每一天 [Chen Anli, Director of the Hubei Province Education Department: 10 Years into the Ranks of Strong Education Province]." http://china.jyb.cn/gnxw/201101/t20110119_411219_1.html (accessed July 19, 2017).

"黄石市人民政府关于加强城镇居民住房保障工作的意见 [Opinions of the People's Government of Huangshi City on Strengthening Housing Security for Urban Residents]." Pub. L., no. 38 (Huangshi: 2007).

# Index

Milton Keynes UK
Ingram Content Group UK Ltd.
UKHW020838110324
439289UK00018B/111

9 781009 066020